"With *Be Thou My Vision*, Jonny Gibson has given us one of the richest resources of Christian devotion for individuals, families, and churches in decades. Now, in *O Come, O Come, Emmanuel*, he has given us a second timeless treasure that can be revisited each Advent season and help us finish the devotional year in a spirit of exultation rather than exhaustion. He inspires our minds and hearts by telling the gospel story at Christmas with simplicity and clarity through beautiful liturgy. By leaning on the finest Christian thinkers and poets in history, Gibson helps to fire the imagination of our souls to repeat the sounding joy like it was the first time. Buy this book and read it to yourself, your spouse, your family, or your friends! Then buy one for your pastor so that it may refresh your corporate celebrations as well. It will make the beauty of Christ's peace the overriding narrative during Advent this year—and every year."

Keith Getty, hymn writer; recording artist; coauthor, *Sing! How Worship Transforms Your Life, Family, and Church*

"Jonny Gibson's *Be Thou My Vision* has become an integral part of my personal worship time with the Lord, as well as a liturgical resource to use in planning for corporate worship. I am elated by the news of his latest project, focusing our attention and preparing our hearts for the Advent season. What a gift to the believer and to the church!"

Laura Story, recording artist; Worship Leader, Perimeter Church, Atlanta, Georgia

"Rich liturgy offers us structure and words to stir our hearts and channel our worship of God. It orients us by the Scriptures and the riches of the Christian tradition so that our minds and hearts begin to run in biblical paths. My prayer is that God will use this book to help many hearts to prepare him room."

Joe Rigney, President, Bethlehem College and Seminary

"With the flurry of activity, sometimes it's hard even for us as believers to 'put Christ back into Christmas.' Expertly selected from our creedal, catechetical, and liturgical heritage, this treasure chest of focused meditation and praise helps us to revel in 'the reason for the season.' I plan on using it and giving it away, especially as a timely opportunity for evangelizing friends and family."

Michael Horton, J. Gresham Machen Professor of Systematic Theology and Apologetics, Westminster Seminary California

"Jonny Gibson provides a rich gift in this collection. Not only has he curated some of the finest prayers and hymns of church history, but he has also arranged them into soul-enriching liturgies that echo the outlines of the gospel message even in their structure. I warmly commend this excellent resource."

Matt Merker, hymn writer; Director of Creative Resources and Training, Getty Music; author, *Corporate Worship*

"In this handsomely produced volume, Gibson has drawn upon the rich heritage of prayers and meditations from Christian leaders of the past, as well as biblical authors, to enhance our daily worship of God. While many Christians may be unaware of this legacy, the judicious choice of Christian creeds, collects, and meditations across twenty centuries, together with selected biblical texts, provides readers with a wealth of resources for their daily devotions from Advent to Epiphany. A rich array of wisdom and insight from our forebears provides a new landmark for Christians as they reflect, meditate, and offer praise to God for the gift of his incarnate Son, our Lord Jesus Christ."

Glenn N. Davies, Archbishop of Sydney (2013–2021)

"Here is a daily liturgy for all who desire to grow in their enjoyment and worship of Christ. The prayers are robust, the meditations thoughtful, the confessions sincere, and the praise stirring. Any Christian would benefit from using it as a help in private and family devotions."

Jason Helopoulos, Senior Pastor, University Reformed Church, East Lansing, Michigan; author, *The Promise: The Amazing Story of Our Long-Awaited Savior*

"If you are weary of the materialistic, sentimental Christmas of our culture, this book will lead you back to heartfelt worship and adoration. While these liturgies are intended for private and family worship, they breathe a communion with the church of all ages. Above all, they will lead you into a deeper appreciation for the glory of the incarnation—and joyful worship of the one who came and is coming again!"

Dale Van Dyke, Pastor, Harvest Orthodox Presbyterian Church, Wyoming, Michigan

"This is a wonderful resource! It gives focus and articulation to the watchful waiting of Advent and, through its thoughtful selection of passages, a sense of the companionship of countless fellow travelers and faithful guides drawn from the entire history of the people of God in our journey through the season."

Alastair J. Roberts, Adjunct Senior Fellow, Theopolis Institute

O Come, O Come, Emmanuel

O Come, O Come, Emmanuel

A Liturgy for Daily Worship from Advent to Epiphany

Jonathan Gibson

:: CROSSWAY®

WHEATON, ILLINOIS

Library of Congress Cataloging-in-Publication Data

Names: Gibson, Jonathan, 1977– author.

Title: O come, o come Emmanuel : a liturgy for daily worship from advent to epiphany / Jonathan Gibson.

Description: Wheaton, Illinois : Crossway, 2023. | Includes bibliographical references.

Identifiers: LCCN 2022035548 (print) | LCCN 2022035549 (ebook) | ISBN 9781433587948 (hardcover) | ISBN 9781433587955 (pdf) | ISBN 9781433587979 (epub)

Subjects: LCSH: Advent. | Devotional exercises.

Classification: LCC BV40 .G495 2023 (print) | LCC BV40 (ebook) | DDC 242/.332—dc23/eng/20221205

LC record available at https://lccn.loc.gov/2022035548

LC ebook record available at https://lccn.loc.gov/2022035549

Crossway is a publishing ministry of Good News Publishers.

RRD		32	31	30	29	28	27	26	25	24	23
15	14	13	12	11	10	9	8	7	6	5	4	3	2	1

May the Lord make you glad during this remembrance of
the birth of His only Son, Jesus Christ;
that as you joyfully receive Him for your redeemer,
you may with sure confidence behold Him
when He shall come to be our judge.

CHRISTMAS COLLECT FROM
BOOK OF COMMON PRAYER (1928)

For
Simon and Rebecca

———

Fellow saints
Fellow servants

Contents

Preface

CHRISTMAS IS MY FAVORITE TIME OF YEAR. For as long as I can remember, I have loved the season of Christmas—the warm open fire on cold winter nights, the twinkling lights outside, the mince pies and mulled wine, the presents wrapped and waiting under the tree, the visits of family and friends. However, it is more than just the seasonal atmosphere and company that I enjoy. I love the Advent services and carol singing; I love listening to (or preaching on) Old Testament prophecies about the coming of Christ or his nativity; I love the "Carols by Candlelight" service on Christmas Eve, in which we remember that holy night in the little town of Bethlehem when the everlasting light began to shine in the dark streets. Yet despite my love for these things and my embrace of the season, I always find myself arriving at Christmas Day somewhat dissatisfied with my personal meditation on the incarnation of Christ. I have tried this or that devotional guide but am still left wanting something more orderly, something more mystery-evoking, something more *worshipful*. The book that you now hold in your hands is my attempt to improve our appreciation of the mystery we celebrate each year at Christmas.

If you are familiar with *Be Thou My Vision: A Liturgy for Daily Worship*,[1] then you will recognize the similarities in this book; but there are also differences. I have incorporated more worshipful elements throughout the daily liturgy to fit the season. The day now begins with a meditation on the incarnation of Christ from a prominent figure in church history; the calls to worship are tailored to the content of the day's liturgy, focused on either the first or second coming of Christ; the element of adoration is a hymn or psalm appropriate to Advent, Christmastide, or Epiphany; three alternative *Gloria Patri* hymns and two alternative Doxologies rotate on a weekly basis; the catechism questions (from Heidelberg Catechism or Westminster Shorter Catechism) are focused on the necessity, accomplishment, and application of Christ's work; the Scripture readings in Advent concern Old Testament types and prophecies of Christ's coming, followed by New Testament Nativity readings in Christmastide, before concluding with some Epiphany readings; a new praise element, in the form of an ancient Christian prayer or hymn focused on the incarnation, follows the Scripture reading; finally, the liturgy closes with a scriptural benediction and a doxological postlude (based on Psalm 72:17–19).

As will be seen, each day's liturgy has been carefully crafted for the purpose of enhancing daily worship during the season of Advent up through Epiphany so that our minds are better fixed on, and our hearts are better affected by, that great mystery of the Christian faith: God "was manifested *in the flesh*" (1 Tim. 3:16). My prayer is that the content, structure, and rhythms of this daily liturgy may help us to be more like

1   Jonathan Gibson, *Be Thou My Vision: A Liturgy for Daily Worship* (Wheaton, IL: Crossway, 2021).

the shepherds and wise men on that first Christmas, who, upon seeing the babe lying in a manger, bowed down and worshiped Christ the newborn King!

Jonathan Gibson, Glenside, PA
Summer 2022
Soli Deo Gloria

Acknowledgments

MY THANKS TO JUSTIN TAYLOR for asking me to write another devotional after *Be Thou My Vision* was received so well. I had already given some thought to designing seasonal ones for Christmas and Paschal (Easter), but Justin's request gave me fresh motivation. As always, the good folk at Crossway have been a pleasure to work with: my thanks to Lydia Brownback for her editorial skill and wisdom, and to Dan Farrell and his team for another beautifully designed cover. I am grateful to my research assistants Jeremy Menicucci, Jiang Ningning, and Bryce Simon for their help with content formation. Mitchell Dixon, Anthony and Lorraine Gosling, Lawrence McErlean, and Jason Patterson each provided valuable feedback, which has further shaped the content and structure of this book. My appreciation is also expressed to Drew Tulloch, musical director at Trinity Church, Aberdeen, who helped to compile the tunes and meter for the hymns and psalms. Todd Rester and Danny Hyde helped to locate some of the prayers in the Old Palatinate Liturgy of 1563.

Many of the meditations I discovered in Justin Holcomb's book *God with Us: 365 Devotions on the Person and Work of*

Christ,[2] though I retrieved original sources in Logos and then made slight adaptions where needed. Other meditations I found in my own reading of original sources. The majority of prayers in this book are taken from the ESV *Prayer Bible*; a dozen or so are taken from *Reformation Worship: Liturgies from the Past for the Present*.[3] These latter prayers were translated by Matthias Mangold and Bernard Aubert. I am grateful to Crossway and New Growth Press for permission to use a select number of prayers from these respective works. Other prayers have been modernized from original sources that are in the public domain, such as Augustine's *Confessions* (c. 400), Gregory the Great's "Seven-Fold Litany" (c. 600), the Anglican Book of Common Prayer (1552 and 1662), the Old Palatinate Liturgy (1563), the Middelburg Liturgy (1586), the Savoy Liturgy (1661), *Preces Ecclesiasticae* (1856), and *A Book of Public Prayer* (1857). The psalms used are from the Free Church of Scotland's *Sing Psalms* (2003 edition) and are used here with permission. The questions and answers from Heidelberg Catechism (1563) are taken from the modern version published by the Christian Reformed Church in North America and are used here with permission. The questions and answers from the Westminster Shorter Catechism (1647) have been modernized, as well as the Collects from the Book of Common Prayer (1552).

I also express gratitude to my wife, Jackie, who lovingly supports me in these projects. Jackie makes our home beau-

2   Justin Holcomb, *God with Us: 365 Devotions on the Person and Work of Christ* (Bloomington, MN: Bethany, 2021).

3   *ESV Prayer Bible: Prayers from the Past, Hope for the Present* (Wheaton, IL: Crossway, 2018); Jonathan Gibson and Mark Earngey, eds., *Reformation Worship: Liturgies from the Past for the Present* (Greensboro, NC: New Growth Press, 2018).

tiful and welcoming each Advent and Christmas, which is one of the reasons I enjoy the season so much. To say that our children Benjamin, Zachary, and Hannah love Christmas would be an understatement. But our prayer is that as they dive into the season, they would also delight in the Savior, pondering by faith the wondrous mystery that "a stable once had something inside it that was bigger than our whole world" (C. S. Lewis).[4]

Amidst the fun and festivities of Christmas we are reminded of the empty space at the table. Our sweet Leila died in the spring, yet Christmas is one of the times we miss her the most. Three "Leila ornaments" hang on the tree in her absence. As they sparkle in the twinkling lights, they make us long for Christ's glorious appearing as we think upon his first humble appearing:

O come, Thou Key of David, come,
and open wide our heav'nly home;
make safe the way that leads on high,
and close the path to misery.

This book is affectionately dedicated to our dear friends Simon and Rebecca. In the Lord's providence, our paths crossed nearly twenty years ago, and we have remained friends and partners in the gospel since. Jackie and I are grateful for their love, prayers, and support over many years and in various ways. It is an honor to dedicate this book to them as fellow saints in Christ's church and fellow servants in Christ's vineyard. My prayer is that this liturgy may enrich

4   C. S. Lewis, *The Last Battle* in The Chronicles of Narnia (London: HarperCollins, 2001), 744.

our worship during the Christmas season as together we celebrate the birth of our Lord Jesus:

Mild he lays his glory by,
born that man no more may die,
born to raise the sons of earth,
born to give them second birth.

PART 1

PREPARATION FOR DAILY WORSHIP FROM ADVENT TO EPIPHANY

1

Waiting for Jesus

AS EARLY AS EDEN, God's people have been a waiting people. Following the fall of our first parents, God made a promise that permanently oriented his people toward the future. God told the serpent directly, and the guilty pair indirectly:

I will put enmity between you and the woman,
   and between your offspring and her offspring;
he shall bruise your head,
   and you shall bruise his heel. (Gen. 3:15)

It was, in short, the promise of a coming, conquering son. The promise encapsulated every promise in the Old Testament and, as such, shaped God's people into a waiting people. This anticipatory posture can be seen throughout the Old Testament, as men and women of faith look forward to what God would do in the future through a promised son. Lamech names his son Noah in the hope that he will rescue the chosen line from the curse of sin and death (Gen. 5:29), yet it is six hundred years before Noah enters the ark at the time of the flood (Gen. 7:6). God promises Abraham that he will make him into a great nation through a son from his own body (Gen. 12:2; 15:4; 17:16), but he has to wait twenty-five years for the birth of Isaac (Gen. 21:1–3). Isaac, in turn, has to wait twenty years for the birth of Esau and Jacob, his twin boys (Gen. 25:20, 26). Jacob works for seven years to get his wife Rachel but in the end is deceived into marrying Leah (Gen. 29:20–30), from whom he receives Judah, the son of the promised line (Gen. 29:35; 49:10). Naomi has to wait to see if her line will continue, following the death of her husband and two sons. Even when her daughter-in-law Ruth faithfully follows her back to the promised land and pursues Boaz at the threshing floor, they both have to wait to see whether Boaz will be the kinsman to redeem Ruth (Ruth 3:12–18). Their godly patience allows Boaz to negotiate his way into marriage with Ruth, from whom comes Obed, the father of Jesse, the father of David (Ruth 4:18–22). It is only in Naomi's old age that her life is restored (Ruth 4:15). Hannah has to endure years of barrenness, like the matriarchs preceding her, before the Lord opens her womb and gives her a son called Samuel (1 Sam. 1:1–20), the one who would anoint David as God's chosen king (1 Sam. 16:1–3). However, David's ascension to the throne does not come immediately. While he is anointed in his youth (1 Sam. 16:10–13), he has to go through several years of humiliation and suffering before his ascension to the throne at thirty years old (2 Sam. 5:4); and God's subsequent promise to David that his son will sit on his throne forever (2 Sam. 7:12–16) is not ultimately fulfilled until the coming of his greater son, Jesus Christ—some one thousand years later. Indeed, adding up the ages in the biblical genealogies reveals that God's promise in Eden of a coming, conquering son takes about four thousand years to become a reality.

Waiting. From the beginning of history, God calls his people to be a people waiting for the coming of his promised Son. New Testament writers capture the relief at Jesus's arrival after the prolonged wait. Luke the evangelist describes Simeon as a righteous and devout man who has been "waiting for the consolation of Israel" (Luke 2:25). Taking Jesus in his arms, Simeon utters words that would become an integral part of Christian liturgy from the early centuries of the church—the *Nunc Dimittis*:

Lord, now you are letting your servant depart in peace,
    according to your word;
for my eyes have seen your salvation
that you have prepared in the presence of all peoples,
a light for revelation to the Gentiles,
    and for glory to your people Israel. (Luke 2:29–32)

The prophetess Anna has a similar experience on the same day, as she gazes upon the baby Jesus. Unable to contain her excitement, she speaks about Christ "to all who were waiting for the redemption of Jerusalem" (Luke 2:38).

The same is true at the end of Christ's life as well as the beginning. Joseph of Arimathea, a respected member of the Jerusalem Council, is described as one who is waiting for the kingdom of God (Luke 23:51). In the events bookending Christ's life, there is a remnant in Israel waiting for the day of salvation, waiting for the kingdom of God. The apostle Paul describes it as the "end of the ages" dawning (1 Cor. 10:11). It is a long, long wait. But it is not a minute too late. As Paul explains: "But when the fullness of time had come,

God sent forth his Son, born of woman, born under the law, to redeem those who were under the law, so that we might receive adoption as sons" (Gal. 4:4–5).

Although the longings, hopes, and expectations of the coming, conquering son are met in Jesus's first coming, it does not change the reality that God's people are a waiting people. Following Jesus's ascension to his Father's right hand, New Testament believers are still called to adopt the same anticipatory posture. In his Farewell Discourse, Jesus tells his disciples that he is going away to prepare a place for them but that he will come again to bring them to that heavenly home prepared for them (John 14:3). He promises, "I will not leave you as orphans; I will come to you" (John 14:18). Jesus also speaks about it in parables:

> Stay dressed for action and keep your lamps burning, and be like men who are waiting for their master to come home from the wedding feast, so that they may open the door to him at once when he comes and knocks. (Luke 12:35–36)

The angels reiterate this truth to the apostles as they gaze upward to the sky following Jesus's departure: "This Jesus, who was taken up from you into heaven, will come in the same way as you saw him go into heaven" (Acts 1:11). This "coming again" shapes the posture of God's New Testament church into an anticipatory people, just like his people in the Old Testament.

The apostles reveal the same mindset when they write plainly of "waiting" for the "revealing of our Lord Jesus Christ" (1 Cor. 1:7), for "the hope of righteousness" (Gal. 5:5), for God's "Son from heaven" (1 Thess. 1:10), for "the appearing of the glory of our great God and Savior Jesus Christ" (Titus 2:13), for "the mercy of our Lord Jesus Christ that leads to eternal life" (Jude 21). Indeed, the apostle John closes the Christian canon with words that remind us of Jesus's promise and our longing: "'Surely I am coming soon.' Amen. Come, Lord Jesus!" (Rev. 22:20)

In both dispensations of redemptive history, the people of God are defined by *waiting*. In the Old Testament, believers wait for Jesus's first coming; in the New Testament, believers wait for his second coming. In both cases, God's people live in the light of Christ's advent.

The observance of Christ's advent has been expressed in the liturgy of the Christian church for over two millennia. Each Lord's Day as the gospel is preached or the sacrament of the Lord's Supper is administered, believers are reminded that Jesus is coming again. Whether it be the threatening word about the "day appointed" or the comforting word "until he comes," each Lord's Day we are reminded of the need to adopt an expectant posture. As Christians, we are waiting for God's Son to be revealed from heaven. This has been so since the days of the apostles.

However, since the days of the early church, Christians have also observed a time in the church calendar for a more focused concentration on the second coming of Christ, known as Advent. Its origins go back to the fourth century when converts prepared themselves for baptism. As the centuries passed, the season of Advent became more directly connected to Christmas—a time to consider Christ's second coming as Christians reflected on his first coming. Often it involved a period of fasting and prayer (Advent is also known as "Little Lent") in preparation for the celebration of Christ's birth on December 25 (in the Western church) or January 6 (in the Eastern church). Contrary to popular opinion, the date of Christ's birth on December 25 is not due to a pagan holiday that has been repurposed by Christians; rather, the date is based on a belief that Christ died around the same time he was conceived. The two dates commonly held for his death are March 25 (in the Western church) and April 6 (in the Eastern church). If this was the date on which he was also conceived, then his birth would have been around December 25 or January 6, depending on the respective church tradition.

Although some of the Reformers stopped the practice of observing feast days and the fasting periods associated with them, some branches of the Reformed church kept the more gospel-oriented feast days. For example, in the Swiss Reformed church in Zürich, Huldrych Zwingli and Heinrich Bullinger continued to observe Christmas, the Circumcision of Christ, Easter, Ascension, and Pentecost. Under the influence of Zacharias Ursinus, one of the authors of the Heidelberg Catechism, the Palatinate church did the same. In Geneva, although he did not want the day to be elevated to the same status as the Lord's Day, John Calvin adopted a "moderate course" of observing Christ's birth on Christmas Day. On one occasion, he suspended his practice of *lectio continua* to preach on Christ's nativity during the Christmas season. At the Synod of Dort in 1618–1619, the Dutch Reformed Church codified the keeping of Christmas, the Circumcision of Christ, Easter, Ascension, and Pentecost in their canons of church order (see articles 63 and 67). Today Christmas is observed in some way in most Protestant denominations, often along with Advent, as a time of meditative preparation for celebrating the birth of Christ. Of course, meditating on the first and second comings of Christ is something we do each Lord's Day; however, there is also spiritual benefit in setting aside a period in the church calendar each year to contemplate more deliberately the two advents of our Lord.

The aim of this devotional liturgy, designed for daily worship from Advent to Epiphany, is to prepare us better for the season in which we wait in earnest for Christ's second coming while we wonder in awe at his first coming. To be clear, the season is not about what we can do for Christ by our work or prayers or fasting; rather, it is about what he has done for us in *his* work and prayers and fasting—a work that began in his first coming in humility and which will conclude in his second coming in glory. In the meantime, as we live between these two advents of Christ, we sing with the hymnwriter of old:

O come, O come, Emmanuel,
and rescue captive Israel.

2

Format of Daily Worship
from Advent to Epiphany

THIS DAILY WORSHIP DEVOTIONAL consists of forty days of set liturgy for the season of Advent, Christmas, and Epiphany. Traditionally, Advent begins on the Sunday between November 27 and December 3 each year, while Epiphany is observed on January 6 or the Sunday during Epiphany week. In this devotional, Advent begins on November 28 and Epiphany ends on January 6, constituting forty days in total. The order of the elements in the liturgy is fixed and repeated each day, while the content of the elements changes each day, except for the Lord's Prayer and postlude. The order and content of the elements is as follows, accompanied by a rubric to make the liturgy interactive:

Meditation
Reflect on these words about the incarnation of the Lord Jesus:
Forty meditations from church history

Call to Worship

Hear God call you to worship through his word:
Forty Scripture readings (alternating Old Testament and New Testament daily)

Adoration

Say or sing this praise to God:
Forty hymns or psalms from church history relevant to Advent, Christmas, and Epiphany (a psalm occurs every seven days, except for Christmas Day)

Reading of the Law

Hear God's law as his will for your life:
Seven Scripture readings (repeated weekly)

Confession of Sin

Confess your sins to God:
Forty prayers from church history (a prayer by Martin Bucer is used on Christmas Day, Circumcision of Christ, and Epiphany)

Assurance of Pardon

Receive these words of comfort from God:
Forty Scripture readings (alternating Old Testament and New Testament daily)

Creed

Confess what you believe about the Christian faith:
Apostles' Creed | Nicene Creed | Athanasian Creed (3 parts) (repeated weekly in a chiasm: Apostles' | Nicene | Athanasian 1, 2, 3 | Nicene | Apostles')

Praise

Say or sing this praise to God:

Gloria Patri (traditional) | Doxology (traditional) | *Gloria Patri* (alternative 1) | Doxology (alternative) | *Gloria Patri* (alternative 2) (each repeated weekly; January 2–6 each repeated daily)

Catechism

Receive this instruction from one of the church's catechisms:

Select Q&As from Heidelberg Catechism and Westminster Shorter Catechism related to the coming of Christ to save us from our sin (1–2 questions daily)

Prayer for Illumination

As you read his word, ask God to enlighten your mind and heart:

Seven prayers from church history (repeated weekly)

Scripture Reading

Read this portion of God's word: . . .

Select Advent, Christmas, and Epiphany readings from Old and New Testaments: Old Testament readings about the coming of Christ prior to December 22; then Nativity readings from December 22 onward, before concluding with some Epiphany readings up to January 6

Praise

Say or sing this praise to God:

November 28–December 16

Liturgical prayers or praises from church history up to December 16 (repeated weekly):

Es ist ein Ros entsprungen (verses 1, 2, 4, 6) | Magnificat | Benedictus | Nunc Dimittis | Sanctus | Phos Hilaron | Corde Natus (verses 1, 2, 6, 7)

December 17–23
Liturgical Advent "O Antiphons" hymns from December 17 to 23 (one each daily)

December 24
"O Holy Night"

December 25–January 6
Liturgical prayers or praises from church history up to January 6 (repeated weekly):
Sileat Omnis Caro Mortalis | *Magnificat* | *Benedictus* | *Nunc Dimittis* and *Sanctus* | *Gloria in Excelsis* | *Phos Hilaron* | *Corde Natus* (verses 3, 4, 5, 9)

Prayer of Intercession
As you make your requests to God, pray this prayer:
Forty prayers from church history

Further Petition
- Personal
- Church
- World

Lord's Prayer
Pray the words that Jesus taught us to pray:
Traditional or modern version (repeated daily)

Benediction
Receive by faith this blessing from God:
Seven benedictions (repeated weekly): Numbers 6:24–26 | Romans 15:13 | 2 Corinthians 13:14 | Ephesians 3:20–21 | 1 Thessalonians 5:23–24 | 2 Peter 1:2 | Jude 24–25

Postlude

In closing, say or sing this praise to God:
Doxology based on Psalm 72:17–19 (repeated daily)

As in *Be Thou My Vision*, the fixed order of the elements is to aid concentration, while the variety of content in the elements is to avoid boredom. The repetition of Scripture readings, prayers, creeds, praises, benedictions, postludes (repeated every seven or forty days) encourages familiarity and memorization. If one follows this liturgy of worship each day throughout the season of Advent to Epiphany, then one will become well acquainted with the creeds of the Christian church and also historic (and seasonal) prayers throughout church history—some of which were written for corporate worship on the Lord's Day, others of which were written for personal or family worship on any day, and still others of which were written for the season. After the set prayer of intercession, there is a time for further petitions covering personal, church, or world matters, as the individual or family desires. The Lord's Prayer, which closes the time of intercessory prayer, may be said in whatever version with which one is most familiar. (The modern version is provided in the liturgy.) Each day's liturgy closes with a scriptural benediction followed by a doxological postlude based on Psalm 72:17–19.

If one is using the liturgy for personal worship, then the rubric may be read silently, as if one is being led in worship. If one is using the liturgy for family worship, then the person leading may read the rubric aloud, while other family members might wish to read some of the prayers or Bible passages to ensure a collective participation. In either case, it is best practice to read the content of the elements *aloud*. This adds a level of formality that will help concentration and deepen a sense of worship. The musical tunes for the three versions of the *Gloria Patri*, the two versions of the Doxology, and the postlude Doxology based on Psalm 72:17–19 are indicated in appendix 1. The ribbons serve to help the worshiper(s): (1) mark the day; (2) mark the appendix for the musical tunes for the hymns or psalms of adoration as well as the different versions of *Gloria Patri* and Doxology; and (3) mark the seasonal reading plan if one wishes to have a comprehensive view of the Scripture readings covered during Advent, Christmas, and Epiphany. In practice, the daily worship time (allowing for the allocated Bible reading, usually a single chapter) will take about 15 to 20 minutes. On days when circumstances may restrict one's time more than other days, the liturgy allows for flexibility by dropping some of the elements, such as the meditation, the creed and/or catechism, and the postlude. If some days are missed in the week or season, then one may use the Lord's Day to catch up on the seasonal Bible readings in order to enjoy the full scriptural focus on the coming, birth, and appearing of Christ.

Since the beginning of time, it has been God's plan to fill heaven and earth with the praise of his name. By grace, we have been swept up into this plan through faith in his Son, Jesus Christ. This liturgy of daily worship from Advent to Epiphany aims to help us worship God by meditating on the first coming of his Son while we wait for the second coming of his Son.

As for me, I will look to the LORD;
I will wait for the God of my salvation. (Mic. 7:7)

PART 2

PRACTICE OF DAILY WORSHIP FROM ADVENT TO EPIPHANY

November 28

Meditation

Reflect on these words about the incarnation of the Lord Jesus:

We preach not one advent only of Christ, but a second also, far more glorious than the former. For the former gave a view of His patience; but the latter brings with it the crown of a divine kingdom. For all things, for the most part, are twofold in our Lord Jesus Christ: a twofold generation: one of God, before the ages; and one, of a virgin, at the close of the ages; His descents twofold: one, the unobserved, like rain on a fleece; and a second, His open coming, which is to be. In His former advent, He was wrapped in swaddling clothes in the manger; in His second, He covers Himself with light as with a garment. In His first coming, He endured the cross, despising shame; in His second, He comes attended by a host of angels, receiving glory. We rest not upon His first advent only, but look also for His second. And as at His first coming, we said, "Blessed is He that comes in the Name of the Lord," so will we repeat the same at His second coming; that when with angels we meet our Master, we may worship Him and say, "Blessed is He that comes in the Name of the Lord."   *Cyril of Jerusalem*

Call to Worship

Hear God call you to worship through his word:

It will be said on that day,
   "Behold, this is our God; we have waited for him, that
         he might save us.
   This is the LORD; we have waited for him;
   let us be glad and rejoice in his salvation."   *Isaiah 25:9*

Adoration

Say or sing the words of this Advent hymn:

Come, Thou long-expected Jesus,
Born to set Thy people free;
From our fears and sins release us,
Let us find our rest in Thee.
Israel's Strength and Consolation,
Hope of all the earth Thou art;
Dear Desire of every nation,
Joy of every longing heart.

Joy to those who long to see Thee,
Dayspring from on high, appear.
Come, Thou promised Rod of Jesse,
Of Thy birth, we long to hear!
O'er the hills the angels singing
News, glad tidings of a birth;
"Go to Him your praises bringing
Christ the Lord has come to earth!"

Come to earth to taste our sadness,
He whose glories knew no end.
By His life He brings us gladness,

Our Redeemer, Shepherd, Friend.
Leaving riches without number,
Born within a cattle stall;
This the everlasting wonder,
Christ was born the Lord of all.

Born Thy people to deliver,
Born a child and yet a King,
Born to reign in us forever,
Now Thy gracious kingdom bring.
By Thine own eternal Spirit
Rule in all our hearts alone;
By Thine all-sufficient merit,
Raise us to Thy glorious throne.   *Charles Wesley*

Reading of the Law
Hear God's law as his will for your life:

The words of our Lord Jesus Christ:

You shall love the Lord your God with all your heart and with
all your soul and with all your mind. This is the great and first
commandment. And a second is like it: You shall love your
neighbor as yourself. On these two commandments depend
all the Law and the Prophets.   *Matthew 22:37–40*

Confession of Sin
Confess your sins to God:

Almighty God,
　　unto whom all hearts are open,
　　all desires known,
　　and from whom no secrets are hidden—

cleanse the thoughts of our hearts
by the inspiration of your Holy Spirit,
so that we may perfectly love you,
and worthily magnify your holy name;
through Christ our Lord. Amen.

Book of Common Prayer (1552)

Assurance of Pardon
Receive these words of comfort from God:

Come to me, all who labor and are heavy laden, and I will give
you rest. Take my yoke upon you, and learn from me, for I am
gentle and lowly in heart, and you will find rest for your souls.
For my yoke is easy, and my burden is light.   *Matthew 11:28–30*

Apostles' Creed
Confess what you believe about the Christian faith:

I believe in God the Father Almighty,
Maker of heaven and earth.

I believe in Jesus Christ, his only-begotten Son, our Lord;
who was conceived by the Holy Spirit, born of the
Virgin Mary;
suffered under Pontius Pilate;
was crucified, dead, and buried;
he descended into hell;
the third day he rose again from the dead;
he ascended into heaven,
and sits at the right hand of God the Father Almighty;
from there he shall come to judge the living and the dead.

I believe in the Holy Spirit;
   the holy catholic church;
   the communion of saints;
   the forgiveness of sins;
   the resurrection of the body;
   and the life everlasting. Amen.

Praise
Say or sing this praise to God:

Glory be to the Father,
   and to the Son,
   and to the Holy Spirit:
As it was in the beginning,
   is now and ever shall be,
   world without end. Amen.   *Gloria Patri*

Catechism
Receive this instruction from the Heidelberg Catechism:

Q. 12. According to God's righteous judgment we deserve punishment both now and in eternity: how then can we escape this punishment and return to God's favor?
A. God requires that his justice be satisfied. Therefore the claims of this justice must be paid in full, either by ourselves or by another.

Q. 13. Can we make this payment ourselves?
A. Certainly not. Actually, we increase our debt every day.

Prayer for Illumination

As you read his word, ask God to enlighten your mind and heart:

Merciful Lord, the comforter and teacher of your faithful people, increase in your church the desires which you have given, and confirm the hearts of those who hope in you by enabling them to understand the depth of your promises, that all of your adopted sons may even now behold, with the eyes of faith, and patiently wait for, the light which as yet you do not openly manifest; through Jesus Christ our Lord. Amen.   *Ambrose*

Scripture Reading

Read this portion of God's word: Genesis 3:1–15

Praise

Say or sing this praise to God:

Es ist ein Ros entsprungen

Lo, how a rose e'er blooming,
From tender stem has sprung.
Of Jesse's lineage coming,
As men of old have sung;
It came, a flow'ret bright,
Amid the cold of winter,
When half spent was the night.

Isaiah 'twas foretold it,
The Rose I have in mind,
With Mary, we behold it,
The virgin mother kind;
To show God's love aright,

She bore to men a Savior,
When half spent was the night.

O Flower, whose fragrance tender
With sweetness fills the air,
Dispel with glorious splendor
The darkness everywhere;
True man, yet very God,
From sin and death now save us,
And share our every load.

O Savior, Child of Mary,
Who felt our human woe;
O Savior, King of Glory,
Who does our weakness know,
Bring us at length we pray,
To the bright courts of Heaven
And to the endless day.   *Anonymous*

Prayer of Intercession

As you make your requests to God, pray this prayer:

Almighty God, give us grace, that we may cast away the works of darkness, and put upon us the armor of light, now in the time of this mortal life, in which your Son Jesus Christ came to visit us in great humility; that in the last day when he shall come again in his glorious majesty to judge both the living and the dead, we may rise to the life immortal, through him who lives and reigns with you and the Holy Spirit, now and forever. Amen.   *Book of Common Prayer (1552)*

Further Petition

- Personal
- Church
- World

Lord's Prayer

Pray the words that Jesus taught us to pray:

Our Father in heaven,
   hallowed be your name;
   your kingdom come;
   your will be done, on earth as it is in heaven.
   Give us this day our daily bread.
   And forgive us our debts, as we forgive our debtors.
   And lead us not into temptation but deliver us from evil.
   For yours is the kingdom, and the power,
   and the glory, forever. Amen.

Benediction

Receive by faith this blessing from God:

The LORD bless you and keep you;
The LORD make his face to shine upon you
   and be gracious to you;
The LORD lift up his countenance upon you
   and give you peace.   *Numbers 6:24–26*

Postlude

In closing, say or sing this praise to God:

His Name for ever shall endure,
   last like the sun it shall;

Men shall be blessed in Him, and blessed
    all nations shall Him call.

Now blessèd be the Lord, our God,
    the God of Israel,
For He alone does wondrous works,
    in glory that excel.

And blessèd be His glorious Name
    to all eternity;
The whole earth let His glory fill.
    Amen, so let it be.   *Based on Psalm 72:17–19*

November 29

Reflect on these words about the incarnation of the Lord Jesus:

What we have said will be clearer once we understand that the role of Mediator was no ordinary one, in the sense that his task was to so restore us to God's grace as to make us, the children of men, children of God, and to make us who were heirs of hell, heirs of the heavenly kingdom. Who could have accomplished that except the Son of God who was made Son of Man, who so took our condition upon himself that he transferred his to us, and who made what was his by nature ours by grace? So we are confident that we are children of God, having this as our guarantee, that God's natural Son took his body from ours, flesh of our flesh and bone of our bone, that he might be united to us. What was ours he took into his own person so that what was his should belong to us, and thus that, in common with us, he might be both Son of God and Son of man. That is why we have hope that the heavenly inheritance is ours, because only God's Son to whom it was wholly due has adopted us as his brothers. Now if we are brothers, we are co-heirs with him.   *John Calvin*

Call to Worship

Hear God call you to worship through his word:

For the grace of God has appeared, bringing salvation for all people, training us to renounce ungodliness and worldly passions, and to live self-controlled, upright, and godly lives in the present age, waiting for our blessed hope, the appearing of the glory of our great God and Savior Jesus Christ, who gave himself for us to redeem us from all lawlessness and to purify for himself a people for his own possession who are zealous for good works.   *Titus 2:11–14*

Adoration

Say or sing this praise to God:

The advent of our King
our prayers must now employ,
and we must hymns of welcome sing
in strains of holy joy.

The everlasting Son
incarnate deigns to be;
himself a servant's form puts on,
to set his servants free.

Daughter of Zion, rise
to meet your lowly King;
nor let your faithless heart despise
the peace he comes to bring.

As judge, on clouds of light,
he soon will come again,
and his true members all unite
with him in heaven to reign.

All glory to the Son
who comes to set us free,
with Father, Spirit, ever One,
through all eternity.   *Charles Coffin*

Reading of the Law
Hear God's law as his will for your life:

Hear, O Israel: The LORD our God, the LORD is one.
You shall love the LORD your God with all your heart and
   with all your soul and with all your might.
And these words that I command you today shall be on
   your heart.
You shall teach them diligently to your children,
 and shall talk of them when you sit in your house,
 and when you walk by the way,
 and when you lie down,
 and when you rise.
You shall bind them as a sign on your hand,
 and they shall be as frontlets between your eyes.
You shall write them on the doorposts of your house and
   on your gates.   *Deuteronomy 6:4–9*

Confession of Sin
Confess your sins to God:

O Lord, in whose hands are life and death, by whose power I
am sustained, and by whose mercy I am spared—look down
upon me with pity. Forgive me that I have until now so much
neglected the duty which you have assigned to me, and suffered the days and hours of which I must give account to pass
away without any endeavor to accomplish your will. Make me

to remember, O God, that every day is your gift, and ought to be used according to your command. Grant me, therefore, so to repent of my negligence, that I may obtain mercy from you, and pass the time which you shall yet allow me in diligent performance of your commands, through Jesus Christ. Amen.   *Samuel Johnson*

Assurance of Pardon
Receive these words of comfort from God:

"The LORD, the LORD, a God merciful and gracious, slow to anger, and abounding in steadfast love and faithfulness, keeping steadfast love for thousands, forgiving iniquity and transgression and sin."   *Exodus 34:6–7*

Nicene Creed
Confess what you believe about the Christian faith:

I believe in one God, the Father Almighty,
    Maker of heaven and earth, and of all things visible and
        invisible.

And in one Lord Jesus Christ, the only-begotten Son of God;
    begotten of the Father before all worlds;
    God of God, Light of Light, very God of very God;
    begotten, not made, being of one substance with the
        Father;
    by whom all things were made.
Who, for us men and for our salvation,
    came down from heaven
    and was incarnate by the Holy Spirit of the Virgin Mary,
    and was made man;
    and was crucified also for us under Pontius Pilate;

he suffered and was buried;
and the third day he rose again, according to the Scriptures;
and ascended into heaven, and sits on the right hand of
      the Father;
and he shall come again, with glory, to judge the living
      and the dead;
whose kingdom shall have no end.

And I believe in the Holy Spirit, the Lord and Giver of life;
who proceeds from the Father and the Son;
who with the Father and the Son together is worshiped
      and glorified;
who spoke by the prophets.

And I believe in one holy catholic and apostolic church.
I acknowledge one baptism for the forgiveness of sins;
and I look for the resurrection of the dead,
and the life of the world to come. Amen.

Praise
Say or sing this praise to God:

Glory be to the Father,
    and to the Son,
    and to the Holy Spirit:
As it was in the beginning,
    is now and ever shall be,
    world without end. Amen.   *Gloria Patri*

Catechism
Receive this instruction from the Heidelberg Catechism:

Q. 14. *Can another creature—any at all—pay this debt for us?*

A. No. To begin with, God will not punish any other creature for what a human is guilty of. Furthermore, no mere creature can bear the weight of God's eternal wrath against sin and deliver others from it.

Prayer for Illumination
As you read his word, ask God to enlighten your mind and heart:

Heavenly Father, may you grant us to comprehend your holy Word according to your divine will, that we may learn from it to put all our confidence in you alone, and withdraw it from all other creatures; moreover, that also our old man with all his lusts may be crucified more and more each day, and that we may offer ourselves to you as a living sacrifice, to the glory of your holy name and to the edification of our neighbor, through our Lord Jesus Christ. Amen.
Zacharias Ursinus

Scripture Reading
Read this portion of God's word: Genesis 22:1–19

Praise
Say this praise to God:

My soul magnifies the Lord.
And my spirit rejoices in God my Savior.
For he has regarded the lowliness of his servant.
For behold, from now on all generations shall call me blessed.
For he who is mighty has magnified me, and holy is his Name.
And his mercy is on them that fear him, throughout all
        generations.
He has showed strength with his arm.

He has scattered the proud in the imagination of their hearts.
He has put down the mighty from their thrones, and has
exalted the humble and meek.
He has filled the hungry with good things, and the rich he
has sent away empty.
He, remembering his mercy, has helped his servant Israel,
as he promised to our forefathers, Abraham and
his seed, forever.

Glory be to the Father, and to the Son, and to the Holy
Spirit:
As it was in the beginning, is now, and ever shall be, world
without end. Amen.   *Magnificat*

Prayer of Intercession
As you make your requests to God, pray this prayer:

O Almighty God, who fills all things with your presence,
and is a God afar off as well as near at hand—you sent your
angel to bless Jacob in his journey and you led the children
of Israel through the Red Sea, making it a wall on the right
hand and on the left. Be pleased to let your angel go out
before me and guide me in my journey, preserving me from
dangers of robbers, from violence of enemies, and sudden and
sad accidents, from falls and errors. And prosper my journey
to your glory, and to all my innocent purposes; and preserve
me from all sin, that I may return in peace and holiness, with
your favor and your blessing, and may serve you in thankful-
ness and obedience all the days of my pilgrimage; and at last
bring me to your country, to the celestial Jerusalem, there to
dwell in your house and to sing praises to you forever. Amen.
Jeremy Taylor

Further Petition
- Personal
- Church
- World

Lord's Prayer
Pray the words that Jesus taught us to pray:

Our Father in heaven,
    hallowed be your name;
    your kingdom come;
    your will be done, on earth as it is in heaven.
    Give us this day our daily bread.
    And forgive us our debts, as we forgive our debtors.
    And lead us not into temptation but deliver us from evil.
    For yours is the kingdom, and the power,
    and the glory, forever. Amen.

Benediction
Receive by faith this blessing from God:

May the God of hope fill you with all joy and peace in believing, so that by the power of the Holy Spirit you may abound in hope.   Romans 15:13

Postlude
In closing, say or sing this praise to God:

His Name for ever shall endure,
    last like the sun it shall;
Men shall be blessed in Him, and blessed
    all nations shall Him call.

Now blessèd be the Lord, our God,
    the God of Israel,
For He alone does wondrous works,
    in glory that excel.

And blessèd be His glorious Name
    to all eternity;
The whole earth let His glory fill.
    Amen, so let it be.   *Based on Psalm 72:17–19*

November 30

Meditation

Reflect on these words about the incarnation of the Lord Jesus:

The infinite became finite, the eternal and supratemporal entered time and became subject to its conditions, the immutable became mutable, the invisible became the visible, the Creator became the created, the Sustainer of all became dependent, the Almighty infirm. All is summed up in the proposition, "God became man."   *John Murray*

———

Call to Worship

Hear God call you to worship through his word:

Oh that you would rend the heavens and come down,
    that the mountains might quake at your presence—
as when fire kindles brushwood
    and the fire causes water to boil—
to make your name known to your adversaries,
    and that the nations might tremble at your presence!
Isaiah 64:1–2

Adoration

Say or sing this praise to God:

O Savior, rend the heavens wide!
Come down, come down with mighty stride.
Unbar the gates, the doors break down;
unbar the way to heaven's crown.

O Dayspring, dew from heaven send.
As gentle dew, O Son, descend.
Drop down, you clouds, and torrents bring,
to Jacob's line rain down a King.

O earth, in flowering bud be seen,
clothe hill and dale in garb of green.
O earth, bring forth this Blossom rare;
O Savior, rise from meadow fair.

Here dreadful doom upon us lies;
Death looms so grim before our eyes.
O come, lead us with mighty hand
from exile to our promised land.

There will we all our praises bring
ever to you, our Savior King.
There will we laud you and adore
forever and forevermore.   *Friedrich von Spee*

Reading of the Law

Hear God's law as his will for your life:

Our Lord Jesus said,

Blessed are the poor in spirit,
    for theirs is the kingdom of heaven.

Blessed are those who mourn,
  for they shall be comforted.
Blessed are the meek,
  for they shall inherit the earth.
Blessed are those who hunger and thirst for righteousness,
  for they shall be satisfied.
Blessed are the merciful,
  for they shall receive mercy.
Blessed are the pure in heart,
  for they shall see God.
Blessed are the peacemakers,
  for they shall be called sons of God.
Blessed are those who are persecuted for righteousness'
    sake,
  for theirs is the kingdom of heaven.   *Matthew 5:3–10*

Confession of Sin
Confess your sins to God:

O Lord, you have mercy upon all—take away from me my
sins, and mercifully kindle in me the fire of your Holy Spirit.
Take away from me the heart of stone, and give me a heart
of flesh, a heart to love and adore you, a heart to delight in
you, to follow and to enjoy you, for Christ's sake. Amen.
Ambrose

Assurance of Pardon
Receive these words of comfort from God:

For God so loved the world, that he gave his only Son, that
whoever believes in him should not perish but have eternal life.   *John 3:16*

Athanasian Creed, Part I
Confess what you believe about the Christian faith:

Whoever desires to be saved should above all hold to the catholic faith. Anyone who does not keep it whole and unbroken will doubtless perish eternally. Now this is the catholic faith:

that we worship one God in Trinity and the Trinity in unity, neither confounding their persons nor dividing the essence.

> For the person of the Father is a distinct person,
>> the person of the Son is another,
>> and that of the Holy Spirit still another.
> But the divinity of the Father, Son, and Holy Spirit is one,
>> the glory equal, the majesty coeternal.
> Such as the Father is, such is the Son and such is the
>> Holy Spirit.
> The Father is uncreated, the Son is uncreated, the Holy
>> Spirit is uncreated.
> The Father is immeasurable, the Son is immeasurable,
>> the Holy Spirit is immeasurable.
> The Father is eternal, the Son is eternal, the Holy Spirit
>> is eternal.
> And yet there are not three eternal beings; there is but
>> one eternal being.
> So too there are not three uncreated or immeasurable
>> beings;
>> there is but one uncreated and immeasurable being.
> Similarly, the Father is almighty, the Son is almighty,
>> the Holy Spirit is almighty.
> Yet there are not three almighty beings; there is but one
>> almighty being.

Thus, the Father is God, the Son is God, the Holy Spirit
is God.
Yet there are not three gods; there is but one God.
Thus, the Father is Lord, the Son is Lord, the Holy Spirit
is Lord.
Yet there are not three lords; there is but one Lord.
Just as Christian truth compels us to confess each person
individually as both God and Lord,
so catholic religion forbids us to say that there are
three gods or lords.

Praise
Say or sing this praise to God:

Glory be to the Father,
and to the Son,
and to the Holy Spirit:
As it was in the beginning,
is now and ever shall be,
world without end. Amen.   *Gloria Patri*

Catechism
Receive this instruction from the Heidelberg Catechism:

Q. 15. *What kind of mediator and deliverer should we look for then?*
A. One who is a true and righteous man, yet more powerful
than all creatures, that is, one who is also true God.

Prayer for Illumination
As you read his word, ask God to enlighten your mind and heart:

Lord, you know what distracted hearts we have, O give us
self-recollection; you know what hard, dead hearts we have,

O touch and awaken us! You know how we yet resist your Word and our lower nature is reluctant to bow to your scepter; therefore, O Lord, show forth your power; send your Spirit on high to work among us, to make our hearts submissive, and ourselves capable of living in true union with you, our salvation, and of yielding totally to your grace. Amen.
Gerhard Tersteegen

Scripture Reading
Read this portion of God's word: Genesis 49:1–12

Praise
Say this praise to God:

Blessed be the Lord God of Israel, for he has visited,
    and redeemed his people;
and has raised up a mighty salvation for us,
    in the house of his servant David;
as he spoke by the mouth of his holy prophets,
    which have been since the world began;
that we should be saved from our enemies,
    and from the hands of all that hate us;
to perform the mercy promised to our forefathers,
    and to remember his holy covenant;
to perform the oath which he swore to our forefather
        Abraham,
    that he would give us;
that we, being delivered out of the hands of our enemies,
    might serve him without fear;
in holiness and righteousness before him,
    all the days of our life.

And you, child, shall be called the prophet of the Most
       High,
   for you shall go before the face of the Lord to prepare his
          ways;
to give knowledge of salvation unto his people,
   for the remission of their sins,
through the tender mercy of our God,
   whereby the Dayspring from on high has visited us;
to give light to them that sit in darkness,
   and in the shadow of death,
and to guide our feet into the way of peace.

Glory be to the Father,
   and to the Son,
   and to the Holy Spirit:
As it was in the beginning,
   is now and ever shall be,
   world without end. Amen.   *Benedictus*

Prayer of Intercession
As you make your requests to God, pray this prayer:

Lord, without you I can do nothing; with you I can do all.
Help me by your grace, that I fall not; help me by your
strength, to resist mightily the very first beginnings of evil,
before it takes hold of me; help me to cast myself at once at
your sacred feet, and lie still there, until storm be overpast;
and, if I lose sight of you, bring me back quickly to you, and
grant me to love you better. Amen.   E. B. *Pusey*

Further Petition

- Personal
- Church
- World

Lord's Prayer

Pray the words that Jesus taught us to pray:

Our Father in heaven,
    hallowed be your name;
    your kingdom come;
    your will be done, on earth as it is in heaven.
    Give us this day our daily bread.
    And forgive us our debts, as we forgive our debtors.
    And lead us not into temptation but deliver us from evil.
    For yours is the kingdom, and the power,
    and the glory, forever. Amen.

Benediction

Receive by faith this blessing from God:

The grace of the Lord Jesus Christ and the love of God and the fellowship of the Holy Spirit be with you all.   *2 Corinthians 13:14*

Postlude

In closing, say or sing this praise to God:

His Name for ever shall endure,
    last like the sun it shall;
Men shall be blessed in Him, and blessed
    all nations shall Him call.

Now blessèd be the Lord, our God,
    the God of Israel,
For He alone does wondrous works,
    in glory that excel.

And blessèd be His glorious Name
    to all eternity;
The whole earth let His glory fill.
    Amen, so let it be.   *Based on Psalm 72:17–19*

December 1

Meditation

Reflect on these words about the incarnation of the Lord Jesus:

Man's Maker was made man, that He, Ruler of the stars, might nurse at His mother's breast; that the Bread might hunger, the Fountain thirst, the Light sleep, the Way be tired on its journey; that the Truth might be accused of false witness, the Teacher be beaten with whips, the Foundation be suspended on wood; that Strength might grow weak; that the Healer might be wounded; that Life might die.   *Augustine*

Call to Worship

Hear God call you to worship through his word:

Who, though he was in the form of God, did not count equality with God a thing to be grasped, but emptied himself, by taking the form of a servant, being born in the likeness of men. And being found in human form, he humbled himself by becoming obedient to the point of death, even death on a cross.   *Philippians 2:6–8*

Adoration

Say or sing this praise to God:

Creator of the starry height,
thy people's everlasting light,
Jesu, redeemer of us all,
hear thou thy servants when they call.

Thou, sorrowing at the helpless cry
of all creation doomed to die,
didst come to save our fallen race
by healing gifts of heavenly grace.

When earth was near its evening hour,
thou didst, in love's redeeming power,
like bridegroom from his chamber, come
forth from a virgin-mother's womb.

At thy great name, exalted now,
all knees in lowly homage bow;
all things in heaven and earth adore,
and own thee King for evermore.

To thee, O Holy One, we pray,
our judge in that tremendous day,
ward off, while yet we dwell below,
the weapons of our crafty foe.

To God the Father, God the Son,
and God the Spirit, Three in One,
praise, honour, might, and glory be
from age to age eternally.   *Anonymous*

Reading of the Law
Hear God's law as his will for your life:

Our Lord said,

As the Father has loved me, so have I loved you. Abide in my love. If you keep my commandments, you will abide in my love, just as I have kept my Father's commandments and abide in his love. These things I have spoken to you, that my joy may be in you, and that your joy may be full. This is my commandment, that you love one another as I have loved you.   *John 15:9–12*

Confession of Sin
Confess your sins to God:

Cleanse me from my secret faults, O Lord, and forgive those offenses to your servant which he has caused in others. I contend not in judgment with you, who are truth; I fear to deceive myself, lest my sin should make me think that I am not sinful. Therefore I contend not in judgment with you; for if you, Lord, should mark iniquities, O Lord, who shall abide it? Amen.   *Augustine*

Assurance of Pardon
Receive these words of comfort from God:

Oh, taste and see that the LORD is good!
  Blessed is the man who takes refuge in him!   *Psalm 34:8*

Athanasian Creed, Part 2

Confess what you believe about the Christian faith:

Whoever desires to be saved should above all hold to the catholic faith. Anyone who does not keep it whole and unbroken will doubtless perish eternally. Now this is the catholic faith:

that we worship one God in Trinity and the Trinity in unity, neither confounding their persons nor dividing the essence....

The Father was neither made nor created nor begotten
　　　from anyone.
The Son was neither made nor created; he was begotten
　　　from the Father alone.
The Holy Spirit was neither made nor created nor
　　　begotten;
　he proceeds from the Father and the Son.
Accordingly, there is one Father, not three fathers;
　there is one Son, not three sons;
　there is one Holy Spirit, not three holy spirits.
None in this Trinity is before or after, none is greater or
　　　smaller;
　in their entirety the three persons are coeternal and
　　　coequal with each other.
So in everything, as was said earlier, the unity in Trinity,
　　　and the Trinity in unity, is to be worshiped.
Anyone then who desires to be saved should think thus
　　　about the Trinity.

Praise
Say or sing this praise to God:

Glory be to the Father,
  and to the Son,
  and to the Holy Spirit:
As it was in the beginning,
  is now and ever shall be,
  world without end. Amen.   *Gloria Patri*

Catechism
Receive this instruction from the Heidelberg Catechism:

Q. 16. *Why must the mediator be a true and righteous man?*
A. Because God's justice requires that human nature, which
has sinned, must pay for its sin; but a sinner could never pay
for others.

Prayer for Illumination
As you read his word, ask God to enlighten your mind and heart:

O God, you instruct us by your Holy Scriptures—we urge you
by your grace to enlighten our minds and cleanse our hearts;
that reading, hearing, and meditating upon them, we may
rightly understand and heartily embrace the things you have
revealed in them. Give efficacy to the reading of the gospel
in your Word, that through the operation of the Holy Spirit,
this holy seed may be received into our hearts as into good
ground; and that we may not only hear your Word but keep
it, living in conformity with your precepts; so that we may
finally attain everlasting salvation, through Jesus Christ our
Lord. Amen.   *Waldensian Liturgy*

Scripture Reading
Read this portion of God's word: Numbers 24:1–19

Praise
Say this praise to God:

Lord, now let your servant depart in peace according to
>your word.
For mine eyes have seen your salvation,
Which you have prepared before the face of all people,
To be a light to lighten the Gentiles and to be the glory of
>your people Israel. Amen.   *Nunc Dimittis*

Prayer of Intercession
As you make your requests to God, pray this prayer:

My life is yours, O God; created by you, redeemed by you and
mine again today, because you have remembered me. And
now the calling of today is upon me, with its work and trial,
and I go forth to it until the evening. Let your blessing go
with me into whatever it brings. I do not trust myself at all. I
am afraid to live, unless you keep me. I am afraid to act or to
speak, unless I am guided by you. Hold me today, that I may
not leave your peace or fall into sin. Amen.   *Henry Wotherspoon*

Further Petition
- Personal
- Church
- World

Lord's Prayer
Pray the words that Jesus taught us to pray:

Our Father in heaven,
 hallowed be your name;
 your kingdom come;
 your will be done, on earth as it is in heaven.
 Give us this day our daily bread.
 And forgive us our debts, as we forgive our debtors.
 And lead us not into temptation but deliver us from evil.
 For yours is the kingdom, and the power,
 and the glory, forever. Amen.

Benediction
Receive by faith this blessing from God:

Now to him who is able to do far more abundantly than all
that we ask or think, according to the power at work within
us, to him be glory in the church and in Christ Jesus throughout all generations, forever and ever. Amen.   *Ephesians 3:20–21*

Postlude
In closing, say or sing this praise to God:

His Name for ever shall endure,
 last like the sun it shall;
Men shall be blessed in Him, and blessed
 all nations shall Him call.

Now blessèd be the Lord, our God,
 the God of Israel,
For He alone does wondrous works,
 in glory that excel.

And blessèd be His glorious Name
    to all eternity;
The whole earth let His glory fill.
    Amen, so let it be.   *Based on Psalm 72:17–19*

December 2

Meditation

Reflect on these words about the incarnation of the Lord Jesus:

The glory of the incarnation is that it presents to our adoring gaze not a humanized God or deified man, but a true God-man—one who is all that God is and at the same time all that man is: on whose mighty arm we can rest, and to whose human sympathy we can appeal. We cannot afford to lose either the God in the man or the man in God; our hearts cry out for the complete God-man, whom the Scriptures offer us.
B. B. Warfield

Call to Worship

Hear God call you to worship through his word:

I saw in the night visions, and behold, with the clouds of heaven there came one like a son of man, and he came to the Ancient of Days and was presented before him. And to him was given dominion and glory and a kingdom, that all peoples, nations, and languages should serve him; his dominion is an everlasting dominion, which shall not pass away, and his kingdom one that shall not be destroyed.   Daniel 7:13–14

Adoration

Say or sing this praise to God:

Lo! He comes with clouds descending,
once for favoured sinner slain;
thousand, thousand saints attending
swell the triumph of his train:
Alleluia, alleluia, alleluia!
God appears on earth to reign.

Every eye shall now behold him
robed in dreadful majesty;
those who set at naught and sold him,
pierced and nailed him to the tree,
deeply wailing, deeply wailing, deeply wailing,
shall their true Messiah see.

Those dear tokens of his passion
still his dazzling body bears,
cause of endless exultation
to his ransomed worshippers.
With what rapture, with what rapture, with what rapture,
gaze we on those glorious scars!

Yea, Amen, let all adore thee
high on thine eternal throne;
Saviour, take the power and glory,
claim the kingdom for thine own.
Alleluia, alleluia, alleluia!
Thou shalt reign, and thou alone!   *Charles Wesley*

Reading of the Law

Hear God's law as his will for your life:

The words of our Lord Jesus Christ:

Unless your righteousness exceeds that of the scribes and Pharisees, you will never enter the kingdom of heaven. . . . You therefore must be perfect, as your heavenly Father is perfect. . . . Beware of practicing your righteousness before other people in order to be seen by them, for then you will have no reward from your Father who is in heaven. . . . Seek first the kingdom of God and his righteousness, and all these things will be added to you. . . . So whatever you wish that others would do to you, do also to them, for this is the Law and the Prophets.   *Matthew 5:20, 48; 6:1, 33; 7:12*

Confession of Sin

Confess your sins to God:

Almighty God and heavenly Father, we poor, miserable sinners confess that from our childhood until this very hour we have sinned against your commandments by evil thoughts, words, will, and works, which we cannot count, and first of all by vast unbelief. Therefore, we are not worthy to be called your children, nor lift our eyes up to heaven. O God and Father, we wish that we had never provoked you to anger. In your mercy and for the sake of your glory, we ask you to receive us into your grace by the forgiveness of our sins. Amen.   *John Oecolampadius*

Assurance of Pardon
Receive these words of comfort from God:

Therefore, since we have been justified by faith, we have peace with God through our Lord Jesus Christ. Through him we have also obtained access by faith into this grace in which we stand, and we rejoice in hope of the glory of God.   *Romans 5:1–2*

Athanasian Creed, Part 3
Confess what you believe about the Christian faith:

Whoever desires to be saved should above all hold to the catholic faith. Anyone who does not keep it whole and unbroken will doubtless perish eternally. Now this is the catholic faith:

that we worship one God in Trinity and the Trinity in unity, neither confounding their persons nor dividing the essence. . . .

But it is necessary for eternal salvation that one also believe in the incarnation of our Lord Jesus Christ faithfully.

Now this is the true faith:

> that we believe and confess that our Lord Jesus Christ,
> God's Son,
>   is both God and man, equally.
> He is God from the essence of the Father, begotten
>   before time;
>   and he is man from the essence of his mother, born
>   in time;
>   completely God, completely man, with a rational soul
>   and human flesh;

equal to the Father as regards divinity,
    less than the Father as regards humanity.
Although he is God and man, yet Christ is not two,
        but one.
He is one, however, not by his divinity being turned
        into flesh,
    but by God's taking humanity to himself.
He is one, certainly not by the blending of his essence,
    but by the unity of his person.
For just as one man is both rational soul and flesh,
    so too the one Christ is both God and man.

He suffered for our salvation;
he descended to hell;
he arose from the dead on the third day;
he ascended to heaven;
he is seated at the Father's right hand;
from there he will come to judge the living and the dead.
At his coming all people will arise bodily and give an
        accounting of their own deeds.
Those who have done good will enter eternal life,
    and those who have done evil will enter eternal fire.

This is the catholic faith: that one cannot be saved without
believing it firmly and faithfully.

Praise
Say or sing this praise to God:

Glory be to the Father,
    and to the Son,
    and to the Holy Spirit:

As it was in the beginning,
   is now and ever shall be,
      world without end. Amen.   *Gloria Patri*

Catechism
Receive this instruction from the Heidelberg Catechism:

Q. 17. Why must he also be true God?
A. So that, by the power of his divinity, he might bear in his humanity the weight of God's wrath, and earn for us and restore to us righteousness and life.

Prayer for Illumination
As you read his word, ask God to enlighten your mind and heart:

Almighty God, I earnestly ask you for such deeper fellowship of the Holy Spirit, who speaks in the blessed Scriptures, that when I open them, I may perceive his mind in what I read, and immediately hear in them his voice to myself. I ask you for a quicker understanding in spiritual things, for more desire to understand, a fuller perception of your promise in the church, that I may become teachable, and may love that by which you will teach me. Amen.   *Henry Wotherspoon*

Scripture Reading
Read this portion of God's word: Deuteronomy 18:1–22

Praise
Say this praise to God:

Holy, holy, holy, Lord God of hosts,
heaven and earth are full of your glory.
Glory be to you, O Lord Most High.

Blessed is he that comes in the name of the Lord.
Hosanna in the highest. Amen.   *Sanctus*

Prayer of Intercession
As you make your requests to God, pray this prayer:

O you who are full of compassion, I commit and commend
myself unto you, in whom I am, and live, and know. Be the
goal of my pilgrimage, and my rest by the way. Let my soul
take refuge from the crowding turmoil of worldly thoughts
beneath the shadow of your wings; let my heart, this sea of
restless waves, find peace in you, O God. Amen.   *Augustine*

Further Petition
- Personal
- Church
- World

Lord's Prayer
Pray the words that Jesus taught us to pray:

Our Father in heaven,
    hallowed be your name;
    your kingdom come;
    your will be done, on earth as it is in heaven.
    Give us this day our daily bread.
    And forgive us our debts, as we forgive our debtors.
    And lead us not into temptation but deliver us from evil.
    For yours is the kingdom, and the power,
    and the glory, forever. Amen.

Benediction

Receive by faith this blessing from God:

Now may the God of peace himself sanctify you completely, and may your whole spirit and soul and body be kept blameless at the coming of our Lord Jesus Christ. He who calls you is faithful; he will surely do it.   *1 Thessalonians 5:23–24*

Postlude

In closing, say or sing this praise to God:

His Name for ever shall endure,
    last like the sun it shall;
Men shall be blessed in Him, and blessed
    all nations shall Him call.

Now blessèd be the Lord, our God,
    the God of Israel,
For He alone does wondrous works,
    in glory that excel.

And blessèd be His glorious Name
    to all eternity;
The whole earth let His glory fill.
    Amen, so let it be.   *Based on Psalm 72:17–19*

December 3

Meditation

Reflect on these words about the incarnation of the Lord Jesus:

If Christ had arrived with trumpets and lain in a cradle of gold, his birth would have been a splendid affair. But it would not be a comfort to me. He was rather to lie in the lap of a poor maiden and be thought of little significance in the eyes of the world. Now I can come to him. Now he reveals himself to the miserable in order not to give any impression that he arrives with great power, splendor, wisdom, and aristocratic manners.   *Martin Luther*

———

Call to Worship

Hear God call you to worship through his word:

And those who went before and those who followed were shouting, "Blessed is the coming kingdom of our father David! Hosanna in the highest!"   *Mark 11: 9–10*

Adoration

Say or sing this praise to God:

Hail to the Lord's anointed,
Great David's greater Son.

Hail in the time appointed
His reign on earth begun!
He comes to break oppression,
To set the captive free,
To take away transgression
And rule in equity.

He comes with succour speedy
To those who suffer wrong;
To help the poor and needy
and bid the weak be strong;
To give them songs for sighing,
Their darkness turn to light,
Whose souls, condemned and dying,
Were precious in his sight.

He shall come down like showers
Upon the fruitful earth;
And love, joy, hope, like flowers
Spring in his path to birth;
Before him, on the mountains
Shall peace, the herald, go;
And righteousness, in fountains
From hill to valley flow.

Kings shall fall down before him,
And gold and incense bring.
All nations shall adore him,
His praise all people sing.
To him shall prayer unceasing
And daily vows ascend;
His kingdom still increasing,
A kingdom without end.   *James Montgomery*

Reading of the Law

Hear God's law as his will for your life:

And God spoke all these words, saying,

"I am the LORD your God, who brought you out of the land of Egypt, out of the house of slavery.

You shall have no other gods before me.

You shall not make for yourself a carved image, or any likeness of anything that is in heaven above, or that is in the earth beneath, or that is in the water under the earth. You shall not bow down to them or serve them, for I the LORD your God am a jealous God, visiting the iniquity of the fathers on the children to the third and the fourth generation of those who hate me, but showing steadfast love to thousands of those who love me and keep my commandments.

You shall not take the name of the LORD your God in vain, for the LORD will not hold him guiltless who takes his name in vain.

Remember the Sabbath day, to keep it holy. Six days you shall labor, and do all your work, but the seventh day is a Sabbath to the LORD your God. On it you shall not do any work, you, or your son, or your daughter, your male servant, or your female servant, or your livestock, or the sojourner who is within your gates. For in six days the LORD made heaven and earth, the sea, and all that is in them, and rested on the seventh day. Therefore the LORD blessed the Sabbath day and made it holy.

Honor your father and your mother, that your days may be long in the land that the LORD your God is giving you.

You shall not murder.

You shall not commit adultery.

You shall not steal.

You shall not bear false witness against your neighbor.

You shall not covet your neighbor's house; you shall not covet your neighbor's wife, or his male servant, or his female servant, or his ox, or his donkey, or anything that is your neighbor's." *Exodus 20:1–17*

Confession of Sin

Confess your sins to God:

O Lord, I do not deserve a glimpse of heaven, and I am unable with my works to redeem myself from sin, death, the devil, and hell. Nevertheless, you have given me your Son, Jesus Christ, who is far more precious and dear than heaven, and much stronger than sin, death, the devil, and hell. For this I rejoice, praise, and thank you, O God. Without cost and out of pure grace you have given me this boundless blessing in your dear Son. Through him you take sin, death, and hell from me, and do grant me all that belongs to him. Amen.   *Martin Luther*

Assurance of Pardon

Receive these words of comfort from God:

Surely he has borne our griefs
   and carried our sorrows;
yet we esteemed him stricken,
   smitten by God, and afflicted.
But he was pierced for our transgressions;
   he was crushed for our iniquities;
upon him was the chastisement that brought us peace,
   and with his wounds we are healed.

All we like sheep have gone astray;
    we have turned—every one—to his own way;
and the Lᴏʀᴅ has laid on him
    the iniquity of us all.   *Isaiah 53:4–6*

Nicene Creed
Confess what you believe about the Christian faith:

I believe in one God, the Father Almighty,
    Maker of heaven and earth, and of all things visible and
        invisible.

And in one Lord Jesus Christ, the only-begotten Son of God;
    begotten of the Father before all worlds;
    God of God, Light of Light, very God of very God;
    begotten, not made, being of one substance with the
        Father;
    by whom all things were made.
Who, for us men and for our salvation,
    came down from heaven
    and was incarnate by the Holy Spirit of the Virgin Mary,
    and was made man;
    and was crucified also for us under Pontius Pilate;
    he suffered and was buried;
    and the third day he rose again, according to the Scriptures;
    and ascended into heaven, and sits on the right hand of
        the Father;
    and he shall come again, with glory, to judge the living
        and the dead;
    whose kingdom shall have no end.

And I believe in the Holy Spirit, the Lord and Giver of life;
    who proceeds from the Father and the Son;

who with the Father and the Son together is worshiped
and glorified;
who spoke by the prophets.

And I believe in one holy catholic and apostolic church.
I acknowledge one baptism for the forgiveness of sins;
and I look for the resurrection of the dead,
and the life of the world to come. Amen.

Praise
Say or sing this praise to God:

Glory be to the Father,
and to the Son,
and to the Holy Spirit:
As it was in the beginning,
is now and ever shall be,
world without end. Amen.   *Gloria Patri*

Catechism
Receive this instruction from the Heidelberg Catechism:

*Q. 18. Then who is this mediator—true God and at the same time a true
and righteous man?*
A. Our Lord Jesus Christ, who was given to us for our complete deliverance and righteousness.

Prayer for Illumination
As you read his word, ask God to enlighten your mind and heart:

Almighty God, enter our hearts, and so fill us with your love,
that, forsaking all evil desires, we may embrace you, our only
good. Show unto us, for your mercies' sake, O Lord our God,

what you are unto us. Say unto our souls, "I am your salvation." So speak that we may hear. Our hearts are before you; open our ears; let us hasten after your voice and take hold of you. Amen.   *Augustine*

Scripture Reading
Read this portion of God's word: 2 Samuel 7:1–16

Praise
Say or sing this praise to God:

Phos Hilaron

O radiant light, O sun divine
Of God the Father's deathless face,
O image of the light sublime
That fills the heav'nly dwelling place.

O Son of God, the source of life,
Praise is your due by night and day;
Our happy lips must raise the strain
Of your esteemed and splendid name.

Lord Jesus Christ, as daylight fades,
As shine the lights of eventide,
We praise the Father with the Son,
The Spirit blest, and with them one.   *Anonymous*

Prayer of Intercession
As you make your requests to God, pray this prayer:

Give us faith in all the truths of your Word; may we be daily warned by the terrors of the Lord, and invited by your mercy. May we meditate on the awful punishments denounced against the wicked, and call to mind the reward which you have promised unto those who please you by patient continuance in well-doing. And thus may we be prepared to make every sacrifice to which you may be pleased to call us. May we cut off the right hand, and pluck out the right eye, when you require us to do it. And may we consider all our interests in this life as of no value compared with the eternal welfare of our souls. May we seek first the kingdom of God, and his righteousness, trusting that all things which are needful for the body shall be added unto us. Amen.   *Henry Thornton*

Further Petition
- Personal
- Church
- World

Lord's Prayer
Pray the words that Jesus taught us to pray:

Our Father in heaven,
 hallowed be your name;
 your kingdom come;
 your will be done, on earth as it is in heaven.
 Give us this day our daily bread.
 And forgive us our debts, as we forgive our debtors.
 And lead us not into temptation but deliver us from evil.
 For yours is the kingdom, and the power,
 and the glory, forever. Amen.

Benediction

Receive by faith this blessing from God:

May grace and peace be multiplied to you in the knowledge
of God and of Jesus our Lord.   *2 Peter 1:2*

Postlude

In closing, say or sing this praise to God:

His Name for ever shall endure,
    last like the sun it shall;
Men shall be blessed in Him, and blessed
    all nations shall Him call.

Now blessèd be the Lord, our God,
    the God of Israel,
For He alone does wondrous works,
    in glory that excel.

And blessèd be His glorious Name
    to all eternity;
The whole earth let His glory fill.
    Amen, so let it be.   *Based on Psalm 72:17–19*

December 4

Meditation

Reflect on these words about the incarnation of the Lord Jesus:

He was poor that he might make us rich. He was born of a virgin that we might be born of God. He took our flesh that he might give us his Spirit. He lay in the manger that we might lie in paradise. He came down from heaven that he might bring us to heaven . . . that the Ancient of Days should be born,—that he who thunders in the heavens should cry in the cradle,—that he who rules the stars should suck the breast,—that a virgin should conceive,—that Christ should be made of a woman, and of that woman which himself made,—that the branch should bear the vine,—that the mother should be younger than the child she bore, and the child in the womb bigger than the mother,—that the human nature should not be God, yet one with God: this was not only amazing but miraculous.   *Thomas Watson*

Call to Worship

Hear God call you to worship through his word:

The Lord reigns; let the peoples tremble!
   He sits enthroned upon the cherubim; let the earth quake!

The LORD is great in Zion;
>he is exalted over all the peoples.
Let them praise your great and awesome name!
>Holy is he!   *Psalm 99:1–3*

Adoration

Say or sing the words of this psalm:

The world and all in it are God's,
>all peoples of the earth,
For it was founded by the LORD
>upon the seas beneath.

Who may ascend the hill of God,
>or in his temple stand?
The one who shuns false gods and lies,
>who's pure in heart and hand.

He will find favour from the LORD,
>and from his Saviour grace.
Thus are they blessed, O Jacob's God,
>who truly seek your face.

You ancient gates, lift up your heads;
>you doors, be opened wide—
So may the King of glory come
>for ever to abide.

But who is this exalted King?
>what glorious King is he?
It is the LORD of strength and might,
>the LORD of victory.

You ancient gates, lift up your heads;
    you doors, be opened wide—
So may the King of glory come
    for ever to abide.

But who is this exalted King?
    who can this sovereign be?
The LORD Almighty, he is King
    of glory, none but he.   *Sing Psalms: 24:1–10*

Reading of the Law
Hear God's law as his will for your life:

Beloved, let us love one another, for love is from God, and whoever loves has been born of God and knows God. Anyone who does not love does not know God, because God is love. In this the love of God was made manifest among us, that God sent his only Son into the world, so that we might live through him. In this is love, not that we have loved God but that he loved us and sent his Son to be the propitiation for our sins. Beloved, if God so loved us, we also ought to love one another.   *1 John 4:7–11*

Confession of Sin
Confess your sins to God:

I, a poor sinful person, confess myself before you, my Lord God and Maker, that sadly I have sinned much, with my senses, thoughts, words, and deeds, as you, eternal God, know very well. I regret them and beg your grace. Amen. *Heinrich Bullinger*

Assurance of Pardon
Receive these words of comfort from God:

What then shall we say to these things? If God is for us, who can be against us? He who did not spare his own Son but gave him up for us all, how will he not also with him graciously give us all things? Who shall bring any charge against God's elect? It is God who justifies. Who is to condemn? Christ Jesus is the one who died—more than that, who was raised—who is at the right hand of God, who indeed is interceding for us.   Romans 8:31–34

Apostles' Creed
Confess what you believe about the Christian faith:

I believe in God the Father Almighty,
    Maker of heaven and earth.

I believe in Jesus Christ, his only-begotten Son, our Lord;
    who was conceived by the Holy Spirit, born of the
           Virgin Mary;
    suffered under Pontius Pilate;
    was crucified, dead, and buried;
    he descended into hell;
    the third day he rose again from the dead;
    he ascended into heaven,
    and sits at the right hand of God the Father Almighty;
    from there he shall come to judge the living and the dead.

I believe in the Holy Spirit;
    the holy catholic church;
    the communion of saints;
    the forgiveness of sins;

100 · December 4

the resurrection of the body;
and the life everlasting. Amen.

Praise
Say or sing this praise to God:

Glory be to the Father,
  and to the Son,
  and to the Holy Spirit:
As it was in the beginning,
  is now and ever shall be,
  world without end. Amen.   *Gloria Patri*

Catechism
Receive this instruction from the Heidelberg Catechism:

Q. 19. *How do you come to know this?*
A. The holy gospel tells me. God himself began to reveal the
gospel already in Paradise; later, he proclaimed it by the holy
patriarchs and prophets and foreshadowed it by the sacrifices
and other ceremonies of the law; and finally, he fulfilled it
through his own beloved Son.

Prayer for Illumination
As you read his word, ask God to enlighten your mind and heart:

Almighty, eternal and merciful God, whose Word is a lamp
unto our feet and a light unto our path, open and illuminate
our minds, that we may purely and perfectly understand
your Word and that our lives may be conformed to what
we have rightly understood, that in nothing we may be
displeasing to your Majesty, through Jesus Christ our Lord.
Amen.   *Huldrych Zwingli*

Scripture Reading

Read this portion of God's word: Psalm 2

Praise

Say or sing this praise to God:

Corde Natus

Of the Father's love begotten,
Ere the worlds began to be,
He is Alpha and Omega,
He the source, the ending He,
Of the things that are, that have been,
And that future years shall see,
Evermore and evermore!

At His Word the worlds were framèd;
He commanded; it was done:
Heaven and earth and depths of ocean
In their threefold order one;
All that grows beneath the shining
Of the moon and burning sun,
Evermore and evermore!

This is He Whom seers in old time
Chanted of with one accord;
Whom the voices of the prophets
Promised in their faithful word;
Now He shines, the long expected,
Let creation praise its Lord,
Evermore and evermore!

Righteous Judge of souls departed,
Righteous King of them that live,

On the Father's throne exalted
None in might with Thee may strive;
Who at last in vengeance coming
Sinners from Thy face shalt drive,
Evermore and evermore!   *Aurelius Prudentius*

Prayer of Intercession
As you make your requests to God, pray this prayer:

Grant, Almighty God, that as you have stretched forth your
helping hand to us by your only begotten Son, not only bind-
ing yourself to us by an oath, but even sealing your eternal
covenant by the blood of the same, your Son—grant that we
in turn may keep our faith toward you so that we persevere
in the undefiled worship of your name, till we attain unto
the reward of our faith in your heavenly kingdom, through
the same, Christ our Lord. Amen.   *John Calvin*

Further Petition
- Personal
- Church
- World

Lord's Prayer
Pray the words that Jesus taught us to pray:

Our Father in heaven,
   hallowed be your name;
   your kingdom come;
   your will be done, on earth as it is in heaven.
   Give us this day our daily bread.
   And forgive us our debts, as we forgive our debtors.

And lead us not into temptation but deliver us from evil.
For yours is the kingdom, and the power,
and the glory, forever. Amen.

Benediction
Receive by faith this blessing from God:

Now to him who is able to keep you from stumbling and to present you blameless before the presence of his glory with great joy, to the only God, our Savior, through Jesus Christ our Lord, be glory, majesty, dominion, and authority, before all time and now and forever. Amen.   *Jude 24–25*

Postlude
In closing, say or sing this praise to God:

His Name for ever shall endure,
    last like the sun it shall;
Men shall be blessed in Him, and blessed
    all nations shall Him call.

Now blessèd be the Lord, our God,
    the God of Israel,
For He alone does wondrous works,
    in glory that excel.

And blessèd be His glorious Name
    to all eternity;
The whole earth let His glory fill.
    Amen, so let it be.   *Based on Psalm 72:17–19*

December 5

Meditation
Reflect on these words about the incarnation of the Lord Jesus:

The Word was not so circumscribed in the body as to be there only and nowhere else. He was still the energizing principle of all things as before. He was in everything, but not essentially identified with everything; being only entirely in the Father alone. The soul by acts of thought can comprehend distant objects, but cannot influence them; not so the Word, for He controlled both His own body and the whole universe, being in all things and yet essentially distinct from them. As man, He fulfilled human duties; as Word, He quickened all things; as Son, He was with the Father.   *Athanasius*

Call to Worship
Hear God call you to worship through his word:

This is evidence of the righteous judgment of God, that you may be considered worthy of the kingdom of God, for which you are also suffering—since indeed God considers it just to repay with affliction those who afflict you, and to grant relief to you who are afflicted as well as to us, when the Lord Jesus is revealed from heaven with his mighty angels

in flaming fire, inflicting vengeance on those who do not
know God and on those who do not obey the gospel of our
Lord Jesus.   *2 Thessalonians 1:5–8*

Adoration

Say or sing the words of this Advent hymn:

Lift up the Advent strain!
Behold the Lord is nigh!
Greet His approach, ye saints, again,
With hymns of holy joy.

The everlasting Son
Incarnate deigns to be;
Our God the form of slave puts on,
A race of slaves to free.

Daughter of Zion, rise
To meet thy lowly King!
Nor let the faithless heart despise
The peace He comes to bring.

As Judge, in clouds of light,
He shall come down again,
And all His scattered saints unite
With Him in heaven to reign.

Before that dreadful day,
May all our sins be gone;
The old man all be put away,
The new man all put on.

Jesu, all praise to Thee,
Our joy and endless rest;

We pray Thee here our guide to be,
Our crown amid the blest.   *Charles Coffin*

Reading of the Law
Hear God's law as his will for your life:

The words of our Lord Jesus Christ:

You shall love the Lord your God with all your heart and with all your soul and with all your mind. This is the great and first commandment. And a second is like it: You shall love your neighbor as yourself. On these two commandments depend all the Law and the Prophets.   *Matthew 22:37–40*

Confession of Sin
Confess your sins to God:

O Lord, *have mercy upon us.*
O Christ, *have mercy upon us.*
O Spirit, *have mercy upon us.*
O God the Father in heaven, *we beseech you, hear us.*
O God the Son, Redeemer of the world, *we beseech you, hear us.*
O God the Holy Spirit, our Comforter, *we beseech you, hear us.*
Be gracious unto us. *Spare us, good Lord.*
Be gracious unto us. *Help us, good Lord.*
Be gracious unto us. *Save us, good Lord,*
    from our sin, from our errors, from all evil.
Good Lord, deliver us.
Lord, *have mercy upon us.* Amen.   *Gregory the Great*

Assurance of Pardon

Receive these words of comfort from God:

"Yet even now," declares the LORD,
    "return to me with all your heart,
with fasting, with weeping, and with mourning;
    and rend your hearts and not your garments."
Return to the LORD your God,
    for he is gracious and merciful,
slow to anger, and abounding in steadfast love;
    and he relents over disaster.   Joel 2:12–13

Apostles' Creed

Confess what you believe about the Christian faith:

I believe in God the Father Almighty,
    Maker of heaven and earth.

I believe in Jesus Christ, his only-begotten Son, our Lord;
    who was conceived by the Holy Spirit, born of the
            Virgin Mary;
    suffered under Pontius Pilate;
    was crucified, dead, and buried;
    he descended into hell;
    the third day he rose again from the dead;
    he ascended into heaven,
    and sits at the right hand of God the Father Almighty;
    from there he shall come to judge the living and the dead.

I believe in the Holy Spirit;
    the holy catholic church;
    the communion of saints;
    the forgiveness of sins;

the resurrection of the body;
and the life everlasting. Amen.

Praise
Say or sing this praise to God:

Praise God from whom all blessings flow;
Praise him all creatures here below;
Praise him above you heavenly host;
Praise Father, Son, and Holy Ghost. Amen.   *Doxology*

Catechism
Receive this instruction from the Heidelberg Catechism:

Q. 29. *Why is the Son of God called "Jesus," meaning "savior"?*
A. Because he saves us from our sins; and because salvation
is not to be sought or found in anyone else.

Prayer for Illumination
As you read his word, ask God to enlighten your mind and heart:

Merciful Lord, the comforter and teacher of your faithful
people, increase in your church the desires which you have
given, and confirm the hearts of those who hope in you by
enabling them to understand the depth of your promises,
that all of your adopted sons may even now behold, with
the eyes of faith, and patiently wait for, the light which as
yet you do not openly manifest; through Jesus Christ our
Lord. Amen.   *Ambrose*

Scripture Reading
Read this portion of God's word: Psalm 16

Praise

Es ist ein Ros entsprungen

Lo, how a rose e'er blooming,
From tender stem has sprung.
Of Jesse's lineage coming,
As men of old have sung;
It came, a flow'ret bright,
Amid the cold of winter,
When half spent was the night.

Isaiah 'twas foretold it,
The Rose I have in mind,
With Mary, we behold it,
The virgin mother kind;
To show God's love aright,
She bore to men a Savior,
When half spent was the night.

O Flower, whose fragrance tender
With sweetness fills the air,
Dispel with glorious splendor
The darkness everywhere;
True man, yet very God,
From sin and death now save us,
And share our every load.

O Savior, Child of Mary,
Who felt our human woe;
O Savior, King of Glory,
Who does our weakness know,
Bring us at length we pray,

To the bright courts of Heaven
And to the endless day.   *Anonymous*

Prayer of Intercession
As you make your requests to God, pray this prayer:

Blessed Lord, who have caused all Holy Scriptures to be
written for our learning; grant us that we may in such a
way hear, read, mark, learn, and inwardly digest them; that
by patience and comfort of your holy Word, we may embrace and ever hold fast the blessed hope of everlasting life,
which you have given us in our Savior Jesus Christ. Amen.
Book of Common Prayer (1552)

Further Petition
- Personal
- Church
- World

Lord's Prayer
Pray the words that Jesus taught us to pray:

Our Father in heaven,
    hallowed be your name;
    your kingdom come;
    your will be done, on earth as it is in heaven.
    Give us this day our daily bread.
    And forgive us our debts, as we forgive our debtors.
    And lead us not into temptation but deliver us from evil.
    For yours is the kingdom, and the power,
    and the glory, forever. Amen.

Benediction

Receive by faith this blessing from God:

The LORD bless you and keep you;
The LORD make his face to shine upon you
    and be gracious to you;
The LORD lift up his countenance upon you
    and give you peace.   *Numbers 6:24–26*

Postlude

In closing, say or sing this praise to God:

His Name for ever shall endure,
    last like the sun it shall;
Men shall be blessed in Him, and blessed
    all nations shall Him call.

Now blessèd be the Lord, our God,
    the God of Israel,
For He alone does wondrous works,
    in glory that excel.

And blessèd be His glorious Name
    to all eternity;
The whole earth let His glory fill.
    Amen, so let it be.   *Based on Psalm 72:17–19*

December 6

Meditation

Reflect on these words about the incarnation of the Lord Jesus:

God, the creator of the universe, made man not only that there might be an image and copy of Himself, but that from among the creatures made from the earth there might be one to enjoy God through fellowship and friendship here, through possession and most intimate contact in the hereafter. Also that He might foreshadow in a sense that intercourse with the world into which He was going to enter through His Son.   *Huldrych Zwingli*

Call to Worship

Hear God call you to worship through his word:

I will greatly rejoice in the LORD;
   my soul shall exult in my God,
for he has clothed me with the garments of salvation;
   he has covered me with the robe of righteousness,
as a bridegroom decks himself like a priest with a beautiful
      headdress,
   and as a bride adorns herself with her jewels.   *Isaiah 61:10*

Adoration

Say or sing the words of this Advent hymn:

"Wake, awake, for night is flying,"
the watchmen on the heights are crying;
"Awake, Jerusalem, arise!"
Midnight hears the welcome voices
and at the thrilling cry rejoices:
"Where are the virgins pure and wise?
The Bridegroom comes: Awake!
Your lamps with gladness take!
Alleluia!
With bridal care and faith's bold prayer,
to meet the Bridegroom, come, prepare!"

Zion hears the watchmen singing,
and in her heart new joy is springing.
She wakes, she rises from her gloom,
For her Lord comes down all-glorious
and strong in grace, in truth victorious.
Her star is risen, her light is come!
Now come, O Blessed One,
Lord Jesus, God's own Son.
Sing hosanna!
We answer all in joy your call;
we follow to the wedding hall.

Lamb of God, the heavens adore you;
the saints and angels sing before you,
with harp and cymbals' clearest tone.
Of one pearl each shining portal,
where, joining with the choir immortal,
we gather round your radiant throne.

No eye has seen that light,
no ear the echoed might
of your glory;
yet there shall we in victory
sing shouts of joy eternally!   *Philipp Nicolai*

Reading of the Law
Hear God's law as his will for your life:

Hear, O Israel: The LORD our God, the LORD is one.
You shall love the LORD your God with all your heart and
         with all your soul and with all your might.
And these words that I command you today shall be on
         your heart.
You shall teach them diligently to your children,
    and shall talk of them when you sit in your house,
    and when you walk by the way,
    and when you lie down,
    and when you rise.
You shall bind them as a sign on your hand,
    and they shall be as frontlets between your eyes.
You shall write them on the doorposts of your house and
         on your gates.   *Deuteronomy 6:4–9*

Confession of Sin
Confess your sins to God:

O Lord, as long as I am apart from you, I am self-satisfied,
because I have no standard by which to measure my low
stature. But when I come near to you, there for the first time
I see myself. In your light, I behold my darkness. In your pu-
rity, I behold my corruption. My very confession of sin is the

fruit of holiness. Oh! Divine Man, let me gaze on you more and more until, in the vision of your brightness, I loathe the sight of my impurity, until in the blaze of that glory which human eye has not seen, I fall prostrate, blinded, broken, to rise again a new man in you. Amen.　*George Matheson*

Assurance of Pardon
Receive these words of comfort from God:

Blessed be the God and Father of our Lord Jesus Christ, who has blessed us in Christ with every spiritual blessing in the heavenly places, even as he chose us in him before the foundation of the world, that we should be holy and blameless before him. In love he predestined us for adoption to himself as sons through Jesus Christ, according to the purpose of his will, to the praise of his glorious grace, with which he has blessed us in the Beloved. In him we have redemption through his blood, the forgiveness of our trespasses, according to the riches of his grace.　*Ephesians 1:3–7*

Nicene Creed
Confess what you believe about the Christian faith:

I believe in one God, the Father Almighty,
　Maker of heaven and earth, and of all things visible and
　　　invisible.

And in one Lord Jesus Christ, the only-begotten Son of God;
　begotten of the Father before all worlds;
　God of God, Light of Light, very God of very God;
　begotten, not made, being of one substance with the
　　　Father;
　by whom all things were made.

Who, for us men and for our salvation,
    came down from heaven
    and was incarnate by the Holy Spirit of the Virgin Mary,
    and was made man;
    and was crucified also for us under Pontius Pilate;
    he suffered and was buried;
    and the third day he rose again, according to the Scriptures;
    and ascended into heaven, and sits on the right hand of
        the Father;
    and he shall come again, with glory, to judge the living
        and the dead;
    whose kingdom shall have no end.

And I believe in the Holy Spirit, the Lord and Giver of life;
    who proceeds from the Father and the Son;
    who with the Father and the Son together is worshiped
        and glorified;
    who spoke by the prophets.

And I believe in one holy catholic and apostolic church.
    I acknowledge one baptism for the forgiveness of sins;
    and I look for the resurrection of the dead,
    and the life of the world to come. Amen.

Praise
Say or sing this praise to God:

Praise God from whom all blessings flow;
Praise him all creatures here below;
Praise him above you heavenly host;
Praise Father, Son, and Holy Ghost. Amen.   *Doxology*

Catechism

Q. 30. Do those who look for their salvation and security in saints, in themselves, or elsewhere really believe in the only savior Jesus?
A. Although they boast of being his, by their actions they deny the only savior, Jesus. Either Jesus is not a perfect savior, or those who in true faith accept this savior have in him all they need for their salvation.

Prayer for Illumination
As you read his word, ask God to enlighten your mind and heart:

Heavenly Father, may you grant us to comprehend your holy Word according to your divine will, that we may learn from it to put all our confidence in you alone, and withdraw it from all other creatures; moreover, that also our old man with all his lusts may be crucified more and more each day, and that we may offer ourselves to you as a living sacrifice, to the glory of your holy name and to the edification of our neighbor, through our Lord Jesus Christ. Amen.   *Zacharias Ursinus*

Scripture Reading
Read this portion of God's word: Psalm 45

Praise
Say this praise to God:

My soul magnifies the Lord.
And my spirit rejoices in God my Savior.
For he has regarded the lowliness of his servant.
For behold, from now on all generations shall call me blessed.
For he who is mighty has magnified me, and holy is his Name.

And his mercy is on them that fear him, throughout all
generations.
He has showed strength with his arm.
He has scattered the proud in the imagination of their hearts.
He has put down the mighty from their thrones, and has
exalted the humble and meek.
He has filled the hungry with good things, and the rich he
has sent away empty.
He, remembering his mercy, has helped his servant Israel,
as he promised to our forefathers, Abraham and
his seed, forever.

Glory be to the Father, and to the Son, and to the Holy Spirit:
As it was in the beginning, is now, and ever shall be, world
without end. Amen.   *Magnificat*

Prayer of Intercession
As you make your requests to God, pray this prayer:

O my God, my Lord, and Father, show unto my poor soul,
that it may perceive that you are my rock, bulwark, shield,
tower, treasure, defense, trust, help, refuge, protection, and
goodness; that I in this my great need and tribulation, may,
through your godly grace, have help and assistance against
my adversaries, and be preserved forever. Lord, upon you do
I trust; let me never be ashamed. Amen.   *Martin Luther*

Further Petition
- Personal
- Church
- World

Lord's Prayer

Pray the words that Jesus taught us to pray:

Our Father in heaven,
  hallowed be your name;
  your kingdom come;
  your will be done, on earth as it is in heaven.
  Give us this day our daily bread.
  And forgive us our debts, as we forgive our debtors.
  And lead us not into temptation but deliver us from evil.
  For yours is the kingdom, and the power,
  and the glory, forever. Amen.

Benediction

Receive by faith this blessing from God:

May the God of hope fill you with all joy and peace in believing, so that by the power of the Holy Spirit you may abound in hope.   *Romans 15:13*

Postlude

In closing, say or sing this praise to God:

His Name for ever shall endure,
  last like the sun it shall;
Men shall be blessed in Him, and blessed
  all nations shall Him call.

Now blessèd be the Lord, our God,
  the God of Israel,
For He alone does wondrous works,
  in glory that excel.

And blessèd be His glorious Name
    to all eternity;
The whole earth let His glory fill.
    Amen, so let it be.   *Based on Psalm 72:17–19*

December 7

Meditation

Reflect on these words about the incarnation of the Lord Jesus:

Sin, our nature demanded to be healed; fallen, to be raised up; dead, to rise again. We had lost the possession of the good; it was necessary for it to be given back to us. Closed in the darkness, it was necessary to bring us the light; captives, we awaited a Savior; prisoners, help; slaves, a liberator. Are these things minor or insignificant? Did they not move God to descend to human nature and visit it, since humanity was in so miserable and unhappy a state?   *Gregory of Nyssa*

Call to Worship

Hear God call you to worship through his word:

Therefore it says, "When he ascended on high he led a host of captives, and he gave gifts to men." (In saying, "He ascended," what does it mean but that he had also descended into the lower regions, the earth? He who descended is the one who also ascended far above all the heavens, that he might fill all things.)   *Ephesians 4:8–10*

Adoration

Say or sing the words of this Advent hymn:

Savior of the nations, come,
virgin's Son, make here thy home!
Marvel now, O heaven and earth,
that the Lord chose such a birth.

Not of flesh and blood the Son,
offspring of the Holy One;
born of Mary ever blest,
God in flesh is manifest.

Wondrous birth! O wondrous Child
of the Virgin undefiled!
Though by all the world disowned,
still to be in heaven enthroned.

From the Father forth he came
and returneth to the same,
captive leading death and hell,
high the song of triumph swell!

Thou, the Father's only Son,
hast over sin the victory won.
Boundless shall thy kingdom be;
when shall we its glories see?

Praise to God the Father sing.
Praise to God the Son, our King.
Praise to God the Spirit be
ever and eternally.   *Ambrose*

Reading of the Law
Hear God's law as his will for your life:

Our Lord Jesus said,

Blessed are the poor in spirit,
    for theirs is the kingdom of heaven.
Blessed are those who mourn,
    for they shall be comforted.
Blessed are the meek,
    for they shall inherit the earth.
Blessed are those who hunger and thirst for righteousness,
    for they shall be satisfied.
Blessed are the merciful,
    for they shall receive mercy.
Blessed are the pure in heart,
    for they shall see God.
Blessed are the peacemakers,
    for they shall be called sons of God.
Blessed are those who are persecuted for righteousness' sake,
    for theirs is the kingdom of heaven.   *Matthew 5:3–10*

Confession of Sin
Confess your sins to God:

Lord God, eternal and Almighty Father, we confess and acknowledge without pretense before your holy Majesty, that we are poor sinners, conceived and born in iniquity and corruption; prone to do what is evil, incapable of any good; and that in our depravity, we endlessly transgress your holy commandments. And so, in your just judgment, we deserve ruin and damnation. But Lord, we are displeased with ourselves for having offended you, and we condemn ourselves and our vices with true repentance, longing for your grace to relieve our distress. May you, therefore, have mercy upon us, most gentle and merciful God and Father, in the name of your Son Jesus Christ our Lord. And as you blot out our vices and blemishes, extend and increase the graces of your Holy Spirit to us day by day, so that as we acknowledge our unrighteousness with all our heart, we might feel the sorrow that gives birth to true penitence, which as we mortify our sins may produce fruits of righteousness and innocence pleasing to you, through Jesus Christ our Lord. Amen.   *John Calvin*

Assurance of Pardon
Receive these words of comfort from God:

The LORD is merciful and gracious,
    slow to anger and abounding in steadfast love.
He will not always chide,
    nor will he keep his anger forever.
He does not deal with us according to our sins,
    nor repay us according to our iniquities.
For as high as the heavens are above the earth,
    so great is his steadfast love toward those who fear him;
as far as the east is from the west,
    so far does he remove our transgressions from us.
Psalm 103:8–12

Athanasian Creed, Part 1
Confess what you believe about the Christian faith:

Whoever desires to be saved should above all hold to the catholic faith. Anyone who does not keep it whole and unbroken will doubtless perish eternally. Now this is the catholic faith:

that we worship one God in Trinity and the Trinity in unity, neither confounding their persons nor dividing the essence.

For the person of the Father is a distinct person,
    the person of the Son is another,
    and that of the Holy Spirit still another.
But the divinity of the Father, Son, and Holy Spirit is one,
    the glory equal, the majesty coeternal.
Such as the Father is, such is the Son and such is the
    Holy Spirit.
The Father is uncreated, the Son is uncreated, the Holy
    Spirit is uncreated.
The Father is immeasurable, the Son is immeasurable,
    the Holy Spirit is immeasurable.
The Father is eternal, the Son is eternal, the Holy Spirit
    is eternal.
And yet there are not three eternal beings; there is but
    one eternal being.
So too there are not three uncreated or immeasurable
    beings;
    there is but one uncreated and immeasurable being.
Similarly, the Father is almighty, the Son is almighty,
    the Holy Spirit is almighty.
Yet there are not three almighty beings; there is but one
    almighty being.
Thus, the Father is God, the Son is God, the Holy Spirit
    is God.
Yet there are not three gods; there is but one God.
Thus, the Father is Lord, the Son is Lord, the Holy Spirit
    is Lord.
Yet there are not three lords; there is but one Lord.

Just as Christian truth compels us to confess each person
individually as both God and Lord,
so catholic religion forbids us to say that there are
three gods or lords.

Praise
Say or sing this praise to God:

Praise God from whom all blessings flow;
Praise him all creatures here below;
Praise him above you heavenly host;
Praise Father, Son, and Holy Ghost. Amen.   *Doxology*

Catechism
Receive this instruction from the Heidelberg Catechism:

Q. 31. Why is he called "Christ," meaning "anointed"?
A. Because he has been ordained by God the Father and has
been anointed with the Holy Spirit to be our chief prophet
and teacher who fully reveals to us the secret counsel and
will of God concerning our deliverance; our only high priest
who has delivered us by the one sacrifice of his body, and
who continually intercedes for us before the Father; and our
eternal king who governs us by his Word and Spirit, and who
guards us and keeps us in the deliverance he has won for us.

Prayer for Illumination
As you read his word, ask God to enlighten your mind and heart:

Lord, you know what distracted hearts we have, O give us
self-recollection; you know what hard, dead hearts we have,
O touch and awaken us! You know how we yet resist your
Word and our lower nature is reluctant to bow to your scep-

ter; therefore, O Lord, show forth your power; send your
Spirit on high to work among us, to make our hearts submissive, and ourselves capable of living in true union with you,
our salvation, and of yielding totally to your grace. Amen.
Gerhard Tersteegen

Scripture Reading
Read this portion of God's word: Psalm 68

Praise
Say this praise to God:

Blessed be the Lord God of Israel, for he has visited,
    and redeemed his people;
and has raised up a mighty salvation for us,
    in the house of his servant David;
as he spoke by the mouth of his holy prophets,
    which have been since the world began;
that we should be saved from our enemies,
    and from the hands of all that hate us;
to perform the mercy promised to our forefathers,
    and to remember his holy covenant;
to perform the oath which he swore to our forefather
        Abraham,
    that he would give us;
that we, being delivered out of the hands of our enemies,
    might serve him without fear;
in holiness and righteousness before him,
    all the days of our life.
And you, child, shall be called the prophet of the Most High,
    for you shall go before the face of the Lord to prepare his
        ways;

to give knowledge of salvation unto his people,
  for the remission of their sins,
through the tender mercy of our God,
  whereby the Dayspring from on high has visited us;
to give light to them that sit in darkness,
  and in the shadow of death,
and to guide our feet into the way of peace.

Glory be to the Father,
  and to the Son,
  and to the Holy Spirit:
As it was in the beginning,
  is now and ever shall be,
    world without end. Amen.   *Benedictus*

Prayer of Intercession
As you make your requests to God, pray this prayer:

Grant Lord, we ask you, that we may learn to have our hopes
and fears, our joys and sorrows, all grounded on your holy
Word, that we may learn to love what you love, and to hate
that which you hate. Amen.   *William Wilberforce*

Further Petition
  · Personal
  · Church
  · World

Lord's Prayer
Pray the words that Jesus taught us to pray:

Our Father in heaven,
  hallowed be your name;

your kingdom come;
your will be done, on earth as it is in heaven.
Give us this day our daily bread.
And forgive us our debts, as we forgive our debtors.
And lead us not into temptation but deliver us from evil.
For yours is the kingdom, and the power,
and the glory, forever. Amen.

Benediction

Receive by faith this blessing from God:

The grace of the Lord Jesus Christ and the love of God and the
fellowship of the Holy Spirit be with you all.   *2 Corinthians 13:14*

Postlude

In closing, say or sing this praise to God:

His Name for ever shall endure,
    last like the sun it shall;
Men shall be blessed in Him, and blessed
    all nations shall Him call.

Now blessèd be the Lord, our God,
    the God of Israel,
For He alone does wondrous works,
    in glory that excel.

And blessèd be His glorious Name
    to all eternity;
The whole earth let His glory fill.
    Amen, so let it be.   *Based on Psalm 72:17–19*

December 8

Meditation

Reflect on these words about the incarnation of the Lord Jesus:

All the works and ways of God have something in them mysterious, above the comprehension of any finite understanding. As this is the case with his works of creation and providence, there is no reason to expect it should be otherwise in the astonishing method of the redemption of the world by Jesus Christ.   *John Witherspoon*

———

Call to Worship

Hear God call you to worship through his word:

As an apple tree among the trees of the forest,
    so is my beloved among the young men.
With great delight I sat in his shadow,
    and his fruit was sweet to my taste.
He brought me to the banqueting house,
    and his banner over me was love.   *Song of Solomon 2:3–4*

Adoration

Say or sing the words of this Advent hymn:

Down in yon forest there stands a hall:
The bells of Paradise I heard them ring;
It's covered all over with purple and pall:
And I love my Lord Jesus above anything.

In that hall there stands a bed:
The bells of Paradise I heard them ring;
It's covered all over with scarlet so red:
And I love my Lord Jesus above anything.

At the bedside there lies a stone:
The bells of Paradise I heard them ring;
Which the sweet Virgin Mary knelt upon:
And I love my Lord Jesus above anything.

Under that bed there runs a flood:
The bells of Paradise I heard them ring;
The one half runs water, the other runs blood:
And I love my Lord Jesus above anything.

At the bed's foot there grows a thorn:
The bells of Paradise I heard them ring;
Which ever blows blossom since he was born:
And I love my Lord Jesus above anything.

Over that bed the moon shines bright:
The bells of Paradise I heard them ring;
Denoting our Saviour was born this night:
And I love my Lord Jesus above anything.   *Anonymous*

Reading of the Law
Hear God's law as his will for your life:

Our Lord said,

As the Father has loved me, so have I loved you. Abide in my love. If you keep my commandments, you will abide in my love, just as I have kept my Father's commandments and abide in his love. These things I have spoken to you, that my joy may be in you, and that your joy may be full. This is my commandment, that you love one another as I have loved you.   John 15:9–12

Confession of Sin
Confess your sins to God:

O Lord my God, light of the blind, and strength of the weak; yes, also light of those that see, and strength of the strong— hearken unto my soul, and hear it crying out of the depths. Woe is me! . . . Lord, help us to turn and seek you; for not as we have forsaken our Creator have you forsaken your creation. Let us turn and seek you, for we know you are here in our heart, when we confess to you, when we cast ourselves upon you, and weep in your bosom, after all our rugged ways; and you gently wipe away our tears, and we weep the more for joy; because you, Lord—not man of flesh and blood—but you, Lord, who made us, remake and comfort us. Amen.   *Augustine*

Assurance of Pardon
Receive these words of comfort from God:

The saying is trustworthy and deserving of full acceptance, that Christ Jesus came into the world to save sinners, of whom I am the foremost. But I received mercy for this reason, that in me, as the foremost, Jesus Christ might display his perfect patience as an example to those who were to believe in him for eternal life. To the King of the ages, immortal, invisible, the only God, be honor and glory forever and ever. Amen.   1 Timothy 1:15–17

Athanasian Creed, Part 2
Confess what you believe about the Christian faith:

Whoever desires to be saved should above all hold to the catholic faith. Anyone who does not keep it whole and unbroken will doubtless perish eternally. Now this is the catholic faith:

that we worship one God in Trinity and the Trinity in unity, neither confounding their persons nor dividing the essence. . . .

> The Father was neither made nor created nor begotten
> > from anyone.
> The Son was neither made nor created; he was begotten
> > from the Father alone.
> The Holy Spirit was neither made nor created nor
> > begotten;
> > he proceeds from the Father and the Son.
> Accordingly, there is one Father, not three fathers;
> > there is one Son, not three sons;
> > there is one Holy Spirit, not three holy spirits.
> None in this Trinity is before or after, none is greater or
> > smaller;
> > in their entirety the three persons are coeternal and
> > > coequal with each other.
> So in everything, as was said earlier, the unity in Trinity,
> > and the Trinity in unity, is to be worshiped.
> Anyone then who desires to be saved should think thus
> > about the Trinity.

Praise
Say or sing this praise to God:

Praise God from whom all blessings flow;
Praise him all creatures here below;
Praise him above you heavenly host;
Praise Father, Son, and Holy Ghost. Amen.   *Doxology*

Catechism
Receive this instruction from the Heidelberg Catechism:

Q. 32. *But why are you called a Christian?*
A. Because by faith I am a member of Christ and so I share in his anointing. I am anointed to confess his name, to present myself to him as a living sacrifice of thanks, to strive with a free conscience against sin and the devil in this life, and afterward to reign with Christ over all creation for eternity.

Prayer for Illumination
As you read his word, ask God to enlighten your mind and heart:

O God, you instruct us by your Holy Scriptures—we urge you by your grace to enlighten our minds and cleanse our hearts; that reading, hearing, and meditating upon them, we may rightly understand and heartily embrace the things you have revealed in them. Give efficacy to the reading of the gospel in your Word, that through the operation of the Holy Spirit, this holy seed may be received into our hearts as into good ground; and that we may not only hear your Word but keep it, living in conformity with your precepts; so that we may finally attain everlasting salvation, through Jesus Christ our Lord. Amen.   *Waldensian Liturgy*

Scripture Reading
Read this portion of God's word: Psalm 89

Praise
Say this praise to God:

Lord, now let your servant depart in peace according to
      your word.
For mine eyes have seen your salvation,
Which you have prepared before the face of all people,
To be a light to lighten the Gentiles and to be the glory of
      your people Israel. Amen.   *Nunc Dimittis*

Prayer of Intercession
As you make your requests to God, pray this prayer:

My Father, gird me still with your presence, both by day and
by night. By day teach me to remember my weakness, and by
night tell me where lies my strength. By day point me down
into Gethsemane, and by night lead me up into the mount
of transfigured glory. By day show me the burden, and by
night reveal to me the crown, so shall my days and nights be
girded about with you. Amen.   *George Matheson*

Further Petition
- Personal
- Church
- World

Lord's Prayer

Pray the words that Jesus taught us to pray:

Our Father in heaven,
   hallowed be your name;
   your kingdom come;
   your will be done, on earth as it is in heaven.
   Give us this day our daily bread.
   And forgive us our debts, as we forgive our debtors.
   And lead us not into temptation but deliver us from evil.
   For yours is the kingdom, and the power,
   and the glory, forever. Amen.

Benediction

Receive by faith this blessing from God:

Now to him who is able to do far more abundantly than all that we ask or think, according to the power at work within us, to him be glory in the church and in Christ Jesus throughout all generations, forever and ever. Amen.   *Ephesians 3:20–21*

Postlude

In closing, say or sing this praise to God:

His Name for ever shall endure,
   last like the sun it shall;
Men shall be blessed in Him, and blessed
   all nations shall Him call.

Now blessèd be the Lord, our God,
   the God of Israel,
For He alone does wondrous works,
   in glory that excel.

And blessèd be His glorious Name
    to all eternity;
The whole earth let His glory fill.
    Amen, so let it be.   *Based on Psalm 72:17–19*

December 9

Meditation

Reflect on these words about the incarnation of the Lord Jesus:

In Christ two natures met to be your cure.   *George Herbert*

———

Call to Worship

Hear God call you to worship through his word:

As he was drawing near—already on the way down the Mount of Olives—the whole multitude of his disciples began to rejoice and praise God with a loud voice for all the mighty works that they had seen, saying, "Blessed is the King who comes in the name of the Lord! Peace in heaven and glory in the highest!"   *Luke 19:37–38*

Adoration

Say or sing the words of this Advent hymn:

Prepare the way, O Zion,
your Christ is drawing near!
Let every hill and valley
a level way appear.
Greet One who comes in glory,
foretold in sacred story.

O blest is Christ who came
in God's most holy name.

He brings God's rule, O Zion;
he comes from heaven above.
His rule is peace and freedom,
and justice, truth, and love.
Lift high your praise resounding,
for grace and joy abounding.

Fling wide your gates, O Zion;
your Savior's rule embrace,
and tidings of salvation
proclaim in every place.
All lands will bow rejoicing,
their adoration voicing.   *Frans Michael Franzén*

Reading of the Law
Hear God's law as his will for your life:

The words of our Lord Jesus Christ:

Unless your righteousness exceeds that of the scribes and
Pharisees, you will never enter the kingdom of heaven. . . .
You therefore must be perfect, as your heavenly Father is
perfect. . . . Beware of practicing your righteousness before
other people in order to be seen by them, for then you will
have no reward from your Father who is in heaven. . . . Seek
first the kingdom of God and his righteousness, and all these
things will be added to you. . . . So whatever you wish that
others would do to you, do also to them, for this is the Law
and the Prophets.   *Matthew 5:20, 48; 6:1, 33; 7:12*

Confession of Sin
Confess your sins to God:

I, poor sinner, confess myself before God Almighty, that I have gravely sinned by the transgression of his commandments; that I have done many things which I should have left undone, and I have left undone that which I should have done, through unbelief and distrust in God and weakness of love toward my fellow servants. God knows the guilt I have incurred, for which I am grieved. Be gracious to me, Lord. Be merciful to me, a poor sinner. Amen.   *Diebold Schwarz*

Assurance of Pardon
Receive these words of comfort from God:

For this is the covenant that I will make with the house of Israel after those days, declares the LORD: I will put my law within them, and I will write it on their hearts. And I will be their God, and they shall be my people. And no longer shall each one teach his neighbor and each his brother, saying, "Know the LORD," for they shall all know me, from the least of them to the greatest, declares the LORD. For I will forgive their iniquity, and I will remember their sin no more.   *Jeremiah 31:33–34*

Athanasian Creed, Part 3
Confess what you believe about the Christian faith:

Whoever desires to be saved should above all hold to the catholic faith. Anyone who does not keep it whole and unbroken will doubtless perish eternally. Now this is the catholic faith:

that we worship one God in Trinity and the Trinity in unity, neither confounding their persons nor dividing the essence. . . .

But it is necessary for eternal salvation that one also believe in the incarnation of our Lord Jesus Christ faithfully.

Now this is the true faith:

> that we believe and confess that our Lord Jesus Christ, God's Son,
>> is both God and man, equally.
> He is God from the essence of the Father, begotten before time;
>> and he is man from the essence of his mother, born in time;
>> completely God, completely man, with a rational soul and human flesh;
>> equal to the Father as regards divinity,
>> less than the Father as regards humanity.
> Although he is God and man, yet Christ is not two, but one.
> He is one, however, not by his divinity being turned into flesh,
>> but by God's taking humanity to himself.
> He is one, certainly not by the blending of his essence,
>> but by the unity of his person.
> For just as one man is both rational soul and flesh,
>> so too the one Christ is both God and man.

> He suffered for our salvation;
> he descended to hell;
> he arose from the dead on the third day;
> he ascended to heaven;
> he is seated at the Father's right hand;
> from there he will come to judge the living and the dead.

At his coming all people will arise bodily and give an
accounting of their own deeds.
Those who have done good will enter eternal life,
and those who have done evil will enter eternal fire.

This is the catholic faith: that one cannot be saved without
believing it firmly and faithfully.

Praise
Say or sing this praise to God:

Praise God from whom all blessings flow;
Praise him all creatures here below;
Praise him above you heavenly host;
Praise Father, Son, and Holy Ghost. Amen.　　Doxology

Catechism
Receive this instruction from the Heidelberg Catechism:

*Q. 33. Why is he called God's "only begotten Son" when we also are God's
children?*
A. Because Christ alone is the eternal, natural Son of God. We,
however, are adopted children of God—adopted by grace for
the sake of Christ.

Prayer for Illumination
As you read his word, ask God to enlighten your mind and heart:

Almighty God, I earnestly ask you for such deeper fellowship
of the Holy Spirit, who speaks in the blessed Scriptures, that
when I open them, I may perceive his mind in what I read,
and immediately hear in them his voice to myself. I ask you
for a quicker understanding in spiritual things, for more

desire to understand, a fuller perception of your promise in the church, that I may become teachable, and may love that by which you will teach me. Amen.   *Henry Wotherspoon*

Scripture Reading
Read this portion of God's word: Psalm 110

Praise
Say this praise to God:

Holy, holy, holy, Lord God of hosts,
heaven and earth are full of your glory.
Glory be to you, O Lord Most High.
Blessed is he that comes in the name of the Lord.
Hosanna in the highest. Amen.   *Sanctus*

Prayer of Intercession
As you make your requests to God, pray this prayer:

Slay utterly, O Lord, and cast down the sin which does so easily beset us; bridle the unholy affection; stay the unlawful thought; chasten the temper; regulate the spirit; correct the tongue; bend the will and the worship of our souls to you, and so sanctify and subdue the whole inward man, that setting up your throne in our hearts, to the dethronement of all our idols, and the things of earth we hold too dear, you may reign there alone in the fullness of your grace, and the consolations of your presence, till the time arrives when we shall reign with you in glory. Amen.   *Richard Brooke*

Further Petition
- Personal
- Church
- World

Lord's Prayer
Pray the words that Jesus taught us to pray:

Our Father in heaven,
   hallowed be your name;
   your kingdom come;
   your will be done, on earth as it is in heaven.
   Give us this day our daily bread.
   And forgive us our debts, as we forgive our debtors.
   And lead us not into temptation but deliver us from evil.
   For yours is the kingdom, and the power,
   and the glory, forever. Amen.

Benediction
Receive by faith this blessing from God:

Now may the God of peace himself sanctify you completely,
and may your whole spirit and soul and body be kept blameless at the coming of our Lord Jesus Christ. He who calls you
is faithful; he will surely do it.   1 Thessalonians 5:23–24

Postlude
In closing, say or sing this praise to God:

His Name for ever shall endure,
   last like the sun it shall;
Men shall be blessed in Him, and blessed
   all nations shall Him call.

Now blessèd be the Lord, our God,
    the God of Israel,
For He alone does wondrous works,
    in glory that excel.

And blessèd be His glorious Name
    to all eternity;
The whole earth let His glory fill.
    Amen, so let it be.   *Based on Psalm 72:17–19*

December 10

Meditation
Reflect on these words about the incarnation of the Lord Jesus:

For we do not sever the man from the Godhead, but we lay down as a dogma the unity and identity of person, who of old was not man but God, and the only Son before all ages, unmingled with body or anything corporeal; but who in these last days has assumed manhood also for our salvation; passible in His flesh, impassible in His Godhead; circumscript in the body, uncircumscript in the Spirit; at once earthly and heavenly, tangible and intangible, comprehensible and incomprehensible; that by one and the same person, who was perfect man and also God, the entire humanity fallen through sin might be created anew.   *Gregory of Nazianzus*

———

Call to Worship
Hear God call you to worship through his word:

My servant David shall be king over them, and they shall all have one shepherd. They shall walk in my rules and be careful to obey my statutes. They shall dwell in the land that I gave to my servant Jacob, where your fathers lived. They and their children and their children's children shall dwell there forever, and David my servant shall be their prince forever.   Ezekiel 37:24–25

Adoration
Say or sing the words of this Advent hymn:

The King shall come when morning dawns
and light triumphant breaks,
when beauty gilds the eastern hills
and life to joy awakes—
not as of old a little child
to bear, and fight, and die,
but crowned with glory like the sun
that lights the morning sky.

Oh, brighter than the rising morn
when Christ, victorious, rose
and left the lonesome place of death
despite the rage of foes.
Shall dawn that glorious, welcome morn
for all who know his grace—
the day when Christ in splendor comes
and we shall see his face.

The King shall come when morning dawns
and earth's dark night is past;
that morning cannot rise too soon,
that day that ever shall last.
Then let the endless bliss begin,
as heaven with praises rings.
Hail, Christ the Lord! Your people pray:
come quickly, King of kings!   *John Brownlie*

Reading of the Law
Hear God's law as his will for your life:

And God spoke all these words, saying,

"I am the LORD your God, who brought you out of the land of Egypt, out of the house of slavery.

You shall have no other gods before me.

You shall not make for yourself a carved image, or any likeness of anything that is in heaven above, or that is in the earth beneath, or that is in the water under the earth. You shall not bow down to them or serve them, for I the LORD your God am a jealous God, visiting the iniquity of the fathers on the children to the third and the fourth generation of those who hate me, but showing steadfast love to thousands of those who love me and keep my commandments.

You shall not take the name of the LORD your God in vain, for the LORD will not hold him guiltless who takes his name in vain.

Remember the Sabbath day, to keep it holy. Six days you shall labor, and do all your work, but the seventh day is a Sabbath to the LORD your God. On it you shall not do any work, you, or your son, or your daughter, your male servant, or your female servant, or your livestock, or the sojourner who is within your gates. For in six days the LORD made heaven and earth, the sea, and all that is in them, and rested on the seventh day. Therefore the LORD blessed the Sabbath day and made it holy.

Honor your father and your mother, that your days may be long in the land that the LORD your God is giving you.

You shall not murder.

You shall not commit adultery.

You shall not steal.

You shall not bear false witness against your neighbor.

You shall not covet your neighbor's house; you shall not covet your neighbor's wife, or his male servant, or his female servant, or his ox, or his donkey, or anything that is your neighbor's." Exodus 20:1–17

Confession of Sin
Confess your sins to God:

Lord Jesus Christ, you carry the lost sheep back into the fold in your arms, and deign to hear the confession of the publican—graciously remit all my guilt and sin. Lord, you hear the penitent thief, you have set a heritage of mercy for your saints, and have not withheld pardon from the sinner—hear the prayers of your servants according to your mercy. Amen. *Wilhelm Loehe*

Assurance of Pardon
Receive these words of comfort from God:

Now to the one who works, his wages are not counted as a gift but as his due. And to the one who does not work but believes in him who justifies the ungodly, his faith is counted as righteousness. *Romans 4:4–5*

Nicene Creed
Confess what you believe about the Christian faith:

I believe in one God, the Father Almighty,
   Maker of heaven and earth, and of all things visible and
           invisible.

And in one Lord Jesus Christ, the only-begotten Son of God;
  begotten of the Father before all worlds;
  God of God, Light of Light, very God of very God;
  begotten, not made, being of one substance with the
        Father;
  by whom all things were made.
Who, for us men and for our salvation,
  came down from heaven
  and was incarnate by the Holy Spirit of the Virgin Mary,
  and was made man;
  and was crucified also for us under Pontius Pilate;
  he suffered and was buried;
  and the third day he rose again, according to the Scriptures;
  and ascended into heaven, and sits on the right hand of
        the Father;
  and he shall come again, with glory, to judge the living
        and the dead;
  whose kingdom shall have no end.

And I believe in the Holy Spirit, the Lord and Giver of life;
  who proceeds from the Father and the Son;
  who with the Father and the Son together is worshiped
        and glorified;
  who spoke by the prophets.

And I believe in one holy catholic and apostolic church.
  I acknowledge one baptism for the forgiveness of sins;
  and I look for the resurrection of the dead,
  and the life of the world to come. Amen.

Praise
Say or sing this praise to God:

Praise God from whom all blessings flow;
Praise him all creatures here below;
Praise him above you heavenly host;
Praise Father, Son, and Holy Ghost. Amen.   Doxology

Catechism
Receive this instruction from the Heidelberg Catechism:

Q. 34. *Why do you call him "our Lord"?*
A. Because—not with gold or silver, but with his precious blood—he has delivered and purchased us body and soul from sin and from the tyranny of the devil, to be his very own.

Prayer for Illumination
As you read his word, ask God to enlighten your mind and heart:

Almighty God, enter our hearts, and so fill us with your love, that, forsaking all evil desires, we may embrace you, our only good. Show unto us, for your mercies' sake, O Lord our God, what you are unto us. Say unto our souls, "I am your salvation." So speak that we may hear. Our hearts are before you; open our ears; let us hasten after your voice and take hold of you. Amen.   *Augustine*

Scripture Reading
Read this portion of God's word: Psalm 118

Praise

Say or sing this praise to God:

Phos Hilaron

O radiant light, O sun divine
Of God the Father's deathless face,
O image of the light sublime
That fills the heav'nly dwelling place.

O Son of God, the source of life,
Praise is your due by night and day;
Our happy lips must raise the strain
Of your esteemed and splendid name.

Lord Jesus Christ, as daylight fades,
As shine the lights of eventide,
We praise the Father with the Son,
The Spirit blest, and with them one.   *Anonymous*

Prayer of Intercession

As you make your requests to God, pray this prayer:

O Almighty God, give to your servant a meek and gentle spirit, that I may be slow to anger, and easy to mercy and forgiveness. Give me a wise and constant heart, that I may never be moved to an intemperate anger for any injury that is done or offered. . . . Let no sickness or cross accident, no employment or weariness, make me angry or ungentle and discontented, or unthankful, or uneasy to them that minister to me; but in all things make me like unto the holy Jesus. Amen.   *Jeremy Taylor*

Further Petition
- Personal
- Church
- World

Lord's Prayer
Pray the words that Jesus taught us to pray:

Our Father in heaven,
> hallowed be your name;
> your kingdom come;
> your will be done, on earth as it is in heaven.
> Give us this day our daily bread.
> And forgive us our debts, as we forgive our debtors.
> And lead us not into temptation but deliver us from evil.
> For yours is the kingdom, and the power,
> and the glory, forever. Amen.

Benediction
Receive by faith this blessing from God:

May grace and peace be multiplied to you in the knowledge of God and of Jesus our Lord.   *2 Peter 1:2*

Postlude
In closing, say or sing this praise to God:

His Name for ever shall endure,
> last like the sun it shall;
Men shall be blessed in Him, and blessed
> all nations shall Him call.

Now blessèd be the Lord, our God,
    the God of Israel,
For He alone does wondrous works,
    in glory that excel.

And blessèd be His glorious Name
    to all eternity;
The whole earth let His glory fill.
    Amen, so let it be.   *Based on Psalm 72:17–19*

December 11

Meditation

Reflect on these words about the incarnation of the Lord Jesus:

For this He clothed Himself with man. For this He voluntarily subjected Himself to the experiences of men, that by bringing Himself to the measure of our weakness whom He loved, He might correspondingly bring us to the measure of His own strength.   *Clement of Alexandria*

Call to Worship

Hear God call you to worship through his word:

Now in putting everything in subjection to him, he left nothing outside his control. At present, we do not yet see everything in subjection to him. But we see him who for a little while was made lower than the angels, namely Jesus, crowned with glory and honor because of the suffering of death, so that by the grace of God he might taste death for everyone.   *Hebrews 2:8–9*

Adoration

Say or sing the words of this psalm:

Why do the heathen nations rage?
Why do the peoples plot in vain?
Earth's kings combine in enmity;
Her rulers join against God's reign.

They take their stand against the LORD
And challenge his anointed one:
"Let us break off their chains from us;
With their restraints let us be done."

The One enthroned in heaven laughs;
The Lord on high derides them all.
Then he rebukes them in his wrath;
His rage and terror on them fall.

The LORD has made it known to them:
"My chosen king I have installed
On Zion, my own holy hill.
He is the one whom I have called."

The king then solemnly declares:
"I will proclaim the LORD's decree.
'Today your father I've become;
You are my son,' he said to me.

"'Ask me, and for your heritage
I'll give you nations near and far.
You'll break them with an iron rod,
And smash them like a potter's jar.'"

Now therefore, kings, true wisdom find;
You judges of the earth, give ear.

With rev'rence come and serve the LORD;
Bow down with joy and trembling fear.

Pay homage to the royal son
Lest you in wrath aside are thrust,
For swiftly can his anger blaze.
Blessèd are all who in him trust.   *Sing Psalms: 2:1–12*

Reading of the Law
Hear God's law as his will for your life:

Beloved, let us love one another, for love is from God, and
whoever loves has been born of God and knows God. Anyone
who does not love does not know God, because God is love.
In this the love of God was made manifest among us, that
God sent his only Son into the world, so that we might live
through him. In this is love, not that we have loved God but
that he loved us and sent his Son to be the propitiation for
our sins. Beloved, if God so loved us, we also ought to love
one another.   *1 John 4:7–11*

Confession of Sin
Confess your sins to God:

O merciful Father, regard not what we have done against
you, but what our blessed Savior has done for us. Regard not
what we have made ourselves; but what he is made unto us of
you, our God. O that Christ may be to every one of our souls,
wisdom and righteousness, sanctification and redemption!
That his precious blood may cleanse us from all our sins;
and that your Holy Spirit may renew and sanctify our souls.
May he crucify our flesh with its affections and lusts, and
mortify all our members which are upon earth. O let not sin

reign in our mortal bodies, that we should obey in the lusts thereof; but being made free from sin, let us be the servants of righteousness. Amen.   *John Wesley*

Assurance of Pardon
Receive these words of comfort from God:

O Israel, hope in the LORD!
   For with the LORD there is steadfast love,
   and with him is plentiful redemption.
And he will redeem Israel
   from all his iniquities.   *Psalm 130:7–8*

Apostles' Creed
Confess what you believe about the Christian faith:

I believe in God the Father Almighty,
   Maker of heaven and earth.

I believe in Jesus Christ, his only-begotten Son, our Lord;
   who was conceived by the Holy Spirit, born of the
         Virgin Mary;
   suffered under Pontius Pilate;
   was crucified, dead, and buried;
   he descended into hell;
   the third day he rose again from the dead;
   he ascended into heaven,
   and sits at the right hand of God the Father Almighty;
   from there he shall come to judge the living and the dead.

I believe in the Holy Spirit;
   the holy catholic church;
   the communion of saints;

the forgiveness of sins;
the resurrection of the body;
and the life everlasting. Amen.

Praise
Say or sing this praise to God:

Praise God from whom all blessings flow;
Praise him all creatures here below;
Praise him above you heavenly host;
Praise Father, Son, and Holy Ghost. Amen.   *Doxology*

Catechism
Receive this instruction from the Heidelberg Catechism:

Q. 35. *What does it mean that he "was conceived by the Holy Spirit, born of the virgin Mary"?*
A. That the eternal Son of God, who is and remains true and eternal God, took to himself, through the working of the Holy Spirit, from the flesh and blood of the virgin Mary, a true human nature so that he might also become David's true descendant, like his brothers in all things except for sin.

Prayer for Illumination
As you read his word, ask God to enlighten your mind and heart:

Almighty, eternal and merciful God, whose Word is a lamp unto our feet and a light unto our path, open and illuminate our minds, that we may purely and perfectly understand your Word and that our lives may be conformed to what we have rightly understood, that in nothing we may be displeasing to your Majesty, through Jesus Christ our Lord. Amen.   *Huldrych Zwingli*

Scripture Reading
Read this portion of God's word: Job 19

Praise
Say or sing this praise to God:

Corde Natus

Of the Father's love begotten,
Ere the worlds began to be,
He is Alpha and Omega,
He the source, the ending He,
Of the things that are, that have been,
And that future years shall see,
Evermore and evermore!

At His Word the worlds were framèd;
He commanded; it was done:
Heaven and earth and depths of ocean
In their threefold order one;
All that grows beneath the shining
Of the moon and burning sun,
Evermore and evermore!

This is He Whom seers in old time
Chanted of with one accord;
Whom the voices of the prophets
Promised in their faithful word;
Now He shines, the long expected,
Let creation praise its Lord,
Evermore and evermore!

Righteous Judge of souls departed,
Righteous King of them that live,

On the Father's throne exalted
None in might with Thee may strive;
Who at last in vengeance coming
Sinners from Thy face shalt drive,
Evermore and evermore!   *Aurelius Prudentius*

Prayer of Intercession
As you make your requests to God, pray this prayer:

We beg you, Lord and Master, to be our help and aid. Save those among us who are in tribulation; have mercy on the lowly; lift up the fallen; show yourself unto the needy; heal the ungodly; convert the wanderers of your people; feed the hungry; release our prisoners; raise up the weak; comfort the fainthearted. Let all the Gentiles know that you are God alone, and Jesus Christ is your Son, and we are your people and the sheep of your pasture. Amen.   *Clement of Rome*

Further Petition
- Personal
- Church
- World

Lord's Prayer
Pray the words that Jesus taught us to pray:

Our Father in heaven,
    hallowed be your name;
    your kingdom come;
    your will be done, on earth as it is in heaven.
    Give us this day our daily bread.
    And forgive us our debts, as we forgive our debtors.

And lead us not into temptation but deliver us from evil.
For yours is the kingdom, and the power,
and the glory, forever. Amen.

Benediction
Receive by faith this blessing from God:

Now to him who is able to keep you from stumbling and to present you blameless before the presence of his glory with great joy, to the only God, our Savior, through Jesus Christ our Lord, be glory, majesty, dominion, and authority, before all time and now and forever. Amen.   *Jude 24–25*

Postlude
In closing, say or sing this praise to God:

His Name for ever shall endure,
    last like the sun it shall;
Men shall be blessed in Him, and blessed
    all nations shall Him call.

Now blessèd be the Lord, our God,
    the God of Israel,
For He alone does wondrous works,
    in glory that excel.

And blessèd be His glorious Name
    to all eternity;
The whole earth let His glory fill.
    Amen, so let it be.   *Based on Psalm 72:17–19*

December 12

Meditation

Reflect on these words about the incarnation of the Lord Jesus:

The spiritual and eternal clothed itself in the form of the natural and temporal. God himself, Elohim, Creator of heaven and earth, as Yahweh, God of the covenant, came down to the level of the creature, entered into history, assumed human language, emotions, and forms, in order to communicate himself with all his spiritual blessings to humans and so to prepare for his incarnation, his permanent and eternal indwelling in humanity.   *Herman Bavinck*

Call to Worship

Hear God call you to worship through his word:

Our help is in the name of the Lord,
  who made heaven and earth.   *Psalm 124:8*

Adoration

Say or sing the words of this Advent hymn:

To earth descending, Word sublime,
Begotten ere the days of time;

Who cam'st a Child, the world to aid,
As years their downward course display'd:

Each breast be lightened from above,
Each heart be kindled with thy love;
That we, who hear thy call today,
At length may cast earth's joys away:

That so—when thou, our Judge, art nigh,
All secret deeds of men to try,
Shalt mete to sin pangs rightly won,
To just men joy for deeds well done—

Thy servants may not be enchain'd
By punishment their guilt has gain'd,
But with the blessèd evermore
May serve and love thee, and adore.

To God the Father, God the Son,
And God the Spirit, Three in One,
Laud, honour, might, and glory be
From age to age eternally. Amen.   *Ambrose*

Reading of the Law
Hear God's law as his will for your life:

The words of our Lord Jesus Christ:

You shall love the Lord your God with all your heart and with
all your soul and with all your mind. This is the great and first
commandment. And a second is like it: You shall love your
neighbor as yourself. On these two commandments depend
all the Law and the Prophets.   *Matthew 22:37–40*

Confession of Sin
Confess your sins to God:

Almighty and most merciful Father, we have erred and strayed from your ways like lost sheep. We have followed too much the devices and desires of our own hearts. We have offended against your holy laws. We have left undone those things which we ought to have done, and we have done those things which we ought not to have done, and there is no health in us. But you, O Lord, have mercy upon us, miserable offenders. Spare those, O God, who confess their faults. Restore those who are repentant, according to your promises declared to mankind, in Christ Jesus our Lord. And grant, O most merciful Father, for his sake, that we may hereafter live a godly, righteous, and sober life, to the glory of your holy name. Amen.   Book of Common Prayer (1552)

Assurance of Pardon
Receive these words of comfort from God:

If we say we have no sin, we deceive ourselves, and the truth is not in us. If we confess our sins, he is faithful and just to forgive us our sins and to cleanse us from all unrighteousness. If we say we have not sinned, we make him a liar, and his word is not in us.   1 John 1:8–10

Apostles' Creed
Confess what you believe about the Christian faith:

I believe in God the Father Almighty,
    Maker of heaven and earth.

I believe in Jesus Christ, his only-begotten Son, our Lord;
    who was conceived by the Holy Spirit, born of the
           Virgin Mary;
    suffered under Pontius Pilate;
    was crucified, dead, and buried;
    he descended into hell;
    the third day he rose again from the dead;
    he ascended into heaven,
    and sits at the right hand of God the Father Almighty;
    from there he shall come to judge the living and the dead.

I believe in the Holy Spirit;
    the holy catholic church;
    the communion of saints;
    the forgiveness of sins;
    the resurrection of the body;
    and the life everlasting. Amen.

Praise
Say or sing this praise to God:

Glory be to God the Father,
Glory be to God the Son,
Glory be to God the Spirit,
ever three and ever one:
As it was in the beginning,
now and evermore shall be.   *Gloria Patri*

Catechism
Receive this instruction from the Heidelberg Catechism:

Q. 36. How does the holy conception and birth of Christ benefit you?

A. He is our mediator and, in God's sight, he covers with his innocence and perfect holiness my sin, in which I was conceived.

Prayer for Illumination
As you read his word, ask God to enlighten your mind and heart:

Merciful Lord, the comforter and teacher of your faithful people, increase in your church the desires which you have given, and confirm the hearts of those who hope in you by enabling them to understand the depth of your promises, that all of your adopted sons may even now behold, with the eyes of faith, and patiently wait for, the light which as yet you do not openly manifest; through Jesus Christ our Lord. Amen. *Ambrose*

Scripture Reading
Read this portion of God's word: Isaiah 7:10–17 and 9:1–7

Praise
Say or sing this praise to God:

Es ist ein Ros entsprungen

Lo, how a rose e'er blooming,
From tender stem has sprung.
Of Jesse's lineage coming,
As men of old have sung;
It came, a flow'ret bright,
Amid the cold of winter,
When half spent was the night.

Isaiah 'twas foretold it,
The Rose I have in mind,
With Mary, we behold it,
The virgin mother kind;
To show God's love aright,
She bore to men a Savior,
When half spent was the night.

O Flower, whose fragrance tender
With sweetness fills the air,
Dispel with glorious splendor
The darkness everywhere;
True man, yet very God,
From sin and death now save us,
And share our every load.

O Savior, Child of Mary,
Who felt our human woe;
O Savior, King of Glory,
Who does our weakness know,
Bring us at length we pray,
To the bright courts of Heaven
And to the endless day.   *Anonymous*

Prayer of Intercession
As you make your requests to God, pray this prayer:

O Lord, let me not henceforth desire health or life, except
to spend them for you, with you, and in you. You alone
know what is good for me; do, therefore, what seems best.
Give to me, or take from me; conform my will to yours; and
grant that, with humble and perfect submission, and in holy
confidence, I may receive the orders of your eternal provi-

dence; and may equally adore all that comes to me from you; through Jesus Christ our Lord. Amen.   *Blaise Pascal*

Further Petition
- Personal
- Church
- World

Lord's Prayer
Pray the words that Jesus taught us to pray:

Our Father in heaven,
    hallowed be your name;
    your kingdom come;
    your will be done, on earth as it is in heaven.
    Give us this day our daily bread.
    And forgive us our debts, as we forgive our debtors.
    And lead us not into temptation but deliver us from evil.
    For yours is the kingdom, and the power,
    and the glory, forever. Amen.

Benediction
Receive by faith this blessing from God:

The LORD bless you and keep you;
The LORD make his face to shine upon you
    and be gracious to you;
The LORD lift up his countenance upon you
    and give you peace.   *Numbers 6:24–26*

Postlude

In closing, say or sing this praise to God:

His Name for ever shall endure,
    last like the sun it shall;
Men shall be blessed in Him, and blessed
    all nations shall Him call.

Now blessèd be the Lord, our God,
    the God of Israel,
For He alone does wondrous works,
    in glory that excel.

And blessèd be His glorious Name
    to all eternity;
The whole earth let His glory fill.
    Amen, so let it be.   *Based on Psalm 72:17–19*

December 13

Meditation

Reflect on these words about the incarnation of the Lord Jesus:

Jesus was God and man in one person, that God and man might be happy together again.   *George Whitefield*

—

Call to Worship

Hear God call you to worship through his word:

Then the angel showed me the river of the water of life, bright as crystal, flowing from the throne of God and of the Lamb through the middle of the street of the city; also, on either side of the river, the tree of life with its twelve kinds of fruit, yielding its fruit each month. The leaves of the tree were for the healing of the nations.   *Revelation 22:1–2*

Adoration

Say or sing the words of this Advent hymn:

The tree of life my soul hath seen,
Laden with fruit, and always green:
The trees of nature fruitless be
Compared with Christ the apple tree.

His beauty doth all things excel:
By faith I know, but ne'er can tell
The glory which I now can see
In Jesus Christ the apple tree.

For happiness I long have sought,
And pleasure dearly I have bought:
I missed of all, but now I see
'Tis found in Christ the apple tree.

I'm weary with my former toil,
Here I will sit and rest awhile:
Under the shadow I will be
Of Jesus Christ the apple tree.

This fruit doth make my soul to thrive,
It keeps my dying faith alive;
Which makes my soul in haste to be
With Jesus Christ the apple tree.   *Richard Hutchins*

Reading of the Law
Hear God's law as his will for your life:

Hear, O Israel: The LORD our God, the LORD is one.
You shall love the LORD your God with all your heart and
        with all your soul and with all your might.
And these words that I command you today shall be on
        your heart.
You shall teach them diligently to your children,
    and shall talk of them when you sit in your house,
    and when you walk by the way,
    and when you lie down,
    and when you rise.
You shall bind them as a sign on your hand,

and they shall be as frontlets between your eyes.
You shall write them on the doorposts of your house and
on your gates.   *Deuteronomy 6:4–9*

Confession of Sin
Confess your sins to God:

O most great, most just and gracious God; you are of purer
eyes than to behold iniquity. You condemn the ungodly,
unrepentant, and unbelievers; but you have promised mercy
through Jesus Christ to all who repent and believe in him.
Therefore we confess that we are sinful by nature and that
we have all sinned and come short of the glory of God. We
have neglected and abused your holy worship and your
holy name. We have dealt unjustly and uncharitably with
our neighbors. We have not sought first your kingdom
and righteousness. We have not been content with our
daily bread. You have revealed your wonderful love to us in
Christ and offered us pardon and salvation in him; but we
have turned away. We have run into temptation; and the sin
that we should have hated, we have committed. Have mercy
upon us, most merciful Father. We confess you alone are our
hope. Make us your children and give us the Spirit of your
Son, our only Savior. Amen.   *Richard Baxter*

Assurance of Pardon
Receive these words of comfort from God:

Come now, let us reason together, says the LORD:
though your sins are like scarlet, they shall be as white
as snow;
though they are red like crimson, they shall become like
wool.   *Isaiah 1:18*

Nicene Creed

Confess what you believe about the Christian faith:

I believe in one God, the Father Almighty,
  Maker of heaven and earth, and of all things visible and
      invisible.

And in one Lord Jesus Christ, the only-begotten Son of God;
  begotten of the Father before all worlds;
  God of God, Light of Light, very God of very God;
  begotten, not made, being of one substance with the
      Father;
  by whom all things were made.
Who, for us men and for our salvation,
  came down from heaven
  and was incarnate by the Holy Spirit of the Virgin Mary,
  and was made man;
  and was crucified also for us under Pontius Pilate;
  he suffered and was buried;
  and the third day he rose again, according to the Scriptures;
  and ascended into heaven, and sits on the right hand of
      the Father;
  and he shall come again, with glory, to judge the living
      and the dead;
  whose kingdom shall have no end.

And I believe in the Holy Spirit, the Lord and Giver of life;
  who proceeds from the Father and the Son;
  who with the Father and the Son together is worshiped
      and glorified;
  who spoke by the prophets.

And I believe in one holy catholic and apostolic church.
  I acknowledge one baptism for the forgiveness of sins;
  and I look for the resurrection of the dead,
  and the life of the world to come. Amen.

Praise
Say or sing this praise to God:

Glory be to God the Father,
Glory be to God the Son,
Glory be to God the Spirit,
ever three and ever one:
As it was in the beginning,
now and evermore shall be.   *Gloria Patri*

Catechism
Receive this instruction from the Heidelberg Catechism:

Q. 37. *What do you understand by the word "suffered"?*
A. That during his whole life on earth, but especially at the
end, Christ sustained in body and soul the wrath of God
against the sin of the whole human race. This he did in order
that, by his suffering as the only atoning sacrifice he might
deliver us, body and soul, from eternal condemnation, and
gain for us God's grace, righteousness, and eternal life.

Prayer for Illumination
As you read his word, ask God to enlighten your mind and heart:

Heavenly Father, may you grant us to comprehend your holy
Word according to your divine will, that we may learn from it
to put all our confidence in you alone, and withdraw it from
all other creatures; moreover, that also our old man with all

his lusts may be crucified more and more each day, and that we may offer ourselves to you as a living sacrifice, to the glory of your holy name and to the edification of our neighbor, through our Lord Jesus Christ. Amen.   *Zacharias Ursinus*

Scripture Reading
Read this portion of God's word: Isaiah 11

Praise
Say this praise to God:

My soul magnifies the Lord.
And my spirit rejoices in God my Savior.
For he has regarded the lowliness of his servant.
For behold, from now on all generations shall call me blessed.
For he who is mighty has magnified me, and holy is his Name.
And his mercy is on them that fear him, throughout all
       generations.
He has showed strength with his arm.
He has scattered the proud in the imagination of their hearts.
He has put down the mighty from their thrones, and has
       exalted the humble and meek.
He has filled the hungry with good things, and the rich he
       has sent away empty.
He, remembering his mercy, has helped his servant Israel,
       as he promised to our forefathers, Abraham and
       his seed, forever.

Glory be to the Father, and to the Son, and to the Holy Spirit:
As it was in the beginning, is now, and ever shall be, world
       without end. Amen.   *Magnificat*

Prayer of Intercession
As you make your requests to God, pray this prayer:

Lord, we ask you, give ear to our prayers, and by your gracious visitation, lighten the darkness of our hearts, by our Lord Jesus Christ. Amen.   *Book of Common Prayer (1552)*

Further Petition
- Personal
- Church
- World

Lord's Prayer
Pray the words that Jesus taught us to pray:

Our Father in heaven,
   hallowed be your name;
   your kingdom come;
   your will be done, on earth as it is in heaven.
   Give us this day our daily bread.
   And forgive us our debts, as we forgive our debtors.
   And lead us not into temptation but deliver us from evil.
   For yours is the kingdom, and the power,
   and the glory, forever. Amen.

Benediction
Receive by faith this blessing from God:

May the God of hope fill you with all joy and peace in believing, so that by the power of the Holy Spirit you may abound in hope.   *Romans 15:13*

Postlude

In closing, say or sing this praise to God:

His Name for ever shall endure,
    last like the sun it shall;
Men shall be blessed in Him, and blessed
    all nations shall Him call.

Now blessèd be the Lord, our God,
    the God of Israel,
For He alone does wondrous works,
    in glory that excel.

And blessèd be His glorious Name
    to all eternity;
The whole earth let His glory fill.
    Amen, so let it be.   *Based on Psalm 72:17–19*

December 14

Meditation

Reflect on these words about the incarnation of the Lord Jesus:

After the fall there is nothing spoken of God in the Old Testament, nothing of his institutions, nothing of the way and manner of dealing with the church, but what has respect unto the future incarnation of Christ. And it had been absurd to bring in God under perpetual anthropopathies, as grieving, repenting, being angry, well pleased, and the like, were it not but that the divine person intended was to take on him the nature wherein such affections do dwell.   John Owen

———

Call to Worship

Hear God call you to worship through his word:

You will say in that day:
    "I will give thanks to you, O LORD,
    for though you were angry with me,
your anger turned away,
    that you might comfort me.

"Behold, God is my salvation;
    I will trust, and will not be afraid;
for the LORD GOD is my strength and my song,
    and he has become my salvation."   *Isaiah 12:1–2*

Adoration
Say or sing the words of this Advent hymn:

"Comfort, comfort all my people;
speak of peace," so says our God.
"Comfort those who sit in darkness,
groaning from their sorrows' load.
Speak to all Jerusalem
of the peace that waits for them;
tell them that their sins I cover,
that their warfare now is over."

All their sins our God will pardon,
blotting out each dark misdeed;
all that well deserved his anger
he no more will see or heed.
They have suffered many a day;
now their griefs have passed away.
God will change their aching sadness
into ever-springing gladness.

John the Baptist's voice is crying
in the desert far and near,
calling people to repentance
for the kingdom now is here.
O that warning cry obey!
Now prepare for God a way;

let the Valleys rise to meet him
and the hills bow down to greet him.

Then make straight the crooked highway;
make the rougher places plain.
Let your hearts be true and humble,
ready for his holy reign.
For the glory of the Lord
now over earth is spread abroad,
and all flesh shall see the token
that his word is never broken.   *Johann Olearius*

Reading of the Law
Hear God's law as his will for your life:

Our Lord Jesus said,

Blessed are the poor in spirit,
    for theirs is the kingdom of heaven.
Blessed are those who mourn,
    for they shall be comforted.
Blessed are the meek,
    for they shall inherit the earth.
Blessed are those who hunger and thirst for righteousness,
    for they shall be satisfied.
Blessed are the merciful,
    for they shall receive mercy.
Blessed are the pure in heart,
    for they shall see God.
Blessed are the peacemakers,
    for they shall be called sons of God.
Blessed are those who are persecuted for righteousness' sake,
    for theirs is the kingdom of heaven.   *Matthew 5:3–10*

Confession of Sin

Confess your sins to God:

Dear God, I cast myself at the foot of the cross, bewailing my exceeding sinfulness and unprofitableness deeply, most deeply aggravated by the infinity of my mercies. I plead your precious promises, and earnestly pray to you to shed abroad in my heart more love, more humility, more faith, more hope, more peace and joy; in short, to fill me with all the fullness of God, and make me worthy to be a partaker of the inheritance of the saints in light. Then I shall also be better in all the relations of life in which I am now so defective, and my light will shine before men, and I shall adorn the doctrine of my Savior in all things. Amen.   *William Wilberforce*

Assurance of Pardon

Receive these words of comfort from God:

Then he opened their minds to understand the Scriptures, and said to them, "Thus it is written, that the Christ should suffer and on the third day rise from the dead, and that repentance for the forgiveness of sins should be proclaimed in his name to all nations, beginning from Jerusalem."   *Luke 24:45–47*

Athanasian Creed, Part 1

Confess what you believe about the Christian faith:

Whoever desires to be saved should above all hold to the catholic faith. Anyone who does not keep it whole and unbroken will doubtless perish eternally. Now this is the catholic faith:

that we worship one God in Trinity and the Trinity in unity, neither confounding their persons nor dividing the essence.

For the person of the Father is a distinct person,
    the person of the Son is another,
    and that of the Holy Spirit still another.
But the divinity of the Father, Son, and Holy Spirit is one,
        the glory equal, the majesty coeternal.
Such as the Father is, such is the Son and such is the
        Holy Spirit.
The Father is uncreated, the Son is uncreated, the Holy
        Spirit is uncreated.
The Father is immeasurable, the Son is immeasurable,
        the Holy Spirit is immeasurable.
The Father is eternal, the Son is eternal, the Holy Spirit
        is eternal.
And yet there are not three eternal beings; there is but
        one eternal being.
So too there are not three uncreated or immeasurable
        beings;
    there is but one uncreated and immeasurable being.
Similarly, the Father is almighty, the Son is almighty,
        the Holy Spirit is almighty.
Yet there are not three almighty beings; there is but one
        almighty being.
Thus, the Father is God, the Son is God, the Holy Spirit
        is God.
Yet there are not three gods; there is but one God.
Thus, the Father is Lord, the Son is Lord, the Holy Spirit
        is Lord.
Yet there are not three lords; there is but one Lord.
Just as Christian truth compels us to confess each person
        individually as both God and Lord,

so catholic religion forbids us to say that there are three gods or lords.

Praise
Say or sing this praise to God:

Glory be to God the Father,
Glory be to God the Son,
Glory be to God the Spirit,
ever three and ever one:
As it was in the beginning,
now and evermore shall be.   *Gloria Patri*

Catechism
Receive this instruction from the Heidelberg Catechism:

Q. 38. Why did he suffer "under Pontius Pilate" as judge?
A. So that he, though innocent, might be condemned by an earthly judge, and so free us from the severe judgment of God that was to fall on us.

Prayer for Illumination
As you read his word, ask God to enlighten your mind and heart:

Lord, you know what distracted hearts we have, O give us self-recollection; you know what hard, dead hearts we have, O touch and awaken us! You know how we yet resist your Word and our lower nature is reluctant to bow to your scepter; therefore, O Lord, show forth your power; send your Spirit on high to work among us, to make our hearts submissive, and ourselves capable of living in true union with you, our salvation, and of yielding totally to your grace. Amen.
Gerhard Tersteegen

Scripture Reading

Read this portion of God's word: Isaiah 40

Praise

Say this praise to God:

Blessed be the Lord God of Israel, for he has visited,
    and redeemed his people;
and has raised up a mighty salvation for us,
    in the house of his servant David;
as he spoke by the mouth of his holy prophets,
    which have been since the world began;
that we should be saved from our enemies,
    and from the hands of all that hate us;
to perform the mercy promised to our forefathers,
    and to remember his holy covenant;
to perform the oath which he swore to our forefather
      Abraham,
    that he would give us;
that we, being delivered out of the hands of our enemies,
    might serve him without fear;
in holiness and righteousness before him,
    all the days of our life.
And you, child, shall be called the prophet of the Most High,
    for you shall go before the face of the Lord to prepare his
        ways;
to give knowledge of salvation unto his people,
    for the remission of their sins,
through the tender mercy of our God,
    whereby the Dayspring from on high has visited us;
to give light to them that sit in darkness,
    and in the shadow of death,

and to guide our feet into the way of peace.

Glory be to the Father,
  and to the Son,
  and to the Holy Spirit:
As it was in the beginning,
  is now and ever shall be,
  world without end. Amen.   *Benedictus*

Prayer of Intercession
As you make your requests to God, pray this prayer:

We pray you to impress upon us a deep sense of the importance of eternity. May we be looking continually to the end of our course; and remembering how soon all in which we here delight shall have passed away forever, may we prepare to give up our account of all things done in the body; and day by day may we have our conversation in heaven, moderating our affections toward the things of this world, and living here below a life of faith in the Son of God. Amen.   *Henry Thornton*

Further Petition
· Personal
· Church
· World

Lord's Prayer
Pray the words that Jesus taught us to pray:

Our Father in heaven,
  hallowed be your name;
  your kingdom come;
  your will be done, on earth as it is in heaven.

Give us this day our daily bread.
And forgive us our debts, as we forgive our debtors.
And lead us not into temptation but deliver us from evil.
For yours is the kingdom, and the power,
and the glory, forever. Amen.

Benediction
Receive by faith this blessing from God:

The grace of the Lord Jesus Christ and the love of God and the
fellowship of the Holy Spirit be with you all.   *2 Corinthians 13:14*

Postlude
In closing, say or sing this praise to God:

His Name for ever shall endure,
    last like the sun it shall;
Men shall be blessed in Him, and blessed
    all nations shall Him call.

Now blessèd be the Lord, our God,
    the God of Israel,
For He alone does wondrous works,
    in glory that excel.

And blessèd be His glorious Name
    to all eternity;
The whole earth let His glory fill.
    Amen, so let it be.   *Based on Psalm 72:17–19*

December 15

Reflect on these words about the incarnation of the Lord Jesus:

The successes of the Saviour, brought about by His incarnation, are of such kind and magnitude that, if one wished to go through them all, it would be like those who gaze at the expanse of the sea and try to count its waves. For as it is impossible to take in all the waves with the eye, their multitudinous approach transcending the perception of him who attempts it, so also is it impossible for him who wishes to take in all the successes of Christ in the body, to grasp the whole even by counting them, those which transcend his apprehension being more than those he thinks he has taken in. Better were it, therefore, not to attempt to speak of the whole, when one cannot give worthy expression even to a part; but to mention yet one, and to leave you to marvel at the whole. For all are equally wonderful, and wherever one turns one's eyes, there one sees the Divine working of the Word, and is beyond measure astonished.   *Athanasius*

Call to Worship
Hear God call you to worship through his word:

Behold, I am coming soon, bringing my recompense with me, to repay each one for what he has done. I am the Alpha and the Omega, the first and the last, the beginning and the end. *Revelation 22:12–13*

Adoration
Say or sing the words of this Advent hymn:

O come, divine Messiah;
The world in silence waits the day
When hope shall sing its triumph
And sadness flee away.

> *Dear Savior, haste! Come, come to earth.*
> *Dispel the night and show your face,*
> *and bid us hail the dawn of grace.*
> *O come, divine Messiah;*
> *the world in silence waits the day*
> *when hope shall sing its triumph*
> *and sadness flee away.*

O Christ, whom nations sigh for,
Whom priest and prophet long foretold,
Come, break the captive's fetters,
Redeem the long-lost fold.

You come in peace and meekness
And lowly will your cradle be;
All clothed in human weakness
Shall we your Godhead see.   *Simon-Joseph Pellegrin*

Reading of the Law

Hear God's law as his will for your life:

Our Lord said,

As the Father has loved me, so have I loved you. Abide in my love. If you keep my commandments, you will abide in my love, just as I have kept my Father's commandments and abide in his love. These things I have spoken to you, that my joy may be in you, and that your joy may be full. This is my commandment, that you love one another as I have loved you.   *John 15:9–12*

Confession of Sin

Confess your sins to God:

Almighty, eternal God! Forgive us our sin and lead us to eternal life, through Jesus Christ our Lord. Amen.   *Huldrych Zwingli*

Assurance of Pardon

Receive these words of comfort from God:

When my life was fainting away,
   I remembered the LORD,
and my prayer came to you,
   into your holy temple.
Those who pay regard to vain idols
   forsake their hope of steadfast love.
But I with the voice of thanksgiving
   will sacrifice to you;
what I have vowed I will pay.
   Salvation belongs to the LORD!   *Jonah 2:7–9*

Athanasian Creed, Part 2

Confess what you believe about the Christian faith:

Whoever desires to be saved should above all hold to the catholic faith. Anyone who does not keep it whole and unbroken will doubtless perish eternally. Now this is the catholic faith:

that we worship one God in Trinity and the Trinity in unity, neither confounding their persons nor dividing the essence. . . .

> The Father was neither made nor created nor begotten
> from anyone.
> The Son was neither made nor created; he was begotten
> from the Father alone.
> The Holy Spirit was neither made nor created nor
> begotten;
> > he proceeds from the Father and the Son.
> Accordingly, there is one Father, not three fathers;
> > there is one Son, not three sons;
> > there is one Holy Spirit, not three holy spirits.
> None in this Trinity is before or after, none is greater or
> smaller;
> > in their entirety the three persons are coeternal and
> > coequal with each other.
> So in everything, as was said earlier, the unity in Trinity,
> and the Trinity in unity, is to be worshiped.
> Anyone then who desires to be saved should think thus
> about the Trinity.

Praise
Say or sing this praise to God:

Glory be to God the Father,
Glory be to God the Son,
Glory be to God the Spirit,
ever three and ever one:
As it was in the beginning,
now and evermore shall be.   *Gloria Patri*

Catechism
Receive this instruction from the Heidelberg Catechism:

Q. 39. Is it significant that he was "crucified" instead of dying some other way?
A. Yes. By this death I am convinced that he shouldered the curse which lay on me since death by crucifixion was cursed by God.

Prayer for Illumination
As you read his word, ask God to enlighten your mind and heart:

O God, you instruct us by your Holy Scriptures—we urge you by your grace to enlighten our minds and cleanse our hearts; that reading, hearing, and meditating upon them, we may rightly understand and heartily embrace the things you have revealed in them. Give efficacy to the reading of the gospel in your Word, that through the operation of the Holy Spirit, this holy seed may be received into our hearts as into good ground; and that we may not only hear your Word but keep it, living in conformity with your precepts; so that we may finally attain everlasting salvation, through Jesus Christ our Lord. Amen.   *Waldensian Liturgy*

Scripture Reading

Read this portion of God's word: Isaiah 42

Praise

Say this praise to God:

Lord, now let your servant depart in peace according to
      your word.
For mine eyes have seen your salvation,
Which you have prepared before the face of all people,
To be a light to lighten the Gentiles and to be the glory of
      your people Israel. Amen.   *Nunc Dimittis*

Prayer of Intercession

As you make your requests to God, pray this prayer:

Lord, you know our weakness, and the temptations to which
we are exposed: our dangers from the enemy of souls, and
from the present world, which is full of snares, and, above all,
from the enemy within, our vile flesh and deceitful hearts, so
apt to betray us into sin. We pray, therefore, that you will arm
us with the whole armor of God, and uphold us with your
free Spirit; and watch over us for good evermore. O make us
experience the strongest aids of your heavenly grace, that we
may never fall a prey to the spiritual adversary that seeks to
devour us. Amen.   *Augustus Toplady*

Further Petition

- Personal
- Church
- World

Lord's Prayer
Pray the words that Jesus taught us to pray:

Our Father in heaven,
   hallowed be your name;
   your kingdom come;
   your will be done, on earth as it is in heaven.
   Give us this day our daily bread.
   And forgive us our debts, as we forgive our debtors.
   And lead us not into temptation but deliver us from evil.
   For yours is the kingdom, and the power,
   and the glory, forever. Amen.

Benediction
Receive by faith this blessing from God:

Now to him who is able to do far more abundantly than all
that we ask or think, according to the power at work within
us, to him be glory in the church and in Christ Jesus throughout all generations, forever and ever. Amen.   *Ephesians 3:20–21*

Postlude
In closing, say or sing this praise to God:

His Name for ever shall endure,
   last like the sun it shall;
Men shall be blessed in Him, and blessed
   all nations shall Him call.

Now blessèd be the Lord, our God,
   the God of Israel,
For He alone does wondrous works,
   in glory that excel.

And blessèd be His glorious Name
    to all eternity;
The whole earth let His glory fill.
    Amen, so let it be.   *Based on Psalm 72:17–19*

December 16

Meditation
Reflect on these words about the incarnation of the Lord Jesus:

In the mystery of His incarnation the only-begotten of the Father increased what was ours, but diminished not what was His.   *Gregory the Great*

———

Call to Worship
Hear God call you to worship through his word:

Oh give thanks to the LORD, for he is good,
   for his steadfast love endures forever!
Let the redeemed of the LORD say so,
   whom he has redeemed from trouble
and gathered in from the lands,
   from the east and from the west,
   from the north and from the south.   *Psalm 107:1–3*

Adoration
Say or sing the words of this Advent hymn:

Hills of the North, rejoice,
river and mountain-spring,

hark to the advent voice;
valley and lowland, sing:
Christ comes in righteousness and love,
he brings salvation from above.

Isles of the Southern seas,
sing to the listening earth,
carry on every breeze
hope of a world's new birth:
In Christ shall all be made anew,
his word is sure, his promise true.

Lands of the East, arise,
he is your brightest morn,
greet him with joyous eyes,
praise shall his path adorn:
Your seers have longed to know their Lord;
to you he comes, the final word.

Shores of the utmost West,
lands of the setting sun,
welcome the heavenly guest
in whom the dawn has come:
He brings a never-ending light
who triumphed o'er our darkest night.

Shout, as you journey home,
songs be in every mouth,
lo, from the North they come,
from East and West and South:
In Jesus all shall find their rest,
in him the universe be blest. *Charles E. Oakley*

Reading of the Law

Hear God's law as his will for your life:

The words of our Lord Jesus Christ:

Unless your righteousness exceeds that of the scribes and Pharisees, you will never enter the kingdom of heaven. . . . You therefore must be perfect, as your heavenly Father is perfect. . . . Beware of practicing your righteousness before other people in order to be seen by them, for then you will have no reward from your Father who is in heaven. . . . Seek first the kingdom of God and his righteousness, and all these things will be added to you. . . . So whatever you wish that others would do to you, do also to them, for this is the Law and the Prophets.   *Matthew 5:20, 48; 6:1, 33; 7:12*

Confession of Sin

Confess your sins to God:

Almighty, everlasting God and Father, we acknowledge and confess that we indeed were conceived and born in sin and, therefore, inclined to all evil and slow to all good; that we unceasingly transgress your holy commandments, and corrupt ourselves more and more. But we are sorry for this and desire your grace and help. Therefore, have mercy upon us, most gracious and merciful God and Father, through your Son our Lord Jesus Christ. Grant to us and increase in us your Holy Spirit, so that we may recognize our sin and unrighteousness from the depth of our heart, feel true contrition and grief for them, die to them completely, and please you wholly in a new, godly life. Amen.   *Martin Bucer*

Assurance of Pardon
Receive these words of comfort from God:

For I delivered to you as of first importance what I also received: that Christ died for our sins in accordance with the Scriptures, that he was buried, that he was raised on the third day in accordance with the Scriptures.   *1 Corinthians 15:3–4*

Athanasian Creed, Part 3
Confess what you believe about the Christian faith:

Whoever desires to be saved should above all hold to the catholic faith. Anyone who does not keep it whole and unbroken will doubtless perish eternally. Now this is the catholic faith:

that we worship one God in Trinity and the Trinity in unity, neither confounding their persons nor dividing the essence. . . .

But it is necessary for eternal salvation that one also believe in the incarnation of our Lord Jesus Christ faithfully.

Now this is the true faith:

> that we believe and confess that our Lord Jesus Christ,
> > God's Son,
> > is both God and man, equally.
> He is God from the essence of the Father, begotten
> > before time;
> > and he is man from the essence of his mother, born
> > > in time;
> > completely God, completely man, with a rational soul
> > > and human flesh;
> > equal to the Father as regards divinity,
> > less than the Father as regards humanity.

Although he is God and man, yet Christ is not two,
  but one.
He is one, however, not by his divinity being turned
  into flesh,
 but by God's taking humanity to himself.
He is one, certainly not by the blending of his essence,
 but by the unity of his person.
For just as one man is both rational soul and flesh,
 so too the one Christ is both God and man.

He suffered for our salvation;
he descended to hell;
he arose from the dead on the third day;
he ascended to heaven;
he is seated at the Father's right hand;
from there he will come to judge the living and the dead.
At his coming all people will arise bodily and give an
  accounting of their own deeds.
Those who have done good will enter eternal life,
 and those who have done evil will enter eternal fire.

This is the catholic faith: that one cannot be saved without
believing it firmly and faithfully.

Praise
Say or sing this praise to God:

Glory be to God the Father,
Glory be to God the Son,
Glory be to God the Spirit,
ever three and ever one:
As it was in the beginning,
now and evermore shall be. *Gloria Patri*

Catechism

Receive this instruction from the Heidelberg Catechism:

Q. 40. Why did Christ have to suffer death?
A. Because God's justice and truth require it: nothing else could pay for our sins except the death of the Son of God.

Prayer for Illumination

As you read his word, ask God to enlighten your mind and heart:

Almighty God, I earnestly ask you for such deeper fellowship of the Holy Spirit, who speaks in the blessed Scriptures, that when I open them, I may perceive his mind in what I read, and immediately hear in them his voice to myself. I ask you for a quicker understanding in spiritual things, for more desire to understand, a fuller perception of your promise in the church, that I may become teachable, and may love that by which you will teach me. Amen.   *Henry Wotherspoon*

Scripture Reading

Read this portion of God's word: Isaiah 49

Praise

Say this praise to God:

Holy, holy, holy, Lord God of hosts,
heaven and earth are full of your glory.
Glory be to you, O Lord Most High.
Blessed is he that comes in the name of the Lord.
Hosanna in the highest. Amen.   *Sanctus*

Prayer of Intercession

As you make your requests to God, pray this prayer:

Till we arrive at heaven, our home, may we gratefully avail ourselves of all the advantages afforded us in our journey. We bless you for wilderness privileges; for the manna; the streams of the smitten rock; the fiery cloudy pillar; the tabernacle and the ark. We bless you for the Sabbath, the sanctuary, and the ministry of the Word. We bless you for the opportunities we have, this day, enjoyed in waiting upon you. Amen.   *William Jay*

Further Petition

- Personal
- Church
- World

Lord's Prayer

Pray the words that Jesus taught us to pray:

Our Father in heaven,
    hallowed be your name;
    your kingdom come;
    your will be done, on earth as it is in heaven.
    Give us this day our daily bread.
    And forgive us our debts, as we forgive our debtors.
    And lead us not into temptation but deliver us from evil.
    For yours is the kingdom, and the power,
    and the glory, forever. Amen.

Benediction

Receive by faith this blessing from God:

Now may the God of peace himself sanctify you completely, and may your whole spirit and soul and body be kept blameless at the coming of our Lord Jesus Christ. He who calls you is faithful; he will surely do it.   *1 Thessalonians 5:23–24*

Postlude

In closing, say or sing this praise to God:

His Name for ever shall endure,
    last like the sun it shall;
Men shall be blessed in Him, and blessed
    all nations shall Him call.

Now blessèd be the Lord, our God,
    the God of Israel,
For He alone does wondrous works,
    in glory that excel.

And blessèd be His glorious Name
    to all eternity;
The whole earth let His glory fill.
    Amen, so let it be.   *Based on Psalm 72:17–19*

December 17

Reflect on these words about the incarnation of the Lord Jesus:

Thanks be to God, He is a Savior who seeks the lost, who with eyes supernaturally farsighted discerns us a long way off, and draws our interest to Himself by the sweet constraint of His grace, till we are face to face with Him and our soul is saved. As once, in the incarnation, He came down from heaven to seek mankind, so He still comes down silently from heaven in the case of each sinner, and pursues his search for that individual soul following it through all the mazes of its waywardness and the devious paths of its folly, sometimes unto the very brink of destruction, till at last His grace overtakes it and says, "I must lodge at your house." For, besides the divine omniscience here manifested, we are made witnesses of the Lord's sovereign and almighty power.   *Geerhardus Vos*

Call to Worship
Hear God call you to worship through his word:

As it is written in Isaiah the prophet,

"Behold, I send my messenger before your face,
    who will prepare your way,
the voice of one crying in the wilderness:
    'Prepare the way of the Lord,
make his paths straight.'"   Mark 1:2–3

Adoration

Say or sing the words of this Advent hymn:

Jesus came, the heavens adoring,
Came with peace from realms on high;
Jesus came for man's redemption,
Lowly came on earth to die;
Alleluia! Alleluia!
Came in deep humility.

Jesus comes again in mercy.
When our hearts are bowed with care;
Jesus comes again in answer
To an earnest, heartfelt prayer;
Alleluia! Alleluia!
Comes to save us from despair.

Jesus comes to hearts rejoicing,
Bringing news of sins forgiven;
Jesus comes in sounds of gladness,
Leading souls redeemed to heaven.
Alleluia! Alleluia!
Now the gate of death is riven.

Jesus comes in joy and sorrow,
Shares alike our hopes and fears;
Jesus comes, whate'er befalls us,

Glads our hearts, and dries our tears;
Alleluia! Alleluia!
Cheering e'en our failing years.

Jesus comes on clouds triumphant
When the heavens shall pass away;
Jesus comes again in glory.
Let us, then, our homage pay,
Alleluia! ever singing
Till the dawn of endless day.   *Godfrey Thring*

Reading of the Law
Hear God's law as his will for your life:

And God spoke all these words, saying,

"I am the LORD your God, who brought you out of the
land of Egypt, out of the house of slavery.

You shall have no other gods before me.

You shall not make for yourself a carved image, or any
likeness of anything that is in heaven above, or that is in
the earth beneath, or that is in the water under the earth.
You shall not bow down to them or serve them, for I the
LORD your God am a jealous God, visiting the iniquity of
the fathers on the children to the third and the fourth
generation of those who hate me, but showing steadfast
love to thousands of those who love me and keep my
commandments.

You shall not take the name of the LORD your God in
vain, for the LORD will not hold him guiltless who takes
his name in vain.

Remember the Sabbath day, to keep it holy. Six days
you shall labor, and do all your work, but the seventh day

is a Sabbath to the LORD your God. On it you shall not do any work, you, or your son, or your daughter, your male servant, or your female servant, or your livestock, or the sojourner who is within your gates. For in six days the LORD made heaven and earth, the sea, and all that is in them, and rested on the seventh day. Therefore the LORD blessed the Sabbath day and made it holy.

Honor your father and your mother, that your days may be long in the land that the LORD your God is giving you.

You shall not murder.

You shall not commit adultery.

You shall not steal.

You shall not bear false witness against your neighbor.

You shall not covet your neighbor's house; you shall not covet your neighbor's wife, or his male servant, or his female servant, or his ox, or his donkey, or anything that is your neighbor's."   Exodus 20:1–17

Confession of Sin
Confess your sins to God:

O Lord, let not your law be a cursing to our consciences, but rather give us grace under this extreme and heavy burden of sin, to be fully persuaded, that you by your death have taken away all our sins, and fulfilled the law for us, and by this means have delivered us from the curse of the law and paid our ransom; and then we, being thus fully persuaded, may have quiet and settled hearts, and a free conscience, and glad desiring wills to forsake this wicked world. Amen.
Henry Smith

Assurance of Pardon

Receive these words of comfort from God:

I will sprinkle clean water on you, and you shall be clean from all your uncleannesses, and from all your idols I will cleanse you. And I will give you a new heart, and a new spirit I will put within you. And I will remove the heart of stone from your flesh and give you a heart of flesh. And I will put my Spirit within you, and cause you to walk in my statutes and be careful to obey my rules.   *Ezekiel 36:25–27*

Nicene Creed

Confess what you believe about the Christian faith:

I believe in one God, the Father Almighty,
    Maker of heaven and earth, and of all things visible and
        invisible.

And in one Lord Jesus Christ, the only-begotten Son of God;
    begotten of the Father before all worlds;
    God of God, Light of Light, very God of very God;
    begotten, not made, being of one substance with the
        Father;
    by whom all things were made.
Who, for us men and for our salvation,
    came down from heaven
    and was incarnate by the Holy Spirit of the Virgin Mary,
    and was made man;
    and was crucified also for us under Pontius Pilate;
    he suffered and was buried;
    and the third day he rose again, according to the Scriptures;
    and ascended into heaven, and sits on the right hand of
        the Father;

and he shall come again, with glory, to judge the living
and the dead;
whose kingdom shall have no end.

And I believe in the Holy Spirit, the Lord and Giver of life;
who proceeds from the Father and the Son;
who with the Father and the Son together is worshiped
and glorified;
who spoke by the prophets.

And I believe in one holy catholic and apostolic church.
I acknowledge one baptism for the forgiveness of sins;
and I look for the resurrection of the dead,
and the life of the world to come. Amen.

Praise
Say or sing this praise to God:

Glory be to God the Father,
Glory be to God the Son,
Glory be to God the Spirit,
ever three and ever one:
As it was in the beginning,
now and evermore shall be.   *Gloria Patri*

Catechism
Receive this instruction from the Heidelberg Catechism:

Q. 41. Why was he "buried"?
A. His burial testifies that he really died.

Prayer for Illumination

As you read his word, ask God to enlighten your mind and heart:

Almighty God, enter our hearts, and so fill us with your love, that, forsaking all evil desires, we may embrace you, our only good. Show unto us, for your mercies' sake, O Lord our God, what you are unto us. Say unto our souls, "I am your salvation." So speak that we may hear. Our hearts are before you; open our ears; let us hasten after your voice and take hold of you. Amen.   *Augustine*

Scripture Reading

Read this portion of God's word: Isaiah 50

Praise

Say this praise to God:

O Sapientia

O Wisdom, coming forth from the mouth of the Most High,
reaching from one end to the other,
mightily and sweetly ordering all things—
come and teach us the way of prudence. Amen.

Prayer of Intercession

As you make your requests to God, pray this prayer:

O Lord, grant that I may dedicate all my hope unto your providence, power, and mercy, only commending all my troubles, miseries, calamities, adversities, and crosses whatsoever unto you only to be relieved and comforted. O let me not so much as think that the hand of man can hold me up in the least of my dangers, and yet my God, since you work sometimes by means, and sometimes without means, let me not refuse the aid of man, whom it may please you to raise and appoint for my good. Amen.   *Henry Smith*

Further Petition
- Personal
- Church
- World

Lord's Prayer
Pray the words that Jesus taught us to pray:

Our Father in heaven,
hallowed be your name;
your kingdom come;
your will be done, on earth as it is in heaven.
Give us this day our daily bread.
And forgive us our debts, as we forgive our debtors.
And lead us not into temptation but deliver us from evil.
For yours is the kingdom, and the power,
and the glory, forever. Amen.

Benediction
Receive by faith this blessing from God:

May grace and peace be multiplied to you in the knowledge of God and of Jesus our Lord.   *2 Peter 1:2*

Postlude
In closing, say or sing this praise to God:

His Name for ever shall endure,
last like the sun it shall;

Men shall be blessed in Him, and blessed
　all nations shall Him call.

Now blessèd be the Lord, our God,
　the God of Israel,
For He alone does wondrous works,
　in glory that excel.

And blessèd be His glorious Name
　to all eternity;
The whole earth let His glory fill.
　Amen, so let it be.　*Based on Psalm 72:17–19*

December 18

Meditation

Reflect on these words about the incarnation of the Lord Jesus:

Christ caused humanity to cleave to and to become one with God. For unless a human being had overcome the enemy of humanity, the enemy would not have been legitimately vanquished. And again, unless it had been God incarnate who had freely given salvation, we could never have possessed it securely. And unless humanity had been joined to God, we could never have become partakers of incorruptibility. For it was incumbent upon the Mediator between God and humanity, by His relationship to both, to bring both to friendship and concord, and present humanity to God, while He revealed God to humanity.   *Irenaeus*

Call to Worship

Hear God call you to worship through his word:

Let the nations be glad and sing for joy,
    for you judge the peoples with equity
    and guide the nations upon earth. *Selah*
Let the peoples praise you, O God;
    let all the peoples praise you!   *Psalm 67:4–5*

Say or sing the words of this psalm:

May God arise, and may his foes
Be scattered far and put to flight.
As smoke is blown before the wind,
So may your foes be blown from sight:
As wax is melted by the fire,
May they before God's wrath expire.

But may the righteous all be glad;
May they rejoice and sing aloud.
Sing praise to God, sing to his name;
Extol the One who rides the cloud;
For he alone is named the LORD—
With joy all praise to him accord.

A father to the fatherless,
Of widows' rights the champion,
Is God within his holy place;
He gives a home to the forlorn.
He leads the captives forth with song;
To rebels barren wastes belong.

O realms of earth, sing to the Lord,
To him who has his throne on high;
All kingdoms, join in praise to God,
Whose chariot rides the ancient sky.
Listen! As he sends out his word,
A mighty thundering is heard.

Proclaim the mighty power of God,
Whose glory shines on Israèl;
His strength is awesome in the heavens

And in the place he comes to dwell.
His people, Isr'el, God will raise
To strength and might. To God be praise!
Sing Psalms: 68:1–6, 32–35

Reading of the Law
Hear God's law as his will for your life:

Beloved, let us love one another, for love is from God, and whoever loves has been born of God and knows God. Anyone who does not love does not know God, because God is love. In this the love of God was made manifest among us, that God sent his only Son into the world, so that we might live through him. In this is love, not that we have loved God but that he loved us and sent his Son to be the propitiation for our sins. Beloved, if God so loved us, we also ought to love one another.   1 John 4:7–11

Confession of Sin
Confess your sins to God:

O Almighty and merciful Father, you pour your benefits upon us—forgive the unthankfulness with which we have requited your goodness. We have remained before you with dead and senseless hearts, unkindled with love of your gentle and enduring goodness. Turn us, O merciful Father, and so shall we be turned. Make us with our whole heart to hunger and thirst after you, and with all our longing to desire you. Amen.   *Anselm*

Assurance of Pardon
Receive these words of comfort from God:

Blessed be the God and Father of our Lord Jesus Christ! According to his great mercy, he has caused us to be born again to a living hope through the resurrection of Jesus Christ from the dead, to an inheritance that is imperishable, undefiled, and unfading, kept in heaven for you, who by God's power are being guarded through faith for a salvation ready to be revealed in the last time.   *1 Peter 1:3–5*

Apostles' Creed
Confess what you believe about the Christian faith:

I believe in God the Father Almighty,
    Maker of heaven and earth.

I believe in Jesus Christ, his only-begotten Son, our Lord;
    who was conceived by the Holy Spirit, born of the
            Virgin Mary;
    suffered under Pontius Pilate;
    was crucified, dead, and buried;
    he descended into hell;
    the third day he rose again from the dead;
    he ascended into heaven,
    and sits at the right hand of God the Father Almighty;
    from there he shall come to judge the living and the dead.

I believe in the Holy Spirit;
    the holy catholic church;
    the communion of saints;
    the forgiveness of sins;
    the resurrection of the body;
    and the life everlasting. Amen.

Praise

Say or sing this praise to God:

Glory be to God the Father,
Glory be to God the Son,
Glory be to God the Spirit,
ever three and ever one:
As it was in the beginning,
now and evermore shall be.   *Gloria Patri*

Catechism

Receive this instruction from the Heidelberg Catechism:

Q. 42. *Since Christ has died for us, why do we still have to die?*
A. Our death is not a payment for our sins, but only a dying
to sins and an entering into eternal life.

Prayer for Illumination

As you read his word, ask God to enlighten your mind and heart:

Almighty, eternal and merciful God, whose Word is a lamp
unto our feet and a light unto our path, open and illuminate
our minds, that we may purely and perfectly understand
your Word and that our lives may be conformed to what
we have rightly understood, that in nothing we may be
displeasing to your Majesty, through Jesus Christ our Lord.
Amen.   *Huldrych Zwingli*

Scripture Reading

Read this portion of God's word: Isaiah 52:13–53:12

Praise

Say this praise to God:

O Adonai

O Adonai, and Captain of the house of Israel,
who appeared to Moses in the fire of the burning bush
and gave him the law on Sinai—
come and redeem us with an outstretched arm. Amen.

Prayer of Intercession

As you make your requests to God, pray this prayer:

We pray, God, our Sovereign, Christ, King forever in the
world of spirits—stretch out your strong hands over your
holy church and over the people that will always be yours.
Defend, protect, preserve them, fight and do battle for them,
subject their enemies to them, subdue the invisible powers
that oppose them, as you have already subdued those that
hate us. Raise now the sign of victory over us and grant that
we may sing with Moses the song of triumph. For yours are
victory and power forever and ever. Amen.   *Hippolytus of Rome*

Further Petition

- Personal
- Church
- World

Lord's Prayer

Pray the words that Jesus taught us to pray:

Our Father in heaven,
   hallowed be your name;
   your kingdom come;

your will be done, on earth as it is in heaven.
Give us this day our daily bread.
And forgive us our debts, as we forgive our debtors.
And lead us not into temptation but deliver us from evil.
For yours is the kingdom, and the power,
and the glory, forever. Amen.

Benediction
Receive by faith this blessing from God:

Now to him who is able to keep you from stumbling and to present you blameless before the presence of his glory with great joy, to the only God, our Savior, through Jesus Christ our Lord, be glory, majesty, dominion, and authority, before all time and now and forever. Amen.   *Jude 24–25*

Postlude
In closing, say or sing this praise to God:

His Name for ever shall endure,
    last like the sun it shall;
Men shall be blessed in Him, and blessed
    all nations shall Him call.

Now blessèd be the Lord, our God,
    the God of Israel,
For He alone does wondrous works,
    in glory that excel.

And blessèd be His glorious Name
    to all eternity;
The whole earth let His glory fill.
    Amen, so let it be.   *Based on Psalm 72:17–19*

December 19

Meditation
Reflect on these words about the incarnation of the Lord Jesus:

What a wonder is it that two natures infinitely distant should be more intimately united than anything in the world, and yet without any confusion! That the same person should have both a glory and a grief; an infinite joy in the Deity, and an inexpressible sorrow in the humanity; that a God upon a throne should be an infant in a cradle; the thundering Creator be a weeping babe and a suffering man. These are such expressions of mighty power, as well as condescending love, that they astonish men upon earth and angels in heaven.   *Stephen Charnock*

———

Call to Worship
Hear God call you to worship through his word:

Rejoice in the Lord always; again I will say, rejoice. Let your reasonableness be known to everyone. The Lord is at hand; do not be anxious about anything, but in everything by prayer and supplication with thanksgiving let your requests be made known to God. And the peace of God, which surpasses

all understanding, will guard your hearts and your minds in
Christ Jesus.   *Philippians 4:4–7*

Adoration
Say or sing the words of this Advent hymn:

Hark! A thrilling voice is sounding!
"Christ is near," we hear it say.
"Cast away the works of darkness,
all you children of the day!"

See, the Lamb, so long expected,
comes with pardon down from heaven.
Let us haste, with tears of sorrow,
one and all, to be forgiven.

So, when next he comes in glory
and the world is wrapped in fear,
he will shield us with his mercy
and with words of love draw near.

Honor, glory, might, dominion
to the Father and the Son
with the everlasting Spirit
while eternal ages run!   *Anonymous*

Reading of the Law
Hear God's law as his will for your life:

The words of our Lord Jesus Christ:

You shall love the Lord your God with all your heart and with
all your soul and with all your mind. This is the great and first
commandment. And a second is like it: You shall love your

neighbor as yourself. On these two commandments depend all the Law and the Prophets.   *Matthew 22:37–40*

Confession of Sin
Confess your sins to God:

Lord, you are our Father and we are but dust and filth; you are our Creator, and we are the work of your hands; you are our Shepherd, we are your flock; you are our Redeemer, we are the people that you have purchased; you are our God, we are your inheritance. Therefore, do not be angry with us to correct us in your fury. No longer remember our iniquity to punish it, but chastise us gently in your kindness. Your wrath is kindled because of our demerits; but remember that your name has been pronounced over us and that we bear your mark and standard. And continue, rather, the work that you have begun in us by your grace, that all the earth might know that you are our God and our Savior. Amen.   *John Calvin*

Assurance of Pardon
Receive these words of comfort from God:

Comfort, comfort my people, says your God.
Speak tenderly to Jerusalem,
   and cry to her
that her warfare is ended,
   that her iniquity is pardoned,
that she has received from the LORD's hand
   double for all her sins.   *Isaiah 40:1–2*

Apostles' Creed

Confess what you believe about the Christian faith:

I believe in God the Father Almighty,
    Maker of heaven and earth.

I believe in Jesus Christ, his only-begotten Son, our Lord;
    who was conceived by the Holy Spirit, born of the
           Virgin Mary;
    suffered under Pontius Pilate;
    was crucified, dead, and buried;
    he descended into hell;
    the third day he rose again from the dead;
    he ascended into heaven,
    and sits at the right hand of God the Father Almighty;
    from there he shall come to judge the living and the dead.

I believe in the Holy Spirit;
    the holy catholic church;
    the communion of saints;
    the forgiveness of sins;
    the resurrection of the body;
    and the life everlasting. Amen.

Praise

Say or sing this praise to God:

Praise and honor to the Father,
Praise and honor to the Son,
Praise and honor to the Spirit,
Ever three and ever one:
One in might and one in glory
While unending ages run!   *Doxology*

Catechism
Receive this instruction from the Heidelberg Catechism:

Q. 43. *What further benefit do we receive from Christ's sacrifice and death on the cross?*
A. By his power our old man is crucified, put to death, and buried with him, so that the evil desires of the flesh may no longer rule us, but that instead we may offer ourselves as a sacrifice of thanksgiving to him.

Prayer for Illumination
As you read his word, ask God to enlighten your mind and heart:

Merciful Lord, the comforter and teacher of your faithful people, increase in your church the desires which you have given, and confirm the hearts of those who hope in you by enabling them to understand the depth of your promises, that all of your adopted sons may even now behold, with the eyes of faith, and patiently wait for, the light which as yet you do not openly manifest; through Jesus Christ our Lord. Amen.   *Ambrose*

Scripture Reading
Read this portion of God's word: Jeremiah 23:1–6 and 33:14–26

Praise
Say this praise to God:

O Radix Jesse

O Root of Jesse, standing as a sign among the peoples;
before you kings will shut their mouths,
to you the nations will make their prayer—
come and deliver us, and delay no longer. Amen.

Prayer of Intercession
As you make your requests to God, pray this prayer:

Lord, raise up, we pray, your power, and come among us, and with great might help us; that whereas through our sins and wickedness, we are obstructed and hindered, your bountiful grace and mercy, through the satisfaction of your Son our Lord, may deliver us, to whom, with you and the Holy Spirit, be honor and glory, world without end. Amen.
Book of Common Prayer (1552)

Further Petition
- Personal
- Church
- World

Lord's Prayer
Pray the words that Jesus taught us to pray:

Our Father in heaven,
hallowed be your name;
your kingdom come;
your will be done, on earth as it is in heaven.
Give us this day our daily bread.
And forgive us our debts, as we forgive our debtors.
And lead us not into temptation but deliver us from evil.
For yours is the kingdom, and the power,
and the glory, forever. Amen.

Benediction

Receive by faith this blessing from God:

The LORD bless you and keep you;
The LORD make his face to shine upon you
    and be gracious to you;
The LORD lift up his countenance upon you
    and give you peace. *Numbers 6:24–26*

Postlude

In closing, say or sing this praise to God:

His Name for ever shall endure,
    last like the sun it shall;
Men shall be blessed in Him, and blessed
    all nations shall Him call.

Now blessèd be the Lord, our God,
    the God of Israel,
For He alone does wondrous works,
    in glory that excel.

And blessèd be His glorious Name
    to all eternity;
The whole earth let His glory fill.
    Amen, so let it be.   *Based on Psalm 72:17–19*

December 20

Meditation
Reflect on these words about the incarnation of the Lord Jesus:

There is another reason why it was necessary for him who was to be our Redeemer to be true God and true man. It was his task to swallow up death. Who could do that but life itself? It was his task to conquer sin. Who could do that but righteousness? It was his task to overcome the powers of the air, that is, the demons. Who could do that but a power greater than world or air? In whom, then, do life, righteousness and the power of heaven reside, but in God alone? Therefore the Lord, in his great kindness, became our Redeemer when he chose to ransom us.   *John Calvin*

Call to Worship
Hear God call you to worship through his word:

How beautiful upon the mountains
    are the feet of him who brings good news,
who publishes peace, who brings good news of happiness,
    who publishes salvation,
        who says to Zion, "Your God reigns."   *Isaiah 52:7*

Adoration

Say or sing the words of this Advent hymn:

Zion's King shall reign victorious;
all the earth shall own his sway;
he will make his kingdom glorious;
he will reign through endless day.
Nations now from God estranged
then shall see a glorious light;
night to day shall then be changed,
heaven shall triumph in the sight.

Then shall Israel, long dispersed,
mourning seek the Lord their God;
look on him whom once they pierced,
own and kiss the chastening rod.
Mighty King, thine arm revealing,
now thy glorious cause maintain;
bring the nations help and healing,
make them subject to thy reign.   *Thomas Kelly*

Reading of the Law

Hear God's law as his will for your life:

Hear, O Israel: The LORD our God, the LORD is one.
You shall love the LORD your God with all your heart and
        with all your soul and with all your might.
And these words that I command you today shall be on
        your heart.
You shall teach them diligently to your children,
    and shall talk of them when you sit in your house,
    and when you walk by the way,

and when you lie down,
    and when you rise.
You shall bind them as a sign on your hand,
    and they shall be as frontlets between your eyes.
You shall write them on the doorposts of your house and
        on your gates.   *Deuteronomy 6:4–9*

Confession of Sin
Confess your sins to God:

Almighty and most merciful Father, you hate nothing that
you have made, nor desire the death of a sinner—look down
with mercy upon me, and grant that I may turn from my
wickedness and live. Forgive the days and years which I have
passed in folly, idleness, and sin. Fill me with such sorrow
for the time misspent, that I may amend my life according
to your holy Word; strengthen me against habitual idleness,
and enable me to direct my thoughts to the performance of
every duty; that while I live I may serve you in the state to
which you shall call me, and at last by a holy and happy death
be delivered from the struggles and sorrows of this life, and
obtain eternal happiness by your mercy, for the sake of Jesus
Christ our Lord. Amen.   *Samuel Johnson*

Assurance of Pardon
Receive these words of comfort from God:

My little children, I am writing these things to you so that
you may not sin. But if anyone does sin, we have an advocate
with the Father, Jesus Christ the righteous. He is the propitiation for our sins, and not for ours only but also for the sins
of the whole world.   *1 John 2:1–2*

Nicene Creed
Confess what you believe about the Christian faith:

I believe in one God, the Father Almighty,
  Maker of heaven and earth, and of all things visible and
    invisible.

And in one Lord Jesus Christ, the only-begotten Son of God;
  begotten of the Father before all worlds;
  God of God, Light of Light, very God of very God;
  begotten, not made, being of one substance with the
    Father;
  by whom all things were made.
Who, for us men and for our salvation,
  came down from heaven
  and was incarnate by the Holy Spirit of the Virgin Mary,
  and was made man;
  and was crucified also for us under Pontius Pilate;
  he suffered and was buried;
  and the third day he rose again, according to the Scriptures;
  and ascended into heaven, and sits on the right hand of
    the Father;
  and he shall come again, with glory, to judge the living
    and the dead;
  whose kingdom shall have no end.

And I believe in the Holy Spirit, the Lord and Giver of life;
  who proceeds from the Father and the Son;
  who with the Father and the Son together is worshiped
    and glorified;
  who spoke by the prophets.

And I believe in one holy catholic and apostolic church.
  I acknowledge one baptism for the forgiveness of sins;
  and I look for the resurrection of the dead,
  and the life of the world to come. Amen.

Praise
Say or sing this praise to God:

Praise and honor to the Father,
Praise and honor to the Son,
Praise and honor to the Spirit,
Ever three and ever one:
One in might and one in glory
While unending ages run!   *Doxology*

Catechism
Receive this instruction from the Heidelberg Catechism:

Q. 44. *Why does the creed add, "He descended to hell"?*
A. To assure me during attacks of deepest dread and temptation that Christ my Lord, by suffering unspeakable anguish, pain, and terror of soul, on the cross but also earlier, has delivered me from hellish anguish and torment.

Prayer for Illumination
As you read his word, ask God to enlighten your mind and heart:

Heavenly Father, may you grant us to comprehend your holy Word according to your divine will, that we may learn from it to put all our confidence in you alone, and withdraw it from all other creatures; moreover, that also our old man with all his lusts may be crucified more and more each day, and that we may offer ourselves to you as a living sacrifice, to the glory of your holy name and to the edification of our neighbor, through our Lord Jesus Christ. Amen.   *Zacharias Ursinus*

Scripture Reading
Read this portion of God's word: Micah 5

Praise
Say this praise to God:

O Clavis David

O Key of David and scepter of the house of Israel,
you open and no one can shut;
you shut and no one can open—
come and lead the prisoners from the prison house,
those who dwell in darkness and the shadow of death. Amen.

Prayer of Intercession
As you make your requests to God, pray this prayer:

Yes, Lord with all my heart and soul, I renounce the vanities of an empty cheating world, and all the pleasures of sin; in your favor stands my life. Whom have I in heaven but you? Whom on earth do I desire besides you? And, O blessed Jesus, Prince of the kings of the earth, who has loved me, and washed me from my sins in your blood, and whom the eternal God has exalted to be a Prince and a Savior, to give repentance and re-mission of sins, I fall before you, my Lord, and my God; I here willingly tender my homage at the footstool of your throne. I take you for the Lord of my life. I absolutely surrender and resign myself to you. Amen.   *John Howe*

Further Petition

- Personal
- Church
- World

Lord's Prayer

Pray the words that Jesus taught us to pray:

Our Father in heaven,
    hallowed be your name;
    your kingdom come;
    your will be done, on earth as it is in heaven.
    Give us this day our daily bread.
    And forgive us our debts, as we forgive our debtors.
    And lead us not into temptation but deliver us from evil.
    For yours is the kingdom, and the power,
    and the glory, forever. Amen.

Benediction

Receive by faith this blessing from God:

May the God of hope fill you with all joy and peace in believing, so that by the power of the Holy Spirit you may abound in hope.   Romans 15:13

Postlude

In closing, say or sing this praise to God:

His Name for ever shall endure,
    last like the sun it shall;
Men shall be blessed in Him, and blessed
    all nations shall Him call.

Now blessèd be the Lord, our God,
    the God of Israel,
For He alone does wondrous works,
    in glory that excel.

And blessèd be His glorious Name
    to all eternity;
The whole earth let His glory fill.
    Amen, so let it be.   *Based on Psalm 72:17–19*

December 21

Meditation

Reflect on these words about the incarnation of the Lord Jesus:

When God creates humans in his image and dwells and works
with his Spirit in them, exerts influence on their heart and
head, speaks to them, and makes himself known to them
and understood by them, that is an act of condescension and
accommodation to his creature, an anthropomorphizing of
God and so, in a sense and to that extent, a humanization of
God. Given with and in creation is the possibility of revelation and incarnation. . . . For while the incarnation is certainly
different from all other revelation, it is also akin to it: it is its
climax, crown, and completion. All revelation tends toward
and groups itself around the incarnation as the highest, richest, and most perfect act of self-revelation.   Herman Bavinck

Call to Worship

Hear God call you to worship through his word:

And the angel said to her, "Do not be afraid, Mary, for you
have found favor with God. And behold, you will conceive in
your womb and bear a son, and you shall call his name Jesus.
He will be great and will be called the Son of the Most High.

And the Lord God will give to him the throne of his father
David, and he will reign over the house of Jacob forever, and
of his kingdom there will be no end."   *Luke 1:30–33*

Adoration
Say or sing the words of this Advent hymn:

This is the truth sent from above,
the truth of God, the God of love;
therefore don't turn me from the door
but hearken all, both rich and poor.

The first thing that I will relate,
that God at first did man create;
the next thing which to you I tell—
woman was made with him to dwell.

Then after that 'twas God's own choice
to place them both in paradise,
there to remain from evil free
except they ate of such a tree.

But they did eat, which was a sin,
and thus their ruin did begin—
ruined themselves, both you and me,
and all of our posterity.

Thus we were heirs to endless woes
till God the Lord did interpose;
and so a promise soon did run:
that he'd redeem us by his Son.

At this season of the year
our blest Redeemer did appear,

and here did live, and here did preach,
and many thousands he did teach.

Thus he in love to us behaved,
to show us how we must be saved;
and if you want to know the way,
be pleased to hear what he did say:

"Go preach the gospel," now he said,
"to all the nations that are made!
And those that do believe on me,
from all their sins I'll set them free."

O seek! O seek of God above
that saving faith that works by love!
And, if he's pleased to grant thee this,
thou't sure to have eternal bliss.

God grant to all within this place
true saving faith, that special grace
which to his people doth belong:
and thus I close my Christmas song.   *Anonymous*

Reading of the Law
Hear God's law as his will for your life:

Our Lord Jesus said,

Blessed are the poor in spirit,
    for theirs is the kingdom of heaven.
Blessed are those who mourn,
    for they shall be comforted.
Blessed are the meek,
    for they shall inherit the earth.

Blessed are those who hunger and thirst for righteousness,
    for they shall be satisfied.
Blessed are the merciful,
    for they shall receive mercy.
Blessed are the pure in heart,
    for they shall see God.
Blessed are the peacemakers,
    for they shall be called sons of God.
Blessed are those who are persecuted for righteousness' sake,
    for theirs is the kingdom of heaven.   Matthew 5:3–10

Confession of Sin
Confess your sins to God:

Almighty God, Father of our Lord Jesus Christ, Maker of all
things, Judge of all men, we acknowledge and bewail our
manifold sins and wickedness, which we from time to time
most grievously have committed, by thought, word, and
deed, against your divine Majesty, provoking most justly your
wrath and indignation against us. We earnestly repent, and
are heartily sorry for these our misdoings. The remembrance
of them is grievous to us, the burden of them is intolerable.
Have mercy upon us, have mercy upon us, most merciful
Father, for your Son our Lord Jesus Christ's sake. Forgive
us all that is past, and grant that we may ever from now on
serve and please you in newness of life, to the honor and
glory of your name, through Jesus Christ our Lord. Amen.
Book of Common Prayer (1552)

Assurance of Pardon
Receive these words of comfort from God:

Have mercy on me, O God,
   according to your steadfast love;
according to your abundant mercy
   blot out my transgressions.
Wash me thoroughly from my iniquity,
   and cleanse me from my sin!   Psalm 51:1–2

Athanasian Creed, Part 1
Confess what you believe about the Christian faith:

Whoever desires to be saved should above all hold to the catholic faith. Anyone who does not keep it whole and unbroken will doubtless perish eternally. Now this is the catholic faith:

that we worship one God in Trinity and the Trinity in unity, neither confounding their persons nor dividing the essence.

   For the person of the Father is a distinct person,
     the person of the Son is another,
     and that of the Holy Spirit still another.
   But the divinity of the Father, Son, and Holy Spirit is one,
     the glory equal, the majesty coeternal.
   Such as the Father is, such is the Son and such is the
     Holy Spirit.
   The Father is uncreated, the Son is uncreated, the Holy
     Spirit is uncreated.
   The Father is immeasurable, the Son is immeasurable,
     the Holy Spirit is immeasurable.
   The Father is eternal, the Son is eternal, the Holy Spirit
     is eternal.

And yet there are not three eternal beings; there is but
  one eternal being.
So too there are not three uncreated or immeasurable
  beings;
 there is but one uncreated and immeasurable being.
Similarly, the Father is almighty, the Son is almighty,
  the Holy Spirit is almighty.
Yet there are not three almighty beings; there is but one
  almighty being.
Thus, the Father is God, the Son is God, the Holy Spirit
  is God.
Yet there are not three gods; there is but one God.
Thus, the Father is Lord, the Son is Lord, the Holy Spirit
  is Lord.
Yet there are not three lords; there is but one Lord.
Just as Christian truth compels us to confess each person
  individually as both God and Lord,
 so catholic religion forbids us to say that there are
   three gods or lords.

Praise
Say or sing this praise to God:

Praise and honor to the Father,
Praise and honor to the Son,
Praise and honor to the Spirit,
Ever three and ever one:
One in might and one in glory
While unending ages run! Doxology

Catechism
Receive this instruction from the Heidelberg Catechism:

Q. 45. How does Christ's resurrection benefit us?
A. First, by his resurrection he has overcome death, so that he might make us share in the righteousness he obtained for us by his death. Second, by his power we too are already raised to a new life. Third, Christ's resurrection is a sure pledge to us of our blessed resurrection.

Prayer for Illumination
As you read his word, ask God to enlighten your mind and heart:

Lord, you know what distracted hearts we have, O give us self-recollection; you know what hard, dead hearts we have, O touch and awaken us! You know how we yet resist your Word and our lower nature is reluctant to bow to your scepter; therefore, O Lord, show forth your power; send your Spirit on high to work among us, to make our hearts submissive, and ourselves capable of living in true union with you, our salvation, and of yielding totally to your grace. Amen.   *Gerhard Tersteegen*

Scripture Reading
Read this portion of God's word: Zechariah 9:9–17; 13:1–9; and Malachi 3:1–4

Praise
Say this praise to God:

O Oriens

O Dayspring, splendor of light eternal and sun of
        righteousness—
come and enlighten those who dwell in darkness and the
        shadow of death. Amen.

Prayer of Intercession

As you make your requests to God, pray this prayer:

I ask you, O Lord, and earnestly entreat you, give me a humble knowledge, which may edify; give me a meek and prudent eloquence, which knows not how to be puffed up, or vaunt itself upon its own worth and endowments above its brethren. Put into my mouth, I ask you, the word of consolation, and edification, and exhortation, that I may be able to exhort those that are good, to go on to greater perfection; and restore those that walk perversely, to the rule of your righteousness, both by my word and by my example. Let the words which you give to your servant be as the sharpest darts and burning arrows, which may penetrate and inflame the minds of my hearers to your fear and love, through Jesus Christ our Lord. Amen.   *Ambrose*

Further Petition

- Personal
- Church
- World

Lord's Prayer

Pray the words that Jesus taught us to pray:

Our Father in heaven,
    hallowed be your name;
    your kingdom come;
    your will be done, on earth as it is in heaven.
    Give us this day our daily bread.
    And forgive us our debts, as we forgive our debtors.
    And lead us not into temptation but deliver us from evil.

For yours is the kingdom, and the power,
and the glory, forever. Amen.

Benediction
Receive by faith this blessing from God:

The grace of the Lord Jesus Christ and the love of God and the
fellowship of the Holy Spirit be with you all.   *2 Corinthians 13:14*

Postlude
In closing, say or sing this praise to God:

His Name for ever shall endure,
   last like the sun it shall;
Men shall be blessed in Him, and blessed
   all nations shall Him call.

Now blessèd be the Lord, our God,
   the God of Israel,
For He alone does wondrous works,
   in glory that excel.

And blessèd be His glorious Name
   to all eternity;
The whole earth let His glory fill.
   Amen, so let it be.   *Based on Psalm 72:17–19*

December 22

Meditation

Reflect on these words about the incarnation of the Lord Jesus:

That Christ should clothe Himself with our flesh, a piece of earth which we tread upon; oh infinite humility! Christ's taking our flesh was one of the lowest steps of His humiliation. He humbled Himself more in lying in the virgin's womb than in hanging on the cross. It was not so much for man to die, but for God to become man was the wonder of humility. "He was made in the likeness of men."   *Thomas Watson*

Call to Worship

Hear God call you to worship through his word:

The people who walked in darkness
    have seen a great light;
those who dwelt in a land of deep darkness,
    on them has light shone.   *Isaiah 9:2*

Adoration

Say or sing the words of this Advent hymn:

O heavenly Word, Eternal Light,
Begotten of the Father's Might,
Who in these latter days art born
For succour to a world forlorn.

Our hearts enlighten from above,
And kindle with Thine own true love,
That we, who hear Thy call today,
May cast earth's vanities away.

And when as Judge Thou drawest nigh
The secrets of our hearts to try,
When sinners meet their awful doom,
And Saints attain their heavenly home.

O let us not, for evil past,
Be driven from Thy Face at last,
But with the blessèd evermore
Behold Thee, love Thee, and adore.

To God the Father, God the Son,
And God the Spirit, Three in One,
Praise, honor, might and glory be
From age to age eternally.   *Ambrose*

Reading of the Law

Hear God's law as his will for your life:

Our Lord said,

As the Father has loved me, so have I loved you. Abide in my
love. If you keep my commandments, you will abide in my love,

just as I have kept my Father's commandments and abide in his love. These things I have spoken to you, that my joy may be in you, and that your joy may be full. This is my commandment, that you love one another as I have loved you.   *John 15:9–12*

Confession of Sin
Confess your sins to God:

We have great reason, O Lord, to be humbled before you, on account of the coldness and insensibility of our hearts, the disorder and irregularity of our lives, and the prevalence of worldly affections within us. Too often have we indulged the tempers which we ought to have subdued, and have left our duty unperformed. O Lord, be merciful to us for your Son Jesus Christ's sake. Produce in us deep repentance, and a lively faith in that Savior who has died for our sins, and risen again for our justification. Amen.   *Henry Thornton*

Assurance of Pardon
Receive these words of comfort from God:

For while we were still weak, at the right time Christ died for the ungodly. For one will scarcely die for a righteous person—though perhaps for a good person one would dare even to die—but God shows his love for us in that while we were still sinners, Christ died for us.   *Romans 5:6–8*

Athanasian Creed, Part 2
Confess what you believe about the Christian faith:

Whoever desires to be saved should above all hold to the catholic faith. Anyone who does not keep it whole and unbroken will doubtless perish eternally. Now this is the catholic faith:

that we worship one God in Trinity and the Trinity in unity, neither confounding their persons nor dividing the essence....

The Father was neither made nor created nor begotten
    from anyone.
The Son was neither made nor created; he was begotten
    from the Father alone.
The Holy Spirit was neither made nor created nor
    begotten;
he proceeds from the Father and the Son.
Accordingly, there is one Father, not three fathers;
    there is one Son, not three sons;
    there is one Holy Spirit, not three holy spirits.
None in this Trinity is before or after, none is greater or
    smaller;
    in their entirety the three persons are coeternal and
        coequal with each other.
So in everything, as was said earlier, the unity in Trinity,
    and the Trinity in unity, is to be worshiped.
Anyone then who desires to be saved should think thus
    about the Trinity.

Praise
Say or sing this praise to God:

Praise and honor to the Father,
Praise and honor to the Son,
Praise and honor to the Spirit,
Ever three and ever one:
One in might and one in glory
While unending ages run!   *Doxology*

Catechism
Receive this instruction from the Heidelberg Catechism:

Q. 46. What do you mean by saying, "He ascended to heaven"?
A. That Christ, while his disciples watched, was taken up from the earth into heaven and remains there on our behalf until he comes again to judge the living and the dead.

Prayer for Illumination
As you read his word, ask God to enlighten your mind and heart:

O God, you instruct us by your Holy Scriptures—we urge you by your grace to enlighten our minds and cleanse our hearts; that reading, hearing, and meditating upon them, we may rightly understand and heartily embrace the things you have revealed in them. Give efficacy to the reading of the gospel in your Word, that through the operation of the Holy Spirit, this holy seed may be received into our hearts as into good ground; and that we may not only hear your Word but keep it, living in conformity with your precepts; so that we may finally attain everlasting salvation, through Jesus Christ our Lord. Amen.   *Waldensian Liturgy*

Scripture Reading
Read this portion of God's word: Luke 1:26–56

Praise
Say this praise to God:

O Rex Gentium

O King of the nations, and their desire,
the cornerstone making both one—

come and save mankind,
whom you fashioned from the dust of the earth. Amen.

Prayer of Intercession
As you make your requests to God, pray this prayer:

Be a pillar of fire unto our hearts and minds always, that these
may follow you even in the darkness; and grant that we be
ever found before you as the children of the light of eternal
day, and not as the children of the darkness of night; through
Jesus Christ our Lord. Amen.   *Wilhelm Loehe*

Further Petition
- Personal
- Church
- World

Lord's Prayer
Pray the words that Jesus taught us to pray:

Our Father in heaven,
    hallowed be your name;
    your kingdom come;
    your will be done, on earth as it is in heaven.
    Give us this day our daily bread.
    And forgive us our debts, as we forgive our debtors.
    And lead us not into temptation but deliver us from evil.
    For yours is the kingdom, and the power,
    and the glory, forever. Amen.

Benediction

Now to him who is able to do far more abundantly than all that we ask or think, according to the power at work within us, to him be glory in the church and in Christ Jesus throughout all generations, forever and ever. Amen.   *Ephesians 3:20–21*

Postlude

His Name for ever shall endure,
 last like the sun it shall;
Men shall be blessed in Him, and blessed
 all nations shall Him call.

Now blessèd be the Lord, our God,
 the God of Israel,
For He alone does wondrous works,
 in glory that excel.

And blessèd be His glorious Name
 to all eternity;
The whole earth let His glory fill.
 Amen, so let it be.   *Based on Psalm 72:17–19*

December 23

Reflect on these words about the incarnation of the Lord Jesus:

Awake, you who lie in the dust, awake and give praise. Behold, the Lord comes with salvation. He comes with salvation, He comes with unction, He comes with glory. Jesus cannot come without salvation, Christ cannot come without unction, nor the Son of God without glory. For He Himself is salvation, He is unction, He is glory, as it is written, "A wise son is the glory of his father."   *Bernard of Clairvaux*

Call to Worship
Hear God call you to worship through his word:

As he considered these things, behold, an angel of the Lord appeared to him in a dream, saying, "Joseph, son of David, do not fear to take Mary as your wife, for that which is conceived in her is from the Holy Spirit. She will bear a son, and you shall call his name Jesus, for he will save his people from their sins."   *Matthew 1:20–21*

Adoration

Say or sing the words of this Christmas carol:

O come, O come, Emmanuel,
and ransom captive Israel,
that mourns in lonely exile here,
until the Son of God appear.

> *Rejoice! Rejoice! Emmanuel*
> *shall come to thee, O Israel.*

O come, Thou Wisdom from on high,
who ordered all things mightily;
to us the path of knowledge show,
and teach us in her ways to go.

O come, O come, great Lord of might,
who to Thy tribes on Sinai's height;
in ancient times didst give the law
in cloud and majesty and awe.

O come, Thou Rod of Jesse, free,
thine own from Satan's tyranny;
from depths of hell thy people save,
and give them vict'ry o'er the grave.

O come, Thou Key of David, come,
and open wide our heavenly home;
make safe the way that leads on high,
and close the path to misery.

O come, Thou Dayspring from on high,
and cheer us by Thy drawing nigh!
Disperse the gloomy clouds of night,
and death's dark shadows put to flight.

O come, Thou Root of Jesse's tree,
an ensign of Thy people be;
before Thee rulers silent fall;
all peoples on Thy mercy call.

O come, Desire of nations, bind,
in one the hearts of all mankind;
bid Thou our sad divisions cease,
and be Thyself our King of Peace.   *Anonymous*

Reading of the Law
Hear God's law as his will for your life:

The words of our Lord Jesus Christ:

Unless your righteousness exceeds that of the scribes and Pharisees, you will never enter the kingdom of heaven. . . . You therefore must be perfect, as your heavenly Father is perfect. . . . Beware of practicing your righteousness before other people in order to be seen by them, for then you will have no reward from your Father who is in heaven. . . . Seek first the kingdom of God and his righteousness, and all these things will be added to you. . . . So whatever you wish that others would do to you, do also to them, for this is the Law and the Prophets.   *Matthew 5:20, 48; 6:1, 33; 7:12*

Confession of Sin
Confess your sins to God:

O Lord, our heavenly Father, seeing you are our Maker, and we are the workmanship of your hands; seeing you are our Pastor, and we your flock; seeing also that you are our Redeemer, and we are the people whom you have bought;

finally, because you are our God, and we are your chosen inheritance—let not your anger be kindled against us, that you should punish us in your wrath, neither remember our wickedness so as to take vengeance for it, but rather chastise us according to your mercy. We confess, O Lord, that our misdeeds have inflamed your wrath against us, yet considering that by your grace we call upon your name, and make profession of your truth—maintain, we ask you, the work that you have begun in us, to the end that all the world may know that you are our God and Savior. You know that those you have destroyed and brought to confusion, do not set forth your praises, but the heavy souls, the humble hearts, the consciences oppressed and laden with the grievous burden of their sins, and therefore thirst after your grace, they shall set forth your praise and glory. Amen.   *Middelburg Liturgy*

Assurance of Pardon
Receive these words of comfort from God:

Sing aloud, O daughter of Zion;
    shout, O Israel!
Rejoice and exult with all your heart,
    O daughter of Jerusalem!
The Lord has taken away the judgments against you;
    he has cleared away your enemies.
The King of Israel, the Lord, is in your midst;
    you shall never again fear evil.   *Zephaniah 3:14–15*

Athanasian Creed, Part 3

Confess what you believe about the Christian faith:

Whoever desires to be saved should above all hold to the catholic faith. Anyone who does not keep it whole and unbroken will doubtless perish eternally. Now this is the catholic faith:

that we worship one God in Trinity and the Trinity in unity, neither confounding their persons nor dividing the essence. . . .

But it is necessary for eternal salvation that one also believe in the incarnation of our Lord Jesus Christ faithfully.

Now this is the true faith:

> that we believe and confess that our Lord Jesus Christ,
> > God's Son,
> > > is both God and man, equally.
> He is God from the essence of the Father, begotten
> > before time;
> > > and he is man from the essence of his mother, born
> > > > in time;
> > > completely God, completely man, with a rational soul
> > > > and human flesh;
> > > equal to the Father as regards divinity,
> > > less than the Father as regards humanity.
> Although he is God and man, yet Christ is not two,
> > but one.
> He is one, however, not by his divinity being turned
> > into flesh,
> > > but by God's taking humanity to himself.
> He is one, certainly not by the blending of his essence,
> > but by the unity of his person.

For just as one man is both rational soul and flesh,
  so too the one Christ is both God and man.

He suffered for our salvation;
he descended to hell;
he arose from the dead on the third day;
he ascended to heaven;
he is seated at the Father's right hand;
from there he will come to judge the living and the dead.
At his coming all people will arise bodily and give an
          accounting of their own deeds.
Those who have done good will enter eternal life,
  and those who have done evil will enter eternal fire.

This is the catholic faith: that one cannot be saved without believing it firmly and faithfully.

Praise
Say or sing this praise to God:

Praise and honor to the Father,
Praise and honor to the Son,
Praise and honor to the Spirit,
Ever three and ever one:
One in might and one in glory
While unending ages run!   Doxology

Catechism
Receive this instruction from the Heidelberg Catechism:

Q. 47. But isn't Christ with us until the end of the world as he promised us?

A. Christ is true man and true God. In his human nature Christ is not now on earth; but in his divinity, majesty, grace, and Spirit he is never absent from us.

Prayer for Illumination
As you read his word, ask God to enlighten your mind and heart:

Almighty God, I earnestly ask you for such deeper fellowship of the Holy Spirit, who speaks in the blessed Scriptures, that when I open them, I may perceive his mind in what I read, and immediately hear in them his voice to myself. I ask you for a quicker understanding in spiritual things, for more desire to understand, a fuller perception of your promise in the church, that I may become teachable, and may love that by which you will teach me. Amen.   *Henry Wotherspoon*

Scripture Reading
Read this portion of God's word: Luke 1:57–80

Praise
Say this praise to God:

O Emmanuel

O Emmanuel, our King and our Lawgiver,
the hope of the nations and their Savior—
come and save us, O Lord our God. Amen.

Prayer of Intercession
As you make your requests to God, pray this prayer:

My God, my strength, in you will I trust, my buckler and the horn of my salvation and my high tower. Therefore, ever faithful God, let your waking eyes be upon me, and prove yourself my defense from the power and attacks of the great enemy; be our watch and guard, surround us with your protection as with a wall, that nothing can harm us, for in you alone is our salvation—to you do I raise my eyes, from you alone comes our help. Amen.   *Johann Habermann*

Further Petition

- Personal
- Church
- World

Lord's Prayer

Pray the words that Jesus taught us to pray:

Our Father in heaven,
   hallowed be your name;
   your kingdom come;
   your will be done, on earth as it is in heaven.
   Give us this day our daily bread.
   And forgive us our debts, as we forgive our debtors.
   And lead us not into temptation but deliver us from evil.
   For yours is the kingdom, and the power,
   and the glory, forever. Amen.

Benediction

Receive by faith this blessing from God:

Now may the God of peace himself sanctify you completely, and may your whole spirit and soul and body be kept blameless at the coming of our Lord Jesus Christ. He who calls you is faithful; he will surely do it.   *1 Thessalonians 5:23–24*

Postlude

In closing, say or sing this praise to God:

His Name for ever shall endure,
    last like the sun it shall;
Men shall be blessed in Him, and blessed
    all nations shall Him call.

Now blessèd be the Lord, our God,
    the God of Israel,
For He alone does wondrous works,
    in glory that excel.

And blessèd be His glorious Name
    to all eternity;
The whole earth let His glory fill.
    Amen, so let it be.   *Based on Psalm 72:17–19*

December 24

Christmas Eve

Meditation

Reflect on these words about the incarnation of the Lord Jesus:

When they [Mary and Joseph] arrived at Bethlehem, they were the most insignificant and despised. . . . No one noticed or was conscious of what God was doing in that stable. He lets the large houses and costly apartments remain empty, lets their inhabitants eat, drink, and be merry; but this comfort and treasure are hidden from them. O what a dark night this was for Bethlehem, that was not conscious of that glorious light! See how God shows that he utterly disregards what the world is, has, or desires; and furthermore, that the world shows how little it knows or notices what God is, has, and does.   Martin Luther

---

Call to Worship

Hear God call you to worship through his word:

On that day it shall be said to Jerusalem:
"Fear not, O Zion;
    let not your hands grow weak.

The LORD your God is in your midst,
    a mighty one who will save;
he will rejoice over you with gladness;
    he will quiet you by his love;
he will exult over you with loud singing." *Zephaniah 3:16–17*

Adoration

Say or sing the words of this Christmas carol:

The darkest midnight in December,
No snow, no hail, nor winter storm,
Shall hinder us for to remember,
The Babe that on this night was born.
With shepherds we are come to see,
This lovely Infant's glorious charms,
Born of a maid as prophets said,
The God of love in Mary's arms.

No earthly gifts can we present Him,
No gold nor myrrh nor odours sweet.
But if with hearts we can content Him,
We humbly lay them at his feet.
'Twas but pure love that from above
Brought Him to save us from all harms.
So let us sing and welcome Him,
The God of Love in Mary's arms.

Four thousand years from the creation
The world lay groaning under sin.
No one could e'er expect salvation,
No one could enter Heaven.
'Twas Adam's fall had damned us all
To Hell, to endless pains forlorn:

'Twas so decreed we'd have ne'er been freed,
Had not this heavenly Babe been born.

But here the best of heads will grumble,
The faithless Jews will not adore
A God so poor, so mean, so humble,
A child they scorn to kneel before.
But, oh, give ear, and you shall hear
How all those wonders came to pass;
Why Christ was born to suffer scorn,
And lodged between an ox and ass.

Have you not heard the sacred story,
How man was made those seats to fill,
Which the fallen angels lost in glory,
By their presumption, pride and will?
They thought us mean for to obtain
Such glorious seats and crowns in heaven,
So through a cheat they got Eve to eat
The fruit, to be avenged on man.

Thus we were lost, our God offended,
The devils triumphing in our shame.
What recompense could be pretended?
No man could ever wipe off the stain.
Till God alone from His high throne,
Becoming Man did us restore.
Let us rejoice in tuneful voice,
Let Satan tremble and adore.

If by a woman we were wounded,
Another woman brings the cure;
If by a fruit we were confounded,

A tree our safety would procure.
They laughed at man, but if they can,
Let Satan with his hellish swarms
Refuse to kneel and honour yield
To the lovely Babe in Mary's arms.

We like beasts lay in a stable,
Our senses blind and dead by sin;
To help ourselves we were not able,
But He brings grace and life again.
Thus conquered hell, confined the devil,
To free our souls from endless harms.
His life He gave and now you have
The God of Love in Mary's arms.

Ye faithful hearts be not offended,
To own your God though seeming mean;
By this from Hell you were defended,
Your joys were purchased by His pain.
The Lord of all comes to a stall,
And to attend Him sends for Kings,
Who by a star are called from far,
To see and hear those joyful things.

Oh, God! although man did offend Thee,
Here is a Man that must Thee please;
Though to compassion none could bend Thee,
Thy anger now must surely cease.
And when our crimes in aftertimes
May Thee to anger justly move,
Pray grant us peace, seeing the face
Of this Thy Son and God of Love.

Ye blessed angels join our voices,
Let your gilded wings beat fluttering over,
Whilst every soul set free rejoices,
And every devil must adore.
We'll sing and pray that He always may
Our Church and clergyman defend;
God grant us grace in all our days,
A merry Christmas and a happy end.   *Anonymous*

Reading of the Law
Hear God's law as his will for your life:

And God spoke all these words, saying,

"I am the LORD your God, who brought you out of the land of Egypt, out of the house of slavery.

You shall have no other gods before me.

You shall not make for yourself a carved image, or any likeness of anything that is in heaven above, or that is in the earth beneath, or that is in the water under the earth. You shall not bow down to them or serve them, for I the LORD your God am a jealous God, visiting the iniquity of the fathers on the children to the third and the fourth generation of those who hate me, but showing steadfast love to thousands of those who love me and keep my commandments.

You shall not take the name of the LORD your God in vain, for the LORD will not hold him guiltless who takes his name in vain.

Remember the Sabbath day, to keep it holy. Six days you shall labor, and do all your work, but the seventh day is a Sabbath to the LORD your God. On it you shall not do any work, you, or your son, or your daughter, your male servant, or your female servant, or your livestock, or the sojourner who is within your gates. For in six days the Lord made heaven and earth, the sea, and all that is in them, and rested on the seventh day. Therefore the Lord blessed the Sabbath day and made it holy.

Honor your father and your mother, that your days may be long in the land that the Lord your God is giving you.

You shall not murder.

You shall not commit adultery.

You shall not steal.

You shall not bear false witness against your neighbor.

You shall not covet your neighbor's house; you shall not covet your neighbor's wife, or his male servant, or his female servant, or his ox, or his donkey, or anything that is your neighbor's." Exodus 20:1–17

Confession of Sin
Confess your sins to God:

O Father, receive again the thing which you have created. O Son, receive the thing which you have governed. O Holy Spirit, fetch the thing which you so bountifully have preserved. Three persons and one very God, I entreat you: remember not my offenses forever. For I cry, Lord God and Father, mercy. Lord God Son, mercy. Lord God Holy Spirit, mercy. Amen. *Martin Luther*

Assurance of Pardon
Receive these words of comfort from God:

But far be it from me to boast except in the cross of our Lord Jesus Christ, by which the world has been crucified to me, and

I to the world. For neither circumcision counts for anything, nor uncircumcision, but a new creation. And as for all who walk by this rule, peace and mercy be upon them, and upon the Israel of God.   *Galatians 6:14–16*

Nicene Creed
Confess what you believe about the Christian faith:

I believe in one God, the Father Almighty,
>   Maker of heaven and earth, and of all things visible and
>>   invisible.

And in one Lord Jesus Christ, the only-begotten Son of God;
>   begotten of the Father before all worlds;
>   God of God, Light of Light, very God of very God;
>   begotten, not made, being of one substance with the
>>   Father;
>   by whom all things were made.

Who, for us men and for our salvation,
>   came down from heaven
>   and was incarnate by the Holy Spirit of the Virgin Mary,
>   and was made man;
>   and was crucified also for us under Pontius Pilate;
>   he suffered and was buried;
>   and the third day he rose again, according to the Scriptures;
>   and ascended into heaven, and sits on the right hand of
>>   the Father;
>   and he shall come again, with glory, to judge the living
>>   and the dead;
>   whose kingdom shall have no end.

And I believe in the Holy Spirit, the Lord and Giver of life;
>   who proceeds from the Father and the Son;

who with the Father and the Son together is worshiped
and glorified;
who spoke by the prophets.

And I believe in one holy catholic and apostolic church.
I acknowledge one baptism for the forgiveness of sins;
and I look for the resurrection of the dead,
and the life of the world to come. Amen.

Praise
Say or sing this praise to God:

Praise and honor to the Father,
Praise and honor to the Son,
Praise and honor to the Spirit,
Ever three and ever one:
One in might and one in glory
While unending ages run!   Doxology

Catechism
Receive this instruction from the Heidelberg Catechism:

*Q. 48. If his humanity is not present wherever his divinity is, then aren't
the two natures of Christ separated from each other?*
A. Certainly not. Since divinity is not limited and is present
everywhere, it is evident that Christ's divinity is surely beyond
the bounds of the humanity that has been taken on, but at
the same time his divinity is in and remains personally united
to his humanity.

Prayer for Illumination

As you read his word, ask God to enlighten your mind and heart:

Almighty God, enter our hearts, and so fill us with your love, that, forsaking all evil desires, we may embrace you, our only good. Show unto us, for your mercies' sake, O Lord our God, what you are unto us. Say unto our souls, "I am your salvation." So speak that we may hear. Our hearts are before you; open our ears; let us hasten after your voice and take hold of you. Amen.   *Augustine*

Scripture Reading

Read this portion of God's word: Luke 2:1–21

Praise

Say or sing this praise to God:

O holy night, the stars are brightly shining,
It is the night of the dear Savior's birth;
Long lay the world in sin and error pining,
'Till he appeared and the soul felt its worth.
A thrill of hope the weary world rejoices,
For yonder breaks a new and glorious morn.

Fall on your knees, Oh hear the angel voices!
O night divine! O night when Christ was born.
O night, O holy night, O night divine.

Prayer of Intercession

As you make your requests to God, pray this prayer:

O God, my God, I am all weakness, but you are my strength; I am ever anew bowed down by any trial, but you can and will lift me up. Let me not fail, O God my strength; let me not be discouraged, O God my hope. Amen.   E. B. *Pusey*

Further Petition

- Personal
- Church
- World

Lord's Prayer

Pray the words that Jesus taught us to pray:

Our Father in heaven,
  hallowed be your name;
  your kingdom come;
  your will be done, on earth as it is in heaven.
  Give us this day our daily bread.
  And forgive us our debts, as we forgive our debtors.
  And lead us not into temptation but deliver us from evil.
  For yours is the kingdom, and the power,
  and the glory, forever. Amen.

Benediction

Receive by faith this blessing from God:

May grace and peace be multiplied to you in the knowledge of God and of Jesus our Lord.   *2 Peter 1:2*

Postlude

In closing, say or sing this praise to God:

His Name for ever shall endure,
  last like the sun it shall;
Men shall be blessed in Him, and blessed

all nations shall Him call.

Now blessèd be the Lord, our God,
    the God of Israel,
For He alone does wondrous works,
    in glory that excel.

And blessèd be His glorious Name
    to all eternity;
The whole earth let His glory fill.
    Amen, so let it be.   *Based on Psalm 72:17–19*

December 25

Christmas Day

Meditation

Reflect on these words about the incarnation of the Lord Jesus:

This day He who is, is born; and He who is becomes what He was not.   *John Chrysostom*

———

Call to Worship

Hear God call you to worship through his word:

And the angel said to them, "Fear not, for behold, I bring you good news of great joy that will be for all the people. For unto you is born this day in the city of David a Savior, who is Christ the Lord. And this will be a sign for you: you will find a baby wrapped in swaddling cloths and lying in a manger." And suddenly there was with the angel a multitude of the heavenly host praising God and saying,

"Glory to God in the highest,
   and on earth peace among those with whom he is
         pleased!"   *Luke 2:10–14*

Adoration

Say or sing the words of this Christmas carol:

Once in royal David's city
stood a lowly cattle shed,
where a mother laid her baby
in a manger for his bed:
Mary was that mother mild,
Jesus Christ, her little child.

He came down to earth from heaven
who is God and Lord of all,
and his shelter was a stable,
and his cradle was a stall;
with the poor and mean and lowly,
lived on earth our Savior holy.

And our eyes at last shall see him,
through his own redeeming love,
for that child, so dear and gentle,
is our Lord in heaven above,
and he leads his children on
to the place where he is gone.

Not in that poor, lowly stable
with the oxen standing by
we shall see him, but in heaven,
set at God's right hand on high.
When like stars his children crowned,
all in white shall wait around.   *Cecil Frances Alexander*

Reading of the Law

Hear God's law as his will for your life:

Beloved, let us love one another, for love is from God, and
whoever loves has been born of God and knows God. Anyone
who does not love does not know God, because God is love.
In this the love of God was made manifest among us, that
God sent his only Son into the world, so that we might live
through him. In this is love, not that we have loved God but
that he loved us and sent his Son to be the propitiation for
our sins. Beloved, if God so loved us, we also ought to love
one another.   *1 John 4:7–11*

Confession of Sin

Confess your sins to God:

O God the Father of heaven, *have mercy upon us.*
O God the Son, Redeemer of the world, *have mercy upon us.*
O God the Holy Spirit, *have mercy upon us.*
Be merciful to us and spare us, O Lord.
Be merciful to us and deliver us, O Lord.
From all sin, from all error, from all evil—*deliver us, O Lord.*
From the wiles of the devil and from everlasting death—
            deliver us, O Lord.

Lord Jesus, by the mystery of your holy incarnation,
by your holy nativity,
by your baptism, fasting, and temptations—*deliver us, O Lord.*
By your agony and bloody sweat,
by your cross and passions,
by your death and burial,
by your resurrection and ascension,

by the coming of the Holy Spirit, the Comforter—
   deliver us, O Lord. Amen.   *Martin Bucer*

Assurance of Pardon
Receive these words of comfort from God:

Seek the LORD while he may be found;
   call upon him while he is near;
let the wicked forsake his way,
   and the unrighteous man his thoughts;
let him return to the LORD, that he may have compassion
      on him,
   and to our God, for he will abundantly pardon.
For my thoughts are not your thoughts,
   neither are your ways my ways, declares the LORD.
For as the heavens are higher than the earth,
   so are my ways higher than your ways
   and my thoughts than your thoughts.   *Isaiah 55:6–9*

Apostles' Creed
Confess what you believe about the Christian faith:

I believe in God the Father Almighty,
   Maker of heaven and earth.

I believe in Jesus Christ, his only-begotten Son, our Lord;
   who was conceived by the Holy Spirit, born of the
         Virgin Mary;
   suffered under Pontius Pilate;
   was crucified, dead, and buried;
   he descended into hell;
   the third day he rose again from the dead;
   he ascended into heaven,

and sits at the right hand of God the Father Almighty;
from there he shall come to judge the living and the dead.

I believe in the Holy Spirit;
the holy catholic church;
the communion of saints;
the forgiveness of sins;
the resurrection of the body;
and the life everlasting. Amen.

Praise
Say or sing this praise to God:

Praise and honor to the Father,
Praise and honor to the Son,
Praise and honor to the Spirit,
Ever three and ever one:
One in might and one in glory
While unending ages run!   Doxology

Catechism
Receive this instruction from the Westminster Shorter Catechism:

Q. 20. Did God leave all mankind to perish in the estate of sin and misery?
A. God having, out of his mere good pleasure, from all eternity, elected some to everlasting life, did enter into a covenant of grace, to deliver them out of the state of sin and misery, and to bring them into a state of salvation by a redeemer.

Prayer for Illumination

As you read his word, ask God to enlighten your mind and heart:

Almighty, eternal and merciful God, whose Word is a lamp unto our feet and a light unto our path, open and illuminate our minds, that we may purely and perfectly understand your Word and that our lives may be conformed to what we have rightly understood, that in nothing we may be displeasing to your Majesty, through Jesus Christ our Lord. Amen.   *Huldrych Zwingli*

Scripture Reading

Read this portion of God's word: Luke 2:22–40

Praise

Say or sing this praise to God:

Sileat Omnis Caro Mortalis

Let all mortal flesh keep silence,
And with fear and trembling stand;
Ponder nothing earthly minded,
For with blessing in His hand,
Christ our God to earth descendeth,
Our full homage to demand.

King of kings, yet born of Mary,
As of old on earth He stood;
Lord of lords, in human vesture,
In the body and the blood;
He will give to all the faithful
His own self for heavenly food.

Rank on rank the host of heaven
Spreads its vanguard on the way,
As the Light of light descendeth
From the realms of endless day,
That the powers of hell may vanish
As the darkness clears away.

At His feet the six-winged seraph,
Cherubim with sleepless eye,
Veil their faces to the presence,
As with ceaseless voice they cry:
"Alleluia, Alleluia,
Alleluia, Lord Most High!"   *Divine Liturgy of St. James*

Prayer of Intercession
As you make your requests to God, pray these prayers:

Almighty God, who have given us your only begotten Son
to take our nature upon him, and this day to be born of a
pure virgin—grant that we, being regenerate and made your
children by adoption and grace, may daily be renewed by your
Holy Spirit, through the same, our Lord Jesus Christ, who
lives and reigns with you and the Holy Spirit, world without
end. Amen.   Book of Common Prayer (1552)

Eternal and Almighty God, we give you most hearty thanks,
that in your great love, you graciously pitied us who were
doomed to eternal death for our sins; and you ordained your
only-begotten Son, before the foundation of the world to be
our Mediator, atonement, and Savior; that he was promised to
our first parents in paradise, after their deplorable fall, and at
the appointed time was sent into the world; that he assumed
our flesh and blood, became our Brother, and in all things

became like us, except without sin. We praise you, that by his death he destroyed him who had the power of death, the devil, and delivered us, who would otherwise have spent our whole life in bondage to the fear of death, from the kingdom of Satan and darkness, and transferred us into the kingdom of light and eternal happiness.

We heartily beseech you to fill us with your grace, that we may rightly know your love and mercy, and Jesus Christ your Son, whom you have made for us wisdom, righteousness, sanctification, and redemption; help us to so love and honor him, as wholly to surrender ourselves up to him, to confide in him, and esteem everything in the world as dross and dung, for the excellency of knowing Jesus Christ. May we cling to this Savior with true faith, the one who forgives all our sins and heals all our diseases, that we may rejoice in all the tribulations of this life, and sing with the heavenly host: "Glory to God in the highest, peace on earth, and goodwill toward men!" And may we finally attain to the end of our faith, even the salvation of our souls; through Jesus Christ our Lord. Amen.   *The Old Palatinate Liturgy (1563)*

Further Petition
- Personal
- Church
- World

Lord's Prayer
Pray the words that Jesus taught us to pray:

Our Father in heaven,
  hallowed be your name;
  your kingdom come;

your will be done, on earth as it is in heaven.
Give us this day our daily bread.
And forgive us our debts, as we forgive our debtors.
And lead us not into temptation but deliver us from evil.
For yours is the kingdom, and the power,
and the glory, forever. Amen.

Benediction
Receive by faith this blessing from God:

Now to him who is able to keep you from stumbling and to
present you blameless before the presence of his glory with
great joy, to the only God, our Savior, through Jesus Christ
our Lord, be glory, majesty, dominion, and authority, before
all time and now and forever. Amen.   *Jude 24–25*

Postlude
In closing, say or sing this praise to God:

His Name for ever shall endure,
   last like the sun it shall;
Men shall be blessed in Him, and blessed
   all nations shall Him call.

Now blessèd be the Lord, our God,
   the God of Israel,
For He alone does wondrous works,
   in glory that excel.

And blessèd be His glorious Name
   to all eternity;
The whole earth let His glory fill.
   Amen, so let it be.   *Based on Psalm 72:17–19*

December 26

Meditation
Reflect on these words about the incarnation of the Lord Jesus:

In our world too, a Stable once had something in it that was
bigger than our whole world.   *C. S. Lewis*

Call to Worship
Hear God call you to worship through his word:

For to us a child is born,
 to us a son is given;
and the government shall be upon his shoulder,
 and his name shall be called
Wonderful Counselor, Mighty God,
 Everlasting Father, Prince of Peace.
Of the increase of his government and of peace
 there will be no end,
on the throne of David and over his kingdom,
 to establish it and to uphold it
with justice and with righteousness
 from this time forth and forevermore.
The zeal of the LORD of hosts will do this.   *Isaiah 9:6–7*

Adoration

Say or sing the words of this Christmas carol:

Hark! the herald angels sing,
"Glory to the newborn King:
peace on earth, and mercy mild,
God and sinners reconciled!"
Joyful, all ye nations, rise,
join the triumph of the skies;
with th'angelic hosts proclaim,
"Christ is born in Bethlehem!"

> *Hark! the herald angels sing,*
> *"Glory to the newborn King!"*

Christ, by highest heaven adored,
Christ, the everlasting Lord,
late in time behold him come,
offspring of the Virgin's womb:
veiled in flesh the Godhead see;
hail the incarnate Deity,
pleased as man with man to dwell,
Jesus, our Emmanuel.

Hail the heaven-born Prince of Peace!
Hail the Sun of Righteousness!
Light and life to all he brings,
ris'n with healing in his wings.
Mild he lays his glory by,
born that man no more may die,
born to raise the sons of earth,
born to give them second birth.   *Charles Wesley*

Reading of the Law
Hear God's law as his will for your life:

The words of our Lord Jesus Christ:

You shall love the Lord your God with all your heart and with all your soul and with all your mind. This is the great and first commandment. And a second is like it: You shall love your neighbor as yourself. On these two commandments depend all the Law and the Prophets.   *Matthew 22:37–40*

Confession of Sin
Confess your sins to God:

Almighty, merciful God, we acknowledge for ourselves and we confess before you that which is the truth; namely, that if you decided to consider our merits and worthiness, we would not be worthy to lift our eyes to heaven and bring our prayer before you. For our consciences accuse us and our sins testify against us. We also know that you are a righteous Judge, who punishes the sins of those who transgress your commandments. But, O Lord, since you commanded us to call upon you in every affliction, and promised in your unspeakable mercy to hear our prayers, not for the sake of our merits—of which there are none—but for the sake of the merits of our Lord Jesus Christ, whom you have set forth as our Mediator and Advocate, so we forsake all other help and take our refuge to your mercy alone. Amen.   *Peter Dathenus*

Assurance of Pardon
Receive these words of comfort from God:

For I am not ashamed of the gospel, for it is the power of God for salvation to everyone who believes, to the Jew first and also to the Greek. For in it the righteousness of God is revealed from faith for faith, as it is written, "The righteous shall live by faith."   *Romans 1:16–17*

Apostles' Creed
Confess what you believe about the Christian faith:

I believe in God the Father Almighty,
    Maker of heaven and earth.

I believe in Jesus Christ, his only-begotten Son, our Lord;
    who was conceived by the Holy Spirit, born of the
            Virgin Mary;
    suffered under Pontius Pilate;
    was crucified, dead, and buried;
    he descended into hell;
    the third day he rose again from the dead;
    he ascended into heaven,
    and sits at the right hand of God the Father Almighty;
    from there he shall come to judge the living and the dead.

I believe in the Holy Spirit;
    the holy catholic church;
    the communion of saints;
    the forgiveness of sins;
    the resurrection of the body;
    and the life everlasting. Amen.

Praise
Say or sing this praise to God:

Glory be to God the Father,
Glory be to God the Son,
Glory be to God the Spirit,
God Almighty, Three in One!
Hallelujah! Hallelujah!
Glory be to him alone.   *Gloria Patri*

Catechism
Receive this instruction from the Westminster Shorter Catechism:

Q. 21. *Who is the redeemer of God's elect?*
A. The only redeemer of God's elect is the Lord Jesus Christ,
who, being the eternal Son of God, became man, and so was,
and continues to be, God and man in two distinct natures,
and one person, forever.

Prayer for Illumination
As you read his word, ask God to enlighten your mind and heart:

Merciful Lord, the comforter and teacher of your faithful
people, increase in your church the desires which you have
given, and confirm the hearts of those who hope in you by
enabling them to understand the depth of your promises,
that all of your adopted sons may even now behold, with
the eyes of faith, and patiently wait for, the light which as
yet you do not openly manifest; through Jesus Christ our
Lord. Amen.   *Ambrose*

Scripture Reading
Read this portion of God's word: Matthew 1:1–25

Praise

Say or sing this praise to God:

My soul magnifies the Lord.
And my spirit rejoices in God my Savior.
For he has regarded the lowliness of his servant.
For behold, from now on all generations shall call me blessed.
For he who is mighty has magnified me, and holy is his Name.
And his mercy is on them that fear him, throughout all
      generations.
He has showed strength with his arm.
He has scattered the proud in the imagination of their hearts.
He has put down the mighty from their thrones, and has
      exalted the humble and meek.
He has filled the hungry with good things, and the rich he
      has sent away empty.
He, remembering his mercy, has helped his servant Israel,
      as he promised to our forefathers, Abraham and
      his seed, forever.

Glory be to the Father, and to the Son, and to the Holy Spirit:
As it was in the beginning, is now, and ever shall be, world
      without end. Amen.   *Magnificat*

Prayer of Intercession

As you make your requests to God, pray this prayer:

Merciful Father, who wills not your children should wander
in darkness; pour the light of your Spirit into our minds
and hearts, that we may discover what is your holy will,
and discern the true from the false, the evil from the good,
that we may henceforth walk in all humility in the paths

of heavenly wisdom and peace, to the glory of your holy name.   *John Hunter*

Further Petition
- Personal
- Church
- World

Lord's Prayer
Pray the words that Jesus taught us to pray:

Our Father in heaven,
  hallowed be your name;
  your kingdom come;
  your will be done, on earth as it is in heaven.
  Give us this day our daily bread.
  And forgive us our debts, as we forgive our debtors.
  And lead us not into temptation but deliver us from evil.
  For yours is the kingdom, and the power,
  and the glory, forever. Amen.

Benediction
Receive by faith this blessing from God:

The Lord bless you and keep you;
The Lord make his face to shine upon you
  and be gracious to you;
The Lord lift up his countenance upon you
  and give you peace. *Numbers 6:24–26*

Postlude

In closing, say or sing this praise to God:

His Name for ever shall endure,
    last like the sun it shall;
Men shall be blessed in Him, and blessed
    all nations shall Him call.

Now blessèd be the Lord, our God,
    the God of Israel,
For He alone does wondrous works,
    in glory that excel.

And blessèd be His glorious Name
    to all eternity;
The whole earth let His glory fill.
    Amen, so let it be.   *Psalm 72:17–19*

December 27

Meditation
Reflect on these words about the incarnation of the Lord Jesus:

Open wide your door to the one who comes. Open your soul, throw open the depths of your heart to see the riches of simplicity, the treasures of peace, the sweetness of grace. Open your heart and run to meet the Sun of eternal light that illuminates all men.   *Ambrose*

———

Call to Worship
Hear God call you to worship through his word:

For God, who said, "Let light shine out of darkness," has shone in our hearts to give the light of the knowledge of the glory of God in the face of Jesus Christ.   *2 Corinthians 4:6*

Adoration
Say or sing the words of this Christmas carol:

Silent night, holy night!
All is calm, all is bright
round yon virgin mother and child.

Holy Infant, so tender and mild,
sleep in heavenly peace,
sleep in heavenly peace.

Silent night, holy night!
Shepherds quake at the sight.
Glories stream from heaven afar,
heav'nly hosts sing, Alleluia!
Christ, the Savior, is born!
Christ, the Savior, is born!

Silent night, holy night!
Son of God, love's pure light
radiant beams from thy holy face
with the dawn of redeeming grace,
Jesus, Lord, at thy birth,
Jesus, Lord, at thy birth.   *Joseph Mohr*

Reading of the Law
Hear God's law as his will for your life:

Hear, O Israel: The LORD our God, the LORD is one.
You shall love the LORD your God with all your heart and
          with all your soul and with all your might.
And these words that I command you today shall be on
          your heart.
You shall teach them diligently to your children,
    and shall talk of them when you sit in your house,
    and when you walk by the way,
    and when you lie down,
    and when you rise.
You shall bind them as a sign on your hand,
    and they shall be as frontlets between your eyes.

You shall write them on the doorposts of your house and
on your gates.   *Deuteronomy 6:4–9*

Confession of Sin
Confess your sins to God:

I pray you heartily to look upon me with the eyes of your
mercy, as you did look upon the evildoer, who was hanged
upon the cross beside you, and did open his heart that he
confessed his sins; and he was mightily afraid of them, but
yet despaired not, but confessed and desired your grace and
mercy which you gave to him willingly and plentifully. . . .
Therefore, dear God and merciful Father, will I strengthen
myself so much and more, and doubt nothing thereof.
Amen.   *Martin Luther*

Assurance of Pardon
Receive these words of comfort from God:

For when I kept silent, my bones wasted away
    through my groaning all day long.
For day and night your hand was heavy upon me;
    my strength was dried up as by the heat of summer. *Selah*

I acknowledged my sin to you,
    and I did not cover my iniquity;
I said, "I will confess my transgressions to the Lord,"
    and you forgave the iniquity of my sin. *Selah.*   *Psalm 32:3–5*

Nicene Creed

Confess what you believe about the Christian faith:

I believe in one God, the Father Almighty,
>	Maker of heaven and earth, and of all things visible and
>>		invisible.

And in one Lord Jesus Christ, the only-begotten Son of God;
>	begotten of the Father before all worlds;
>	God of God, Light of Light, very God of very God;
>	begotten, not made, being of one substance with the
>>		Father;
>	by whom all things were made.

Who, for us men and for our salvation,
>	came down from heaven
>	and was incarnate by the Holy Spirit of the Virgin Mary,
>	and was made man;
>	and was crucified also for us under Pontius Pilate;
>	he suffered and was buried;
>	and the third day he rose again, according to the Scriptures;
>	and ascended into heaven, and sits on the right hand of
>>		the Father;
>	and he shall come again, with glory, to judge the living
>>		and the dead;
>	whose kingdom shall have no end.

And I believe in the Holy Spirit, the Lord and Giver of life;
>	who proceeds from the Father and the Son;
>	who with the Father and the Son together is worshiped
>>		and glorified;
>	who spoke by the prophets.

And I believe in one holy catholic and apostolic church.
I acknowledge one baptism for the forgiveness of sins;
and I look for the resurrection of the dead,
and the life of the world to come. Amen.

Praise
Say or sing this praise to God:

Glory be to God the Father,
Glory be to God the Son,
Glory be to God the Spirit,
God Almighty, Three in One!
Hallelujah! Hallelujah!
Glory be to him alone.   *Gloria Patri*

Catechism
Receive this instruction from the Westminster Shorter Catechism:

Q. 22. How did Christ, being the Son of God, become man?
A. Christ, the Son of God, became man, by taking to himself
a true body and a reasonable soul, being conceived by the
power of the Holy Spirit in the womb of the virgin Mary,
and born of her, yet without sin.

Prayer for Illumination
As you read his word, ask God to enlighten your mind and heart:

Heavenly Father, may you grant us to comprehend your holy
Word according to your divine will, that we may learn from it
to put all our confidence in you alone, and withdraw it from
all other creatures; moreover, that also our old man with all
his lusts may be crucified more and more each day, and that
we may offer ourselves to you as a living sacrifice, to the glory

of your holy name and to the edification of our neighbor, through our Lord Jesus Christ. Amen.   *Zacharias Ursinus*

Scripture Reading
Read this portion of God's word: John 1:1–18

Praise
Say this praise to God:

Blessed be the Lord God of Israel, for he has visited,
   and redeemed his people;
and has raised up a mighty salvation for us,
   in the house of his servant David;
as he spoke by the mouth of his holy prophets,
   which have been since the world began;
that we should be saved from our enemies,
   and from the hands of all that hate us;
to perform the mercy promised to our forefathers,
   and to remember his holy covenant;
to perform the oath which he swore to our forefather
     Abraham,
   that he would give us;
that we, being delivered out of the hands of our enemies,
   might serve him without fear;
in holiness and righteousness before him,
   all the days of our life.
And you, child, shall be called the prophet of the Most High,
   for you shall go before the face of the Lord to prepare his
     ways;
to give knowledge of salvation unto his people,
   for the remission of their sins,

through the tender mercy of our God,
    whereby the Dayspring from on high has visited us;
to give light to them that sit in darkness,
    and in the shadow of death,
and to guide our feet into the way of peace.

Glory be to the Father,
    and to the Son,
    and to the Holy Spirit:
As it was in the beginning,
    is now and ever shall be,
    world without end. Amen.   *Benedictus*

Prayer of Intercession

As you make your requests to God, pray this prayer:

Be light to our darkness, wisdom to our folly, and manifest
your strength in our weakness. Remember us according to
the favor which you bear to your own people; stir us up to
seek your face, and to lay hold on your covenant; and make
us find that it is indeed good for us to draw nigh unto you,
and to wait upon you in and through the name and merits of Jesus Christ, our only mediator and advocate. Amen.
Augustus Toplady

Further Petition

- Personal
- Church
- World

Lord's Prayer

Pray the words that Jesus taught us to pray:

Our Father in heaven,
    hallowed be your name;
    your kingdom come;
    your will be done, on earth as it is in heaven.
    Give us this day our daily bread.
    And forgive us our debts, as we forgive our debtors.
    And lead us not into temptation but deliver us from evil.
    For yours is the kingdom, and the power,
    and the glory, forever. Amen.

Benediction

Receive by faith this blessing from God:

May the God of hope fill you with all joy and peace in believing, so that by the power of the Holy Spirit you may abound in hope.   Romans 15:13

Postlude

In closing, say or sing this praise to God:

His Name for ever shall endure,
    last like the sun it shall;
Men shall be blessed in Him, and blessed
    all nations shall Him call.

Now blessèd be the Lord, our God,
    the God of Israel,
For He alone does wondrous works,
    in glory that excel.

And blessèd be His glorious Name
    to all eternity;
The whole earth let His glory fill.
    Amen, so let it be.   *Based on Psalm 72:17–19*

December 28

Meditation

Reflect on these words about the incarnation of the Lord Jesus:

Christ is born, glorify Him! Christ from heaven, go out to meet Him! Christ on earth, be exalted! Sing to the Lord all the whole earth; and that I may join both in one word: Let the heavens rejoice, and let the earth be glad, for Him who is of heaven and then of earth. Christ in the flesh, rejoice with trembling and with joy; with trembling because of your sins, with joy because of your hope.   *Gregory Nazianzus*

———

Call to Worship

Hear God call you to worship through his word:

But you, O Bethlehem Ephrathah,
    who are too little to be among the clans of Judah,
from you shall come forth for me
    one who is to be ruler in Israel,
whose coming forth is from of old,
    from ancient days.   *Micah 5:2*

Say or sing the words of this Christmas carol:

O little town of Bethlehem,
how still we see thee lie!
Above thy deep and dreamless sleep
the silent stars go by;
yet in thy dark streets shineth
the everlasting light;
the hopes and fears of all the years
are met in thee tonight.

For Christ is born of Mary,
and, gathered all above
while mortals sleep, the angels keep
their watch of wond'ring love.
O morning stars, together
proclaim the holy birth,
and praises sing to God the King
and peace to all the earth.

How silently, how silently,
the wondrous gift is giv'n!
So God imparts to human hearts
the blessings of his heav'n.
No ear may hear his coming,
but in this world of sin,
where meek souls will receive him, still
the dear Christ enters in.

O holy Child of Bethlehem,
descend to us, we pray,
cast out our sin and enter in,

be born in us today.
We hear the Christmas angels
the great glad tidings tell;
O come to us, abide with us,
our Lord Immanuel!   *Phillips Brooks*

Reading of the Law
Hear God's law as his will for your life:

Our Lord Jesus said,

Blessed are the poor in spirit,
    for theirs is the kingdom of heaven.
Blessed are those who mourn,
    for they shall be comforted.
Blessed are the meek,
    for they shall inherit the earth.
Blessed are those who hunger and thirst for righteousness,
    for they shall be satisfied.
Blessed are the merciful,
    for they shall receive mercy.
Blessed are the pure in heart,
    for they shall see God.
Blessed are the peacemakers,
    for they shall be called sons of God.
Blessed are those who are persecuted for righteousness' sake,
    for theirs is the kingdom of heaven.   *Matthew 5:3–10*

Confession of Sin
Confess your sins to God:

I, a poor sinner, confess before you, my God and Creator, that
I have sinned gravely and in various ways against you, not

only with outward gross sins, but much more with internal, innate blindness, unbelief, doubts, faintheartedness, impatience, pride, evil greed, secret envy, hatred and jealousy, as well as other evil emotions. You, my Lord and God, recognize this in me very well, but sadly I cannot recognize them sufficiently. I feel sorrow and regret for them and wholeheartedly desire grace through your dear Son Jesus Christ. Amen.
Zacharias Ursinus

Assurance of Pardon
Receive these words of comfort from God:

For we do not have a high priest who is unable to sympathize with our weaknesses, but one who in every respect has been tempted as we are, yet without sin. Let us then with confidence draw near to the throne of grace, that we may receive mercy and find grace to help in time of need.   *Hebrews 4:15–16*

Athanasian Creed, Part 1
Confess what you believe about the Christian faith:

Whoever desires to be saved should above all hold to the catholic faith. Anyone who does not keep it whole and unbroken will doubtless perish eternally. Now this is the catholic faith:

that we worship one God in Trinity and the Trinity in unity, neither confounding their persons nor dividing the essence.

> For the person of the Father is a distinct person,
>   the person of the Son is another,
>   and that of the Holy Spirit still another.
> But the divinity of the Father, Son, and Holy Spirit is one,
>   the glory equal, the majesty coeternal.

Such as the Father is, such is the Son and such is the
Holy Spirit.
The Father is uncreated, the Son is uncreated, the Holy
Spirit is uncreated.
The Father is immeasurable, the Son is immeasurable,
the Holy Spirit is immeasurable.
The Father is eternal, the Son is eternal, the Holy Spirit
is eternal.
And yet there are not three eternal beings; there is but
one eternal being.
So too there are not three uncreated or immeasurable
beings;
there is but one uncreated and immeasurable being.
Similarly, the Father is almighty, the Son is almighty,
the Holy Spirit is almighty.
Yet there are not three almighty beings; there is but one
almighty being.
Thus, the Father is God, the Son is God, the Holy Spirit
is God.
Yet there are not three gods; there is but one God.
Thus, the Father is Lord, the Son is Lord, the Holy Spirit
is Lord.
Yet there are not three lords; there is but one Lord.
Just as Christian truth compels us to confess each person
individually as both God and Lord,
so catholic religion forbids us to say that there are
three gods or lords.

Praise
Say or sing this praise to God:

Glory be to God the Father,
Glory be to God the Son,
Glory be to God the Spirit,
God Almighty, Three in One!
Hallelujah! Hallelujah!
Glory be to him alone.   *Gloria Patri*

Catechism
Receive this instruction from the Westminster Shorter Catechism:

Q. 23. What offices does Christ execute as our redeemer?
A. Christ, as our redeemer, executes the offices of a prophet,
of a priest, and of a king, both in his state of humiliation
and exaltation.

Prayer for Illumination
As you read his word, ask God to enlighten your mind and heart:

Lord, you know what distracted hearts we have, O give us
self-recollection; you know what hard, dead hearts we have,
O touch and awaken us! You know how we yet resist your
Word and our lower nature is reluctant to bow to your scepter; therefore, O Lord, show forth your power; send your
Spirit on high to work among us, to make our hearts submissive, and ourselves capable of living in true union with you,
our salvation, and of yielding totally to your grace. Amen.
Gerhard Tersteegen

Scripture Reading
Read this portion of God's word: Colossians 1:1–20

Praise

Say these praises to God:

Lord, now let your servant depart in peace according to
      your word.
For mine eyes have seen your salvation,
Which you have prepared before the face of all people,
To be a light to lighten the Gentiles and to be the glory of
      your people Israel. Amen.   *Nunc Dimittis*

Holy, holy, holy, Lord God of hosts,
heaven and earth are full of your glory.
Glory be to you, O Lord Most High.
Blessed is he that comes in the name of the Lord.
Hosanna in the highest. Amen.   *Sanctus*

Prayer of Intercession

As you make your requests to God, pray this prayer:

Lord, I lack wisdom, counsel, strength, understanding,
prudence in your holy fear. The fullness of these are in you;
Lord, it is for your glory to help your poor servant, and bestow some measure of these upon me to do your own work
with. Lo! Lord, I lay myself down to you to work by me. I
have an angry spirit, full of tossings and turmoilings, but
you are the Prince of Peace, abounding in meekness. Oh
bestow on me such a meek and peaceable spirit, as, learning from you, I may be meek and lowly in heart. Amen.
Richard Sibbes

Further Petition
- Personal
- Church
- World

Lord's Prayer
Pray the words that Jesus taught us to pray:

Our Father in heaven,
    hallowed be your name;
    your kingdom come;
    your will be done, on earth as it is in heaven.
    Give us this day our daily bread.
    And forgive us our debts, as we forgive our debtors.
    And lead us not into temptation but deliver us from evil.
    For yours is the kingdom, and the power,
    and the glory, forever. Amen.

Benediction
Receive by faith this blessing from God:

The grace of the Lord Jesus Christ and the love of God and the fellowship of the Holy Spirit be with you all.   *2 Corinthians 13:14*

Postlude
In closing, say or sing this praise to God:

His Name for ever shall endure,
    last like the sun it shall;
Men shall be blessed in Him, and blessed
    all nations shall Him call.

Now blessèd be the Lord, our God,
    the God of Israel,
For He alone does wondrous works,
    in glory that excel.

And blessèd be His glorious Name
    to all eternity;
The whole earth let His glory fill.
    Amen, so let it be.   *Based on Psalm 72:17–19*

December 29

.

Meditation
Reflect on these words about the incarnation of the Lord Jesus:

He, through whom time was made, was made in time; and He, older by eternity than the world itself, was younger in age than many of His servants in the world; He, who made man, was made man; He was given existence by a mother whom He brought into existence; He was carried in hands which He formed; He nursed at breasts which He filled; He cried like a babe in the manger in speechless infancy—this Word without which human eloquence is speechless!   *Augustine*

Call to Worship
Hear God call you to worship through his word:

Great indeed, we confess, is the mystery of godliness:

He was manifested in the flesh,
   vindicated by the Spirit,
   seen by angels,

proclaimed among the nations,
  believed on in the world,
  taken up in glory.   1 Timothy 3:16

Adoration

Say or sing the words of this Christmas carol:

O come, all ye faithful, joyful and triumphant!
O come ye, O come ye to Bethlehem!
Come and behold him,
born the King of angels:

> *O come, let us adore him,*
> *O come, let us adore him,*
> *O come, let us adore him,*
> *Christ the Lord!*

God of God, Light from Light,
Lo, He abhors not the virgin's womb!
Very God,
Begotten, not created.

Sing, choirs of angels, sing in exultation;
Sing, all ye citizens of heaven above!
Glory to God,
glory in the highest.

Yea, Lord, we greet thee, born this happy morning;
Jesus, to thee be all glory given!
Word of the Father,
now in flesh appearing.   *John Francis Wade*

Reading of the Law

God's law as his will for your life:

Our Lord said,

As the Father has loved me, so have I loved you. Abide in my love. If you keep my commandments, you will abide in my love, just as I have kept my Father's commandments and abide in his love. These things I have spoken to you, that my joy may be in you, and that your joy may be full. This is my commandment, that you love one another as I have loved you.   John 15:9–12

Confession of Sin

Confess your sins to God:

Remember, O Lord, that we are a parcel of your portion, your flock, the inheritors of your kingdom, the sheep of your pasture, and the members of your Son our Savior Jesus Christ. Deal with us therefore according to the multitude of your mercies, that all nations, tribes, and languages may celebrate your praises in the restoring of your ruined church to perfection again; for it is your work, O Lord, and not man's, and from you do we with patience look for the same, and not from the fleshly arm of man, and therefore to you only is due all dominion, power, and thanksgiving, now in our days and forevermore. Amen.   John Bradford

Assurance of Pardon

Receive these words of comfort from God:

Remember your mercy, O LORD, and your steadfast love,
    for they have been from of old.

Remember not the sins of my youth or my transgressions;
according to your steadfast love remember me,
for the sake of your goodness, O Lord!   *Psalm 25:6–7*

Athanasian Creed, Part 2
Confess what you believe about the Christian faith:

Whoever desires to be saved should above all hold to the catholic faith. Anyone who does not keep it whole and unbroken will doubtless perish eternally. Now this is the catholic faith:

that we worship one God in Trinity and the Trinity in unity, neither confounding their persons nor dividing the essence. . . .

> The Father was neither made nor created nor begotten
> from anyone.
> The Son was neither made nor created; he was begotten
> from the Father alone.
> The Holy Spirit was neither made nor created nor
> begotten;
> he proceeds from the Father and the Son.
> Accordingly, there is one Father, not three fathers;
> there is one Son, not three sons;
> there is one Holy Spirit, not three holy spirits.
> None in this Trinity is before or after, none is greater or
> smaller;
> in their entirety the three persons are coeternal and
> coequal with each other.
> So in everything, as was said earlier, the unity in Trinity,
> and the Trinity in unity, is to be worshiped.
> Anyone then who desires to be saved should think thus
> about the Trinity.

Praise

Say or sing this praise to God:

Glory be to God the Father,
Glory be to God the Son,
Glory be to God the Spirit,
God Almighty, Three in One!
Hallelujah! Hallelujah!
Glory be to him alone.   *Gloria Patri*

Catechism

Receive this instruction from the Westminster Shorter Catechism:

Q. 24. How does Christ execute the office of a prophet?
A. Christ executes the office of a prophet, in revealing to us, by his word and Spirit, the will of God for our salvation.

Prayer for Illumination

As you read his word, ask God to enlighten your mind and heart:

O God, you instruct us by your Holy Scriptures—we urge you by your grace to enlighten our minds and cleanse our hearts; that reading, hearing, and meditating upon them, we may rightly understand and heartily embrace the things you have revealed in them. Give efficacy to the reading of the gospel in your Word, that through the operation of the Holy Spirit, this holy seed may be received into our hearts as into good ground; and that we may not only hear your Word but keep it, living in conformity with your precepts; so that we may finally attain everlasting salvation, through Jesus Christ our Lord. Amen.   *Waldensian Liturgy*

Scripture Reading

Read this portion of God's word: Ephesians 3:1–12

Praise

Say this praise to God:

Glory to God in the highest,
and peace to his people on earth.

Lord God, heavenly King,
almighty God and Father,
we worship you, we give you thanks,
we praise you for your glory.

Lord Jesus Christ, only Son of the Father,
Lord God, Lamb of God,
you take away the sin of the world:
have mercy on us;
you are seated at the right hand of the Father:
receive our prayer.

For you alone are the Holy One,
you alone are the Lord,
you alone are the Most High, Jesus Christ,
with the Holy Spirit,
in the glory of God the Father.
Amen.   *Gloria in Excelsis*

Prayer of Intercession

As you make your requests to God, pray this prayer:

Give us, this day, our daily bread. Feed us with food convenient for us. If it be your pleasure to cause us to abound with the good things of this life, give us a compassionate spirit, that we may be ready to relieve the wants of others; but let neither riches nor poverty estrange our hearts from you, nor cause us to become negligent of those treasures in heaven which can never be taken from us. And, into whatever circumstances of life we may be brought, teach us to be cheerful and content. In our affliction, let us remember how often we have been helped; and, in our prosperity, may we acknowledge from whose hand our blessings are received. Amen.   *Henry Thornton*

Further Petition

- Personal
- Church
- World

Lord's Prayer

Pray the words that Jesus taught us to pray:

Our Father in heaven,
  hallowed be your name;
  your kingdom come;
  your will be done, on earth as it is in heaven.
  Give us this day our daily bread.
  And forgive us our debts, as we forgive our debtors.
  And lead us not into temptation but deliver us from evil.
  For yours is the kingdom, and the power,
  and the glory, forever. Amen.

Benediction

Receive by faith this blessing from God:

Now to him who is able to do far more abundantly than all that we ask or think, according to the power at work within us, to him be glory in the church and in Christ Jesus throughout all generations, forever and ever. Amen.   *Ephesians 3:20–21*

Postlude

In closing, say or sing this praise to God:

His Name for ever shall endure,
    last like the sun it shall;
Men shall be blessed in Him, and blessed
    all nations shall Him call.

Now blessèd be the Lord, our God,
    the God of Israel,
For He alone does wondrous works,
    in glory that excel.

And blessèd be His glorious Name
    to all eternity;
The whole earth let His glory fill.
    Amen, so let it be.   *Based on Psalm 72:17–19*

December 30

Meditation

Reflect on these words about the incarnation of the Lord Jesus:

Here is something marvelous: the Son of God descended from
heaven in such a way that, without leaving heaven, he willed
to be borne in the virgin's womb, to go about the earth, and
to hang upon the cross; yet he continuously filled the world
even as he had done from the beginning!   *John Calvin*

———

Call to Worship

Hear God call you to worship through his word:

Go on up to a high mountain,
   O Zion, herald of good news;
lift up your voice with strength,
   O Jerusalem, herald of good news;
   lift it up, fear not;
say to the cities of Judah,
   "Behold your God!"   *Isaiah 40:9*

Adoration

Say or sing the words of this Christmas carol:

See in yonder manger low,
Born for us on earth below,
See the gentle Lamb appears,
Promised from eternal years.

Hail the ever blessed morn;
Hail redemption's happy dawn;
Sing through all Jerusalem:
"Christ is born in Bethlehem!"

Lo, within a stable lies
He who built the starry skies,
He who, throned in height sublime,
Sits amid the cherubim.

Sacred Infant, all divine,
What a tender love was Thine,
Thus to come from highest bliss
Down to such a world as this.

Teach, oh, teach us, holy Child,
By Thy face so meek and mild,
Teach us to resemble Thee
In Thy sweet humility.   Edward Caswall

Reading of the Law

Hear God's law as his will for your life:

The words of our Lord Jesus Christ:

Unless your righteousness exceeds that of the scribes and
Pharisees, you will never enter the kingdom of heaven. . . .

You therefore must be perfect, as your heavenly Father is perfect. . . . Beware of practicing your righteousness before other people in order to be seen by them, for then you will have no reward from your Father who is in heaven. . . . Seek first the kingdom of God and his righteousness, and all these things will be added to you. . . . So whatever you wish that others would do to you, do also to them, for this is the Law and the Prophets.   *Matthew 5:20, 48; 6:1, 33; 7:12*

Confession of Sin
Confess your sins to God:

So long, Lord, have I lived in this world of yours, which you made, and not I, as if I might do in it, and with myself, what I pleased! I have usurped upon your unquestionable right in me, have lived to myself and not to you; I am now convinced this was a very undutiful, unlawful way of living. . . . Turn me and I shall be turned; you are the Lord my God. Amen.   *John Howe*

Assurance of Pardon
Receive these words of comfort from God:

For there is no distinction: for all have sinned and fall short of the glory of God, and are justified by his grace as a gift, through the redemption that is in Christ Jesus, whom God put forward as a propitiation by his blood, to be received by faith. This was to show God's righteousness, because in his divine forbearance he had passed over former sins. *Romans 3:22–25*

Athanasian Creed, Part 3
Confess what you believe about the Christian faith:

Whoever desires to be saved should above all hold to the catholic faith. Anyone who does not keep it whole and unbroken will doubtless perish eternally. Now this is the catholic faith:

that we worship one God in Trinity and the Trinity in unity, neither confounding their persons nor dividing the essence. . . .

But it is necessary for eternal salvation that one also believe in the incarnation of our Lord Jesus Christ faithfully.

Now this is the true faith:

> that we believe and confess that our Lord Jesus Christ,
>   God's Son,
>   is both God and man, equally.
> He is God from the essence of the Father, begotten
>   before time;
>   and he is man from the essence of his mother, born
>   in time;
>   completely God, completely man, with a rational soul
>   and human flesh;
>   equal to the Father as regards divinity,
>   less than the Father as regards humanity.
> Although he is God and man, yet Christ is not two, but one.
> He is one, however, not by his divinity being turned
>   into flesh,
>   but by God's taking humanity to himself.
> He is one, certainly not by the blending of his essence,
>   but by the unity of his person.
> For just as one man is both rational soul and flesh,
>   so too the one Christ is both God and man.

He suffered for our salvation;
he descended to hell;
he arose from the dead on the third day;
he ascended to heaven;
he is seated at the Father's right hand;
from there he will come to judge the living and the dead.
At his coming all people will arise bodily and give an
　　　accounting of their own deeds.
Those who have done good will enter eternal life,
　　and those who have done evil will enter eternal fire.

This is the catholic faith: that one cannot be saved without
believing it firmly and faithfully.

Praise
Say or sing this praise to God:

Glory be to God the Father,
Glory be to God the Son,
Glory be to God the Spirit,
God Almighty, Three in One!
Hallelujah! Hallelujah!
Glory be to him alone.　　*Gloria Patri*

Catechism
Receive this instruction from the Westminster Shorter Catechism:

Q. 25. *How does Christ execute the office of a priest?*
A. Christ executes the office of a priest, in his once offering up
of himself a sacrifice to satisfy divine justice, and reconcile us
to God; and in making continual intercession for us.

Prayer for Illumination

As you read his word, ask God to enlighten your mind and heart:

Almighty God, I earnestly ask you for such deeper fellowship of the Holy Spirit, who speaks in the blessed Scriptures, that when I open them, I may perceive his mind in what I read, and immediately hear in them his voice to myself. I ask you for a quicker understanding in spiritual things, for more desire to understand, a fuller perception of your promise in the church, that I may become teachable, and may love that by which you will teach me. Amen.   *Henry Wotherspoon*

Scripture Reading

Read this portion of God's word: Romans 1:1–17

Praise

Say or sing this praise to God:

Phos Hilaron

O radiant light, O sun divine
Of God the Father's deathless face,
O image of the light sublime
That fills the heav'nly dwelling place.

O Son of God, the source of life,
Praise is your due by night and day;
Our happy lips must raise the strain
Of your esteemed and splendid name.

Lord Jesus Christ, as daylight fades,
As shine the lights of eventide,
We praise the Father with the Son,
The Spirit blest, and with them one.   *Anonymous*

Prayer of Intercession

As you make your requests to God, pray this prayer:

O Lord our God, teach us, we pray, to ask aright for the right blessings. Steer the vessel of our life toward yourself, the tranquil haven of all storm-tossed souls. Show us the course wherein we should go. Renew a willing spirit within us. Let your Spirit curb our wayward senses, and guide and enable us unto that which is our true good, to keep your laws, and in all our works evermore to rejoice in your glorious and gladdening presence. Amen.   *Basil of Caesarea*

Further Petition
- Personal
- Church
- World

Lord's Prayer

Pray the words that Jesus taught us to pray:

Our Father in heaven,
   hallowed be your name;
   your kingdom come;
   your will be done, on earth as it is in heaven.
   Give us this day our daily bread.
   And forgive us our debts, as we forgive our debtors.
   And lead us not into temptation but deliver us from evil.
   For yours is the kingdom, and the power,
   and the glory, forever. Amen.

Benediction

Receive by faith this blessing from God:

Now may the God of peace himself sanctify you completely, and may your whole spirit and soul and body be kept blameless at the coming of our Lord Jesus Christ. He who calls you is faithful; he will surely do it.   *1 Thessalonians 5:23–24*

Postlude

In closing, say or sing this praise to God:

His Name for ever shall endure,
    last like the sun it shall;
Men shall be blessed in Him, and blessed
    all nations shall Him call.

Now blessèd be the Lord, our God,
    the God of Israel,
For He alone does wondrous works,
    in glory that excel.

And blessèd be His glorious Name
    to all eternity;
The whole earth let His glory fill.
    Amen, so let it be.   *Based on Psalm 72:17–19*

December 31

Meditation
Reflect on these words about the incarnation of the Lord Jesus:

Perhaps . . . one who exactly understands the mystery would be justified rather in saying that, instead of the death occurring in consequence of the birth, the birth on the contrary was accepted by Him for the sake of the death; for He who lives for ever did not sink down into the conditions of a bodily birth from any need to live, but to call us back from death to life.   *Gregory of Nyssa*

Call to Worship
Hear God call you to worship through his word:

For you know the grace of our Lord Jesus Christ, that though he was rich, yet for your sake he became poor, so that you by his poverty might become rich.   *2 Corinthians 8:9*

Adoration
Say or sing the words of this Christmas carol:

Joy to the world, the Lord is come!
Let earth receive her King;

Let every heart prepare him room,
and heaven and nature sing,
and heaven and nature sing,
and heaven, and heaven and nature sing.

Joy to the earth, the Savior reigns!
Let men their songs employ,
while fields and floods, rocks, hills, and plains,
repeat the sounding joy,
repeat the sounding joy,
repeat, repeat the sounding joy.

No more let sins and sorrows grow,
nor thorns infest the ground;
he comes to make his blessings flow
far as the curse is found,
far as the curse is found,
far as, far as the curse is found.

He rules the world with truth and grace
and makes the nations prove
the glories of his righteousness
and wonders of his love,
and wonders of his love,
and wonders, wonders of his love.   *Isaac Watts*

Reading of the Law
Hear God's law as his will for your life:

And God spoke all these words, saying,
> "I am the LORD your God, who brought you out of the
> land of Egypt, out of the house of slavery.
> You shall have no other gods before me.

You shall not make for yourself a carved image, or any likeness of anything that is in heaven above, or that is in the earth beneath, or that is in the water under the earth. You shall not bow down to them or serve them, for I the Lord your God am a jealous God, visiting the iniquity of the fathers on the children to the third and the fourth generation of those who hate me, but showing steadfast love to thousands of those who love me and keep my commandments.

You shall not take the name of the Lord your God in vain, for the Lord will not hold him guiltless who takes his name in vain.

Remember the Sabbath day, to keep it holy. Six days you shall labor, and do all your work, but the seventh day is a Sabbath to the Lord your God. On it you shall not do any work, you, or your son, or your daughter, your male servant, or your female servant, or your livestock, or the sojourner who is within your gates. For in six days the Lord made heaven and earth, the sea, and all that is in them, and rested on the seventh day. Therefore the Lord blessed the Sabbath day and made it holy.

Honor your father and your mother, that your days may be long in the land that the Lord your God is giving you.

You shall not murder.

You shall not commit adultery.

You shall not steal.

You shall not bear false witness against your neighbor.

You shall not covet your neighbor's house; you shall not covet your neighbor's wife, or his male servant, or his female servant, or his ox, or his donkey, or anything that is your neighbor's." *Exodus 20:1–17*

Confession of Sin
Confess your sins to God:

You have given me a whole life to serve you in, and to advance my hopes of heaven; and this precious time I have thrown away upon my sins and vanities, being improvident of my time and of my talent, and of your grace and my own advantages, resisting your Spirit and quenching him. I have been a great lover of myself, and yet used many ways to destroy myself. I have pursued my temporal ends with greediness and indirect means. I am revengeful and unthankful, forgetting benefits, but not so soon forgetting injuries; curious and murmuring, a great breaker of promises. I have not loved my neighbor's good, nor advanced it in all things, where I could. I have been unlike you in all things. I am unmerciful and unjust, a foolish admirer of things below, and careless of heaven and the ways that lead there. But for your name's sake, O Lord, be merciful unto my sin, for it is great. Amen.   *Jeremy Taylor*

Assurance of Pardon
Receive these words of comfort from God:

Our fathers, when they were in Egypt,
     did not consider your wondrous works;
they did not remember the abundance of your steadfast love,
     but rebelled by the sea, at the Red Sea.
Yet he saved them for his name's sake,
     that he might make known his mighty power.
Psalm 106:7–8

Nicene Creed

Confess what you believe about the Christian faith:

I believe in one God, the Father Almighty,
> Maker of heaven and earth, and of all things visible and
>> invisible.

And in one Lord Jesus Christ, the only-begotten Son of God;
> begotten of the Father before all worlds;
> God of God, Light of Light, very God of very God;
> begotten, not made, being of one substance with the
>> Father;
> by whom all things were made.

Who, for us men and for our salvation,
> came down from heaven
> and was incarnate by the Holy Spirit of the Virgin Mary,
> and was made man;
> and was crucified also for us under Pontius Pilate;
> he suffered and was buried;
> and the third day he rose again, according to the Scriptures;
> and ascended into heaven, and sits on the right hand of
>> the Father;
> and he shall come again, with glory, to judge the living
>> and the dead;
> whose kingdom shall have no end.

And I believe in the Holy Spirit, the Lord and Giver of life;
> who proceeds from the Father and the Son;
> who with the Father and the Son together is worshiped
>> and glorified;
> who spoke by the prophets.

And I believe in one holy catholic and apostolic church.
   I acknowledge one baptism for the forgiveness of sins;
   and I look for the resurrection of the dead,
   and the life of the world to come. Amen.

Praise
Say or sing this praise to God:

Glory be to God the Father,
Glory be to God the Son,
Glory be to God the Spirit,
God Almighty, Three in One!
Hallelujah! Hallelujah!
Glory be to him alone.   *Gloria Patri*

Catechism
Receive this instruction from the Westminster Shorter Catechism:

Q. 26. How does Christ execute the office of a king?
A. Christ executes the office of a king, in subduing us to himself, in ruling and defending us, and in restraining and conquering all his and our enemies.

Prayer for Illumination
As you read his word, ask God to enlighten your mind and heart:

Almighty God, enter our hearts, and so fill us with your love, that, forsaking all evil desires, we may embrace you, our only good. Show unto us, for your mercies' sake, O Lord our God, what you are unto us. Say unto our souls, "I am your salvation." So speak that we may hear. Our hearts are before you; open our ears; let us hasten after your voice and take hold of you. Amen.   *Augustine*

Scripture Reading

Read this portion of God's word: Philippians 2:1–11

Praise

Say or sing this praise to God:

Corde Natus

He is found in human fashion,
Death and sorrow here to know,
That the race of Adam's children
Doomed by law to endless woe,
May not henceforth die and perish
In the dreadful gulf below,
Evermore and evermore!

O that birth forever blessèd,
When the virgin, full of grace,
By the Holy Ghost conceiving,
Bore the Saviour of our race;
And the Babe, the world's Redeemer,
First revealed His sacred face,
Evermore and evermore!

O ye heights of heaven adore Him;
Angel hosts, His praises sing;
Powers, dominions, bow before Him,
And extol our God and King!
Let no tongue on earth be silent,
Every voice in concert sing,
Evermore and evermore!

Christ, to Thee with God the Father,
And, O Holy Ghost, to Thee,

Hymn and chant with high thanksgiving,
And unwearied praises be:
Honour, glory, and dominion,
And eternal victory,
Evermore and evermore!   *Aurelius Prudentius*

Prayer of Intercession
As you make your requests to God, pray this prayer:

Spirit of Christ, who of old did make men soldiers for the times of war, make me now a soldier for the times of peace. Nerve me for the trials of the marketplace, more arduous than the marches of the field. Make me strong, not with the strength of recklessness, but with that strength which comes from an increased burden of care. Inspire me with your sacrificial love, and I shall be a stranger to selfish fear; I shall have the courage to dare all things when I am made a captain in your band. Amen.   *George Matheson*

Further Petition
- Personal
- Church
- World

Lord's Prayer
Pray the words that Jesus taught us to pray:

Our Father in heaven,
    hallowed be your name;
    your kingdom come;
    your will be done, on earth as it is in heaven.
    Give us this day our daily bread.

And forgive us our debts, as we forgive our debtors.
And lead us not into temptation but deliver us from evil.
For yours is the kingdom, and the power,
and the glory, forever. Amen.

Benediction
Receive by faith this blessing from God:

May grace and peace be multiplied to you in the knowledge
of God and of Jesus our Lord.   *2 Peter 1:2*

Postlude
In closing, say or sing this praise to God:

His Name for ever shall endure,
    last like the sun it shall;
Men shall be blessed in Him, and blessed
    all nations shall Him call.

Now blessèd be the Lord, our God,
    the God of Israel,
For He alone does wondrous works,
    in glory that excel.

And blessèd be His glorious Name
    to all eternity;
The whole earth let His glory fill.
    Amen, so let it be.   *Based on Psalm 72:17–19*

January 1

Circumcision of Christ

Meditation
Reflect on these words about the incarnation of the Lord Jesus:

[The] suffering of the Mediator does not date from the end of His stay on earth. . . . The blood of the Savior's circumcision is as much atoning blood for us as is the blood shed on Golgotha. His entire life was a continual suffering.   *Geerhardus Vos*

———

Call to Worship
Hear God call you to worship through his word:

You are the most handsome of the sons of men;
　　grace is poured upon your lips;
　　therefore God has blessed you forever.   *Psalm 45:2*

Adoration
Say or sing the words of this psalm:

Endow the king with justice, LORD,
The royal son with righteousness.
Your people, your afflicted ones,

He'll judge with truth and uprightness.

The mountains will bring peace to them,
The hills the fruit of righteousness.
He will defend and save the poor,
And crush all those who them oppress.

As long as sun and moon endure,
So will he live time without end.
He'll be like showers on the earth,
Like rains that on the mown fields descend.

The righteous then will blossom forth
Throughout his everlasting reign;
Until the moon no longer shines,
Peace in abundance will remain.

From sea to sea he will hold sway
And from the River to earth's end.
His enemies will lick the dust
And desert tribes the knee will bend.

All kings will humbly bow to him;
And nations worship him with fear.
He'll save the needy when they call,
The poor for whom no help is near.

He will take pity on the weak
And save them from oppressive might.
He'll rescue them from violence;
Their blood is precious in his sight.
Sing Psalms: 72:1–9, 11–14

Reading of the Law

Hear God's law as his will for your life:

Beloved, let us love one another, for love is from God, and whoever loves has been born of God and knows God. Anyone who does not love does not know God, because God is love. In this the love of God was made manifest among us, that God sent his only Son into the world, so that we might live through him. In this is love, not that we have loved God but that he loved us and sent his Son to be the propitiation for our sins. Beloved, if God so loved us, we also ought to love one another. *1 John 4:7–11*

Confession of Sin

Confess your sins to God:

O God the Father of heaven, *have mercy upon us.*
O God the Son, Redeemer of the world, *have mercy upon us.*
O God the Holy Spirit, *have mercy upon us.*
Be merciful to us and spare us, O Lord.
Be merciful to us and deliver us, O Lord.
From all sin, from all error, from all evil—*deliver us, O Lord.*
From the wiles of the devil and from everlasting death—
       deliver us, O Lord.

Lord Jesus, by the mystery of your holy incarnation,
by your holy nativity,
by your baptism, fasting, and temptations—*deliver us, O Lord.*
By your agony and bloody sweat,
by your cross and passions,
by your death and burial,
by your resurrection and ascension,

by the coming of the Holy Spirit, the Comforter—
>   *deliver us, O Lord. Amen.*   Martin Bucer

Assurance of Pardon
Receive these words of comfort from God:

But God, being rich in mercy, because of the great love with
which he loved us, even when we were dead in our trespasses,
made us alive together with Christ—by grace you have been
saved—and raised us up with him and seated us with him
in the heavenly places in Christ Jesus, so that in the coming
ages he might show the immeasurable riches of his grace in
kindness toward us in Christ Jesus.   *Ephesians 2:4–7*

Apostles' Creed
Confess what you believe about the Christian faith:

I believe in God the Father Almighty,
>   Maker of heaven and earth.

I believe in Jesus Christ, his only-begotten Son, our Lord;
>   who was conceived by the Holy Spirit, born of the
>   Virgin Mary;
>   suffered under Pontius Pilate;
>   was crucified, dead, and buried;
>   he descended into hell;
>   the third day he rose again from the dead;
>   he ascended into heaven,
>   and sits at the right hand of God the Father Almighty;
>   from there he shall come to judge the living and the dead.

I believe in the Holy Spirit;
>   the holy catholic church;

the communion of saints;
the forgiveness of sins;
the resurrection of the body;
and the life everlasting. Amen.

Praise
Say or sing this praise to God:

Glory be to God the Father,
Glory be to God the Son,
Glory be to God the Spirit,
God Almighty, Three in One!
Hallelujah! Hallelujah!
Glory be to him alone.   *Gloria Patri*

Catechism
Receive this instruction from the Westminster Shorter Catechism:

Q. 27. In what did Christ's humiliation consist?
A. Christ's humiliation consisted in his being born, and that in a low condition, made under the law, undergoing the miseries of this life, the wrath of God, and the cursed death of the cross; in being buried, and continuing under the power of death for a time.

Prayer for Illumination
As you read his word, ask God to enlighten your mind and heart:

Almighty, eternal and merciful God, whose Word is a lamp unto our feet and a light unto our path, open and illuminate our minds, that we may purely and perfectly understand your Word and that our lives may be conformed to what we have rightly understood, that in nothing we may be

displeasing to your Majesty, through Jesus Christ our Lord.
Amen.   *Huldrych Zwingli*

Scripture Reading
Read this portion of God's word: Isaiah 60

Praise
Say or sing this praise to God:

Sileat Omnis Caro Mortalis

Let all mortal flesh keep silence,
And with fear and trembling stand;
Ponder nothing earthly minded,
For with blessing in His hand,
Christ our God to earth descendeth,
Our full homage to demand.

King of kings, yet born of Mary,
As of old on earth He stood;
Lord of lords, in human vesture,
In the body and the blood;
He will give to all the faithful
His own self for heavenly food.

Rank on rank the host of heaven
Spreads its vanguard on the way,
As the Light of light descendeth
From the realms of endless day,
That the powers of hell may vanish
As the darkness clears away.

At His feet the six-winged seraph,
Cherubim with sleepless eye,

Veil their faces to the presence,
As with ceaseless voice they cry:
"Alleluia, Alleluia,
Alleluia, Lord Most High!"   *Divine Liturgy of St. James*

Prayer of Intercession
As you make your requests to God, pray this prayer:

Almighty God, you made your blessed Son to be circumcised and obedient to the law for man—grant us the true circumcision of your Spirit, that our hearts and all our members, being mortified from all worldly and carnal lusts, may in all things obey your blessed will, through the same, your Son, Jesus Christ our Lord. Amen.   *Book of Common Prayer (1552)*

Further Petition
- Personal
- Church
- World

Lord's Prayer
Pray the words that Jesus taught us to pray:

Our Father in heaven,
    hallowed be your name;
    your kingdom come;
    your will be done, on earth as it is in heaven.
    Give us this day our daily bread.
    And forgive us our debts, as we forgive our debtors.
    And lead us not into temptation but deliver us from evil.
    For yours is the kingdom, and the power,
    and the glory, forever. Amen.

Benediction

Receive by faith this blessing from God:

Now to him who is able to keep you from stumbling and to present you blameless before the presence of his glory with great joy, to the only God, our Savior, through Jesus Christ our Lord, be glory, majesty, dominion, and authority, before all time and now and forever. Amen.   *Jude 24–25*

Postlude

In closing, say or sing this praise to God:

His Name for ever shall endure,
    last like the sun it shall;
Men shall be blessed in Him, and blessed
    all nations shall Him call.

Now blessèd be the Lord, our God,
    the God of Israel,
For He alone does wondrous works,
    in glory that excel.

And blessèd be His glorious Name
    to all eternity;
The whole earth let His glory fill.
    Amen, so let it be.   *Based on Psalm 72:17–19*

January 2

Meditation
Reflect on these words about the incarnation of the Lord Jesus:

The love of Christ in the incarnation was great; for herein he did set a pattern without a parallel; in clothing himself with our flesh, which is but walking ashes, he has sewed, as it were, sackcloth to cloth of gold, the humanity to the Deity. . . . It is a sacred depth, how it transcends reason, and even puzzles faith! We know but in part, we see this only in a glass darkly, but in heaven our knowledge shall be cleared up, we shall fully understand this divine riddle.   *Thomas Watson*

———

Call to Worship
Hear God call you to worship through his word:

Concerning this salvation, the prophets who prophesied about the grace that was to be yours searched and inquired carefully, inquiring what person or time the Spirit of Christ in them was indicating when he predicted the sufferings of Christ and the subsequent glories. It was revealed to them that they were serving not themselves but you, in the things that have now been announced to you through those who

preached the good news to you by the Holy Spirit sent from
heaven, things into which angels long to look.   1 Peter 1:10–12

Adoration

Say or sing the words of this Epiphany hymn:

As with gladness men of old
did the guiding star behold,
as with joy they hailed its light,
leading onward, beaming bright,
so, most gracious Lord, may we
evermore be led by thee.

As with joyful steps they sped,
Savior, to thy lowly bed,
there to bend the knee before
thee, whom heaven and earth adore,
so may we with willing feet
ever seek thy mercy seat.

As they offered gifts most rare
at thy cradle, rude and bare,
so may we with holy joy,
pure and free from sin's alloy,
all our costliest treasures bring,
Christ, to thee, our heavenly King.

Holy Jesus, every day
keep us in the narrow way;
and, when earthly things are past,
bring our ransomed souls at last
where they need no star to guide,
where no clouds thy glory hide.

In the heavenly country bright
need they no created light;
thou its light, its joy, its crown,
thou its sun which goes not down.
There forever may we sing
alleluias to our King!   *W. Chatterton Dix*

Reading of the Law
Hear God's law as his will for your life:

The words of our Lord Jesus Christ:

You shall love the Lord your God with all your heart and with
all your soul and with all your mind. This is the great and first
commandment. And a second is like it: You shall love your
neighbor as yourself. On these two commandments depend
all the Law and the Prophets.   *Matthew 22:37–40*

Confession of Sin
Confess your sins to God:

O merciful God, full of compassion, long-suffering and
of great pity, make me earnestly repent, and heartily to be
sorry for all my misdoings; make the remembrance of them
so burdensome and painful that I may flee to you with a
troubled spirit and a contrite heart; and, O merciful Lord,
visit, comfort, and relieve me; excite in me true repentance;
give me in this world knowledge of your truth and confidence
in your mercy, and, in the world to come, life everlasting.
Amen.   *Samuel Johnson*

Assurance of Pardon
Receive these words of comfort from God:

O LORD, is not this what I said when I was yet in my country? That is why I made haste to flee to Tarshish; for I knew that you are a gracious God and merciful, slow to anger and abounding in steadfast love, and relenting from disaster.   *Jonah 4:2*

Apostles' Creed
Confess what you believe about the Christian faith:

I believe in God the Father Almighty,
    Maker of heaven and earth.

I believe in Jesus Christ, his only-begotten Son, our Lord;
    who was conceived by the Holy Spirit, born of the
            Virgin Mary;
    suffered under Pontius Pilate;
    was crucified, dead, and buried;
    he descended into hell;
    the third day he rose again from the dead;
    he ascended into heaven,
    and sits at the right hand of God the Father Almighty;
    from there he shall come to judge the living and the dead.

I believe in the Holy Spirit;
    the holy catholic church;
    the communion of saints;
    the forgiveness of sins;
    the resurrection of the body;
    and the life everlasting. Amen.

Praise
Say or sing this praise to God:

Glory be to the Father,
    and to the Son,
    and to the Holy Spirit:
As it was in the beginning,
    is now and ever shall be,
    world without end. Amen.   *Gloria Patri*

Catechism
Receive this instruction from the Westminster Shorter Catechism:

Q. 28. In what consists Christ's exaltation?
A. Christ's exaltation consists in his rising again from the dead on the third day, in ascending up into heaven, in sitting at the right hand of God the Father, and in coming to judge the world at the last day.

Prayer for Illumination
As you read his word, ask God to enlighten your mind and heart:

Merciful Lord, the comforter and teacher of your faithful people, increase in your church the desires which you have given, and confirm the hearts of those who hope in you by enabling them to understand the depth of your promises, that all of your adopted sons may even now behold, with the eyes of faith, and patiently wait for, the light which as yet you do not openly manifest; through Jesus Christ our Lord. Amen.   *Ambrose*

Scripture Reading
Read this portion of God's word: Hebrews 1

Praise
Say this praise to God:

My soul magnifies the Lord.
And my spirit rejoices in God my Savior.
For he has regarded the lowliness of his servant.
For behold, from now on all generations shall call me blessed.
For he who is mighty has magnified me, and holy is his Name.
And his mercy is on them that fear him, throughout all
      generations.
He has showed strength with his arm.
He has scattered the proud in the imagination of their hearts.
He has put down the mighty from their thrones, and has
      exalted the humble and meek.
He has filled the hungry with good things, and the rich he
      has sent away empty.
He, remembering his mercy, has helped his servant Israel,
      as he promised to our forefathers, Abraham and
      his seed, forever.

Glory be to the Father, and to the Son, and to the Holy Spirit:
As it was in the beginning, is now, and ever shall be, world
      without end. Amen.   *Magnificat*

Prayer of Intercession
As you make your requests to God, pray this prayer:

Grant, O Lord, that from this hour I may know only that
which is worthy to be known; that I may love only that
which is truly lovely; that I may praise only that which chiefly
pleases you; and that I may esteem what you esteem, and
despise that which is contemptible in your sight! Suffer me
no longer to judge by the imperfect perception of my own

senses, or of the senses of men ignorant like myself; but enable me to judge both of visible and invisible things, by the Spirit of truth; and, above all, to know and to obey your will. Amen.   *Thomas à Kempis*

Further Petition

- Personal
- Church
- World

Lord's Prayer

Pray the words that Jesus taught us to pray:

Our Father in heaven,
    hallowed be your name;
    your kingdom come;
    your will be done, on earth as it is in heaven.
    Give us this day our daily bread.
    And forgive us our debts, as we forgive our debtors.
    And lead us not into temptation but deliver us from evil.
    For yours is the kingdom, and the power,
    and the glory, forever. Amen.

Benediction

Receive by faith this blessing from God:

The LORD bless you and keep you;
The LORD make his face to shine upon you
    and be gracious to you;
The LORD lift up his countenance upon you
    and give you peace.   *Numbers 6:24–26*

Postlude

His Name for ever shall endure,
    last like the sun it shall;
Men shall be blessed in Him, and blessed
    all nations shall Him call.

Now blessèd be the Lord, our God,
    the God of Israel,
For He alone does wondrous works,
    in glory that excel.

And blessèd be His glorious Name
    to all eternity;
The whole earth let His glory fill.
    Amen, so let it be.   *Based on Psalm 72:17–19*

January 3

Meditation
Reflect on these words about the incarnation of the Lord Jesus:

The Lord's generation received testimony not only from angels and prophets, from shepherds and parents, but also from the aged and the righteous. Every age and both sexes, as well as the miraculous occurrences, build up faith: a virgin bears Him, a barren woman gives birth, a dumb man speaks, Elizabeth prophesies, the magi adore, the one enclosed in the womb leaps for joy, the widow confesses Him, and the righteous awaits Him.   *Ambrose*

Call to Worship
Hear God call you to worship through his word:

May he have dominion from sea to sea,
    and from the River to the ends of the earth!
May desert tribes bow down before him,
    and his enemies lick the dust!
May the kings of Tarshish and of the coastlands
    render him tribute;
may the kings of Sheba and Seba
    bring gifts!

May all kings fall down before him,
all nations serve him!   *Psalm 72:8–11*

Adoration

Say or sing the words of this Epiphany hymn:

We three kings of Orient are;
bearing gifts we traverse afar,
field and fountain, moor and mountain,
following yonder star.

> *O star of wonder, star of light,*
> *star with royal beauty bright,*
> *westward leading, still proceeding,*
> *guide us to thy perfect light.*

Born a King on Bethlehem's plain,
gold I bring to crown him again;
King forever, ceasing never,
over us all to reign.

Frankincense to offer have I;
incense owns a Deity nigh;
prayer and praising, voices raising,
worshiping God on high.

Myrrh is mine; its bitter perfume
breathes a life of gathering gloom;
sorrowing, sighing, bleeding, dying,
sealed in the stone-cold tomb.

Glorious now behold him arise;
King and God and sacrifice:

Alleluia, Alleluia,
sounds through the earth and skies.   *John H. Hopkins*

Reading of the Law
Hear God's law as his will for your life:

Hear, O Israel: The LORD our God, the LORD is one.
You shall love the LORD your God with all your heart and
       with all your soul and with all your might.
And these words that I command you today shall be on
       your heart.
You shall teach them diligently to your children,
   and shall talk of them when you sit in your house,
   and when you walk by the way,
   and when you lie down,
   and when you rise.
You shall bind them as a sign on your hand,
   and they shall be as frontlets between your eyes.
You shall write them on the doorposts of your house and
       on your gates.   *Deuteronomy 6:4–9*

Confession of Sin
Confess your sins to God:

Renew and sanctify us thoroughly by the Spirit: take from
us the old and stony hearts, and give us hearts more tender
and tractable. Amen.   *Richard Baxter*

Assurance of Pardon
Receive these words of comfort from God:

For through the law I died to the law, so that I might live to
God. I have been crucified with Christ. It is no longer I who

live, but Christ who lives in me. And the life I now live in the flesh I live by faith in the Son of God, who loved me and gave himself for me.   *Galatians 2:19–20*

Nicene Creed

Confess what you believe about the Christian faith:

I believe in one God, the Father Almighty,
    Maker of heaven and earth, and of all things visible and
        invisible.

And in one Lord Jesus Christ, the only-begotten Son of God;
    begotten of the Father before all worlds;
    God of God, Light of Light, very God of very God;
    begotten, not made, being of one substance with the
        Father;
    by whom all things were made.
Who, for us men and for our salvation,
    came down from heaven
    and was incarnate by the Holy Spirit of the Virgin Mary,
    and was made man;
    and was crucified also for us under Pontius Pilate;
    he suffered and was buried;
    and the third day he rose again, according to the Scriptures;
    and ascended into heaven, and sits on the right hand of
        the Father;
    and he shall come again, with glory, to judge the living
        and the dead;
    whose kingdom shall have no end.

And I believe in the Holy Spirit, the Lord and Giver of life;
    who proceeds from the Father and the Son;

who with the Father and the Son together is worshiped
      and glorified;
who spoke by the prophets.

And I believe in one holy catholic and apostolic church.
   I acknowledge one baptism for the forgiveness of sins;
   and I look for the resurrection of the dead,
   and the life of the world to come. Amen.

Praise
Say or sing this praise to God:

Praise God from whom all blessings flow;
Praise him all creatures here below;
Praise him above you heavenly host;
Praise Father, Son, and Holy Ghost. Amen.   Doxology

Catechism
Receive this instruction from the Westminster Shorter Catechism:

Q. 29. How are we made partakers of the redemption purchased by Christ?
A. We are made partakers of the redemption purchased by
Christ, by the effectual application of it to us by his Holy
Spirit.

Prayer for Illumination
As you read his word, ask God to enlighten your mind and heart:

Heavenly Father, may you grant us to comprehend your holy
Word according to your divine will, that we may learn from it
to put all our confidence in you alone, and withdraw it from
all other creatures; moreover, that also our old man with all
his lusts may be crucified more and more each day, and that

we may offer ourselves to you as a living sacrifice, to the glory of your holy name and to the edification of our neighbor, through our Lord Jesus Christ. Amen.   *Zacharias Ursinus*

Scripture Reading
Read this portion of God's word: Hebrews 2

Praise
Say this praise to God:

Blessed be the Lord God of Israel, for he has visited,
    and redeemed his people;
and has raised up a mighty salvation for us,
    in the house of his servant David;
as he spoke by the mouth of his holy prophets,
    which have been since the world began;
that we should be saved from our enemies,
    and from the hands of all that hate us;
to perform the mercy promised to our forefathers,
    and to remember his holy covenant;
to perform the oath which he swore to our forefather
        Abraham,
    that he would give us;
that we, being delivered out of the hands of our enemies,
    might serve him without fear;
in holiness and righteousness before him,
    all the days of our life.
And you, child, shall be called the prophet of the Most High,
    for you shall go before the face of the Lord to prepare his
        ways;
to give knowledge of salvation unto his people,
    for the remission of their sins,

through the tender mercy of our God,
    whereby the Dayspring from on high has visited us;
to give light to them that sit in darkness,
    and in the shadow of death,
and to guide our feet into the way of peace.

Glory be to the Father,
    and to the Son,
    and to the Holy Spirit:
As it was in the beginning,
    is now and ever shall be,
    world without end. Amen.   *Benedictus*

Prayer of Intercession
As you make your requests to God, pray this prayer:

Most merciful and gracious Father, I bless and magnify your name that you have adopted me into the inheritance of sons, and have given me a portion of my elder Brother. You who are the God of patience and consolation, strengthen me that I may bear the yoke and burden of the Lord, without any uneasy and useless murmurs, or ineffective unwillingness. Lord, I am unable to stand under the cross, unable of myself, but be pleased to ease this load by fortifying my spirit, that I may be strongest when I am weakest, and may be able to do and suffer everything that you please, through Christ who strengthens me. Let me pass through the valley of tears, and the valley of the shadow of death with safety and peace, with a meek spirit, and a sense of the divine mercies, through Jesus Christ. Amen.   *Jeremy Taylor*

Further Petition
- Personal
- Church
- World

Lord's Prayer
Pray the words that Jesus taught us to pray:

Our Father in heaven,
    hallowed be your name;
    your kingdom come;
    your will be done, on earth as it is in heaven.
    Give us this day our daily bread.
    And forgive us our debts, as we forgive our debtors.
    And lead us not into temptation but deliver us from evil.
    For yours is the kingdom, and the power,
    and the glory, forever. Amen.

Benediction
Receive by faith this blessing from God:

May the God of hope fill you with all joy and peace in believing, so that by the power of the Holy Spirit you may abound in hope.   Romans 15:13

Postlude
In closing, say or sing this praise to God:

His Name for ever shall endure,
    last like the sun it shall;
Men shall be blessed in Him, and blessed
    all nations shall Him call.

Now blessèd be the Lord, our God,
    the God of Israel,
For He alone does wondrous works,
    in glory that excel.

And blessèd be His glorious Name
    to all eternity;
The whole earth let His glory fill.
    Amen, so let it be.   *Based on Psalm 72:17–19*

January 4

Meditation

Reflect on these words about the incarnation of the Lord Jesus:

For that which He has not assumed He has not healed; but that which is united to His Godhead is also saved. If only half Adam fell, then that which Christ assumes and saves may be half also; but if the whole of his nature fell, it must be united to the whole nature of Him that was begotten, and so be saved as a whole.   *Gregory Nazianzus*

Call to Worship

Hear God call you to worship through his word:

But when the fullness of time had come, God sent forth his Son, born of woman, born under the law, to redeem those who were under the law, so that we might receive adoption as sons. And because you are sons, God has sent the Spirit of his Son into our hearts, crying, "Abba! Father!" So you are no longer a slave, but a son, and if a son, then an heir through God. *Galatians 4:4–7*

Adoration

Say or sing the words of this Epiphany hymn:

Angels from the realms of glory,
Wing your flight o'er all the earth;
Ye who sang creation's story
Now proclaim Messiah's birth:

> *Come and worship, come and worship,*
> *Worship Christ, the newborn King.*

Shepherds, in the field abiding,
Watching over your flocks by night,
God with us is now residing;
Yonder shines the infant light:

Sages, leave your contemplations,
Brighter visions beam afar;
Seek the great Desire of nations;
Ye have seen His natal star:

Saints, before the altar bending,
Watching long in hope and fear;
Suddenly the Lord, descending,
In His temple shall appear:

Sinners, wrung with true repentance,
Doomed for guilt to endless pains,
Justice now revokes the sentence,
Mercy calls you; break your chains:

Though an Infant now we view Him,
He shall fill His Father's throne;
Gather all the nations to Him;
Every knee shall then bow down:

All creation, join in praising
God, the Father, Spirit, Son;
Evermore your voices raising
To th'eternal Three in One: *Anonymous*

Reading of the Law
Hear God's law as his will for your life:

Our Lord Jesus said,

Blessed are the poor in spirit,
    for theirs is the kingdom of heaven.
Blessed are those who mourn,
    for they shall be comforted.
Blessed are the meek,
    for they shall inherit the earth.
Blessed are those who hunger and thirst for righteousness,
    for they shall be satisfied.
Blessed are the merciful,
    for they shall receive mercy.
Blessed are the pure in heart,
    for they shall see God.
Blessed are the peacemakers,
    for they shall be called sons of God.
Blessed are those who are persecuted for righteousness' sake,
    for theirs is the kingdom of heaven.   *Matthew 5:3–10*

Confession of Sin
Confess your sins to God:

I will "confess my transgressions unto the Lord," and acknowledge my infirmity. How small are the afflictions by which I am often cast down, and plunged in sorrow! I resolve to act with fortitude, but by the slightest evil am confounded and distressed. From the most inconsiderable events the most grievous temptations rise against me; and while I think myself established in security and peace, the smallest blast, if it be sudden, has power to bear me down. Behold, therefore, O Lord, my abject state, and pity the infirmity which you know infinitely better than myself! Have mercy upon me that I sink not; that the deep may not swallow me up forever! Amen.   *Thomas à Kempis*

Assurance of Pardon
Receive these words of comfort from God:

Purge me with hyssop, and I shall be clean;
   wash me, and I shall be whiter than snow.
Let me hear joy and gladness;
   let the bones that you have broken rejoice.   *Psalm 51:7–8*

Athanasian Creed, Part I
Confess what you believe about the Christian faith:

Whoever desires to be saved should above all hold to the catholic faith. Anyone who does not keep it whole and unbroken will doubtless perish eternally. Now this is the catholic faith:

that we worship one God in Trinity and the Trinity in unity, neither confounding their persons nor dividing the essence.

For the person of the Father is a distinct person,
   the person of the Son is another,
   and that of the Holy Spirit still another.
But the divinity of the Father, Son, and Holy Spirit is one,
   the glory equal, the majesty coeternal.

Such as the Father is, such is the Son and such is the
Holy Spirit.

The Father is uncreated, the Son is uncreated, the Holy
Spirit is uncreated.

The Father is immeasurable, the Son is immeasurable,
the Holy Spirit is immeasurable.

The Father is eternal, the Son is eternal, the Holy Spirit
is eternal.

And yet there are not three eternal beings; there is but
one eternal being.

So too there are not three uncreated or immeasurable
beings;

there is but one uncreated and immeasurable being.

Similarly, the Father is almighty, the Son is almighty,
the Holy Spirit is almighty.

Yet there are not three almighty beings; there is but one
almighty being.

Thus, the Father is God, the Son is God, the Holy Spirit
is God.

Yet there are not three gods; there is but one God.

Thus, the Father is Lord, the Son is Lord, the Holy Spirit
is Lord.

Yet there are not three lords; there is but one Lord.

Just as Christian truth compels us to confess each person
individually as both God and Lord,

so catholic religion forbids us to say that there are
three gods or lords.

Praise

Say or sing this praise to God:

Glory be to God the Father,
Glory be to God the Son,
Glory be to God the Spirit,
ever three and ever one:
As it was in the beginning,
now and evermore shall be.   *Gloria Patri*

Catechism

Receive this instruction from the Westminster Shorter Catechism:

Q. 30. How does the Spirit apply to us the redemption purchased by Christ?
A. The Spirit applies to us the redemption purchased by Christ, by working faith in us, and thereby uniting us to Christ in our effectual calling.

Prayer for Illumination

As you read his word, ask God to enlighten your mind and heart:

Lord, you know what distracted hearts we have, O give us self-recollection; you know what hard, dead hearts we have, O touch and awaken us! You know how we yet resist your Word and our lower nature is reluctant to bow to your scepter; therefore, O Lord, show forth your power; send your Spirit on high to work among us, to make our hearts submissive, and ourselves capable of living in true union with you, our salvation, and of yielding totally to your grace. Amen.
Gerhard Tersteegen

Scripture Reading

Read this portion of God's word: John 5

Praise

Say these praises to God:

Lord, now let your servant depart in peace according to
  your word.
For mine eyes have seen your salvation,
Which you have prepared before the face of all people,
To be a light to lighten the Gentiles and to be the glory of
  your people Israel. Amen. *Nunc Dimittis*

Holy, holy, holy, Lord God of hosts,
heaven and earth are full of your glory.
Glory be to you, O Lord Most High.
Blessed is he that comes in the name of the Lord.
Hosanna in the highest. Amen. *Sanctus*

Prayer of Intercession

As you make your requests to God, pray this prayer:

Lord, make our service acceptable to you while we live, and
our souls ready for you when we die. As long as we are in the
world, keep us from the evil of it, and from the snares and
dangers to which we are continually exposed in our passage
through it. O make our pilgrimage safe and sure through all
the troubles, changes, and temptations of this mortal life, to
the unchangeable glories and felicities of the life everlasting.
Be merciful to us this day. Keep us in all our ways, bless all our
lawful undertakings, and grant that we may take nothing in
hand but what is warranted by your Word, and agreeable to
your will concerning us. Set your fear before our eyes all the
day long; and put your love into our hearts, that we may not
depart from you. Bless and preserve us in our going out and

coming in. May the angel of your presence save us from all sin and danger. Amen.   *Augustus Toplady*

Further Petition
- Personal
- Church
- World

Lord's Prayer
Pray the words that Jesus taught us to pray:

Our Father in heaven,
  hallowed be your name;
  your kingdom come;
  your will be done, on earth as it is in heaven.
  Give us this day our daily bread.
  And forgive us our debts, as we forgive our debtors.
  And lead us not into temptation but deliver us from evil.
  For yours is the kingdom, and the power,
  and the glory, forever. Amen.

Benediction
Receive by faith this blessing from God:

The grace of the Lord Jesus Christ and the love of God and the fellowship of the Holy Spirit be with you all.   *2 Corinthians 13:14*

Postlude
In closing, say or sing this praise to God:

His Name for ever shall endure,
  last like the sun it shall;

Men shall be blessed in Him, and blessed
    all nations shall Him call.

Now blessèd be the Lord, our God,
    the God of Israel,
For He alone does wondrous works,
    in glory that excel.

And blessèd be His glorious Name
    to all eternity;
The whole earth let His glory fill.
    Amen, so let it be.   *Based on Psalm 72:17–19*

January 5

Meditation

Reflect on these words about the incarnation of the Lord Jesus:

When Christ himself appeared, he declared that the reason for his advent was by appeasing God to gather us from death unto life.   *John Calvin*

———

Call to Worship

Hear God call you to worship through his word:

I see him, but not now;
   I behold him, but not near:
a star shall come out of Jacob,
   and a scepter shall rise out of Israel;
it shall crush the forehead of Moab
   and break down all the sons of Sheth.
Edom shall be dispossessed;
   Seir also, his enemies, shall be dispossessed.
   Israel is doing valiantly.
And one from Jacob shall exercise dominion
   and destroy the survivors of cities!   *Numbers 24:17–19*

Adoration

Say or sing the words of this Epiphany hymn:

What star is this, with beams so bright,
more lovely than the noonday light?
'Tis sent to announce a newborn king,
glad tidings of our God to bring.

'Tis now fulfilled what God decreed,
"From Jacob shall a star proceed";
and lo! the eastern sages stand
to read in heaven the Lord's command.

While outward signs the star displays,
an inward light the Lord conveys
and urges them, with tender might,
to seek the giver of the light.

O Jesus, while the star of grace
impels us on to seek your face,
let not our slothful hearts refuse
the guidance of your light to use.   *Charles Coffin*

Reading of the Law

Hear God's law as his will for your life:

Our Lord said,

As the Father has loved me, so have I loved you. Abide in my love. If you keep my commandments, you will abide in my love, just as I have kept my Father's commandments and abide in his love. These things I have spoken to you, that my joy may be in you, and that your joy may be full. This is my commandment, that you love one another as I have loved you.   *John 15:9–12*

Confession of Sin

Confess your sins to God:

We appeal, O Lord, to your mercies, knowing them to be much more greater than our sins; and you came not to call the righteous but the sinners to repentance, to whom you say, "Come unto me all you that are overladen and diseased with the burden of sins, and I will ease you and refresh you." Yes, Lord, you are that God who wills not the death of a sinner, but rather that he should turn and live. You are our Savior, who wishes all men to be saved and to come to the knowledge of your truth. Therefore, O Lord, we humbly ask you not to withdraw your mercies from us because of our sins, but rather, O Lord, lay upon us your saving health, that you may show yourself toward us to be a Savior: for what greater praise can there be to a Physician, than to heal the sick; neither can there be any greater glory to you being a Savior, than to save sinners. Amen.   *Henry Smith*

Assurance of Pardon

Receive these words of comfort from God:

If then you have been raised with Christ, seek the things that are above, where Christ is, seated at the right hand of God. Set your minds on things that are above, not on things that are on earth. For you have died, and your life is hidden with Christ in God. When Christ who is your life appears, then you also will appear with him in glory.   *Colossians 3:1–4*

Athanasian Creed, Part 2
Confess what you believe about the Christian faith:

Whoever desires to be saved should above all hold to the catholic faith. Anyone who does not keep it whole and unbroken will doubtless perish eternally. Now this is the catholic faith:

that we worship one God in Trinity and the Trinity in unity, neither confounding their persons nor dividing the essence. . . .

> The Father was neither made nor created nor begotten
> from anyone.
> The Son was neither made nor created; he was begotten
> from the Father alone.
> The Holy Spirit was neither made nor created nor begotten;
> he proceeds from the Father and the Son.
> Accordingly, there is one Father, not three fathers;
> there is one Son, not three sons;
> there is one Holy Spirit, not three holy spirits.
> None in this Trinity is before or after, none is greater or
> smaller;
> in their entirety the three persons are coeternal and
> coequal with each other.
> So in everything, as was said earlier, the unity in Trinity,
> and the Trinity in unity, is to be worshiped.
> Anyone then who desires to be saved should think thus
> about the Trinity.

Praise
Say or sing this praise to God:

Praise and honor to the Father,
Praise and honor to the Son,

Praise and honor to the Spirit,
Ever three and ever one:
One in might and one in glory
While unending ages run!   Doxology

Catechism
Receive this instruction from the Westminster Shorter Catechism:

Q. 31. *What is effectual calling?*
A. Effectual calling is the work of God's Spirit, whereby, convincing us of our sin and misery, enlightening our minds in the knowledge of Christ, and renewing our wills, he does persuade and enable us to embrace Jesus Christ, freely offered to us in the gospel.

Prayer for Illumination
As you read his word, ask God to enlighten your mind and heart:

O God, you instruct us by your Holy Scriptures—we urge you by your grace to enlighten our minds and cleanse our hearts; that reading, hearing, and meditating upon them, we may rightly understand and heartily embrace the things you have revealed in them. Give efficacy to the reading of the gospel in your Word, that through the operation of the Holy Spirit, this holy seed may be received into our hearts as into good ground; and that we may not only hear your Word but keep it, living in conformity with your precepts; so that we may finally attain everlasting salvation, through Jesus Christ our Lord. Amen.   *Waldensian Liturgy*

Scripture Reading
Read this portion of God's word: Psalm 72

Praise

Say this praise to God:

Glory to God in the highest,
and peace to his people on earth.

Lord God, heavenly King,
almighty God and Father,
we worship you, we give you thanks,
we praise you for your glory.

Lord Jesus Christ, only Son of the Father,
Lord God, Lamb of God,
you take away the sin of the world:
have mercy on us;
you are seated at the right hand of the Father:
receive our prayer.

For you alone are the Holy One,
you alone are the Lord,
you alone are the Most High, Jesus Christ,
with the Holy Spirit,
in the glory of God the Father.
Amen.   *Gloria in Excelsis*

Prayer of Intercession

As you make your requests to God, pray this prayer:

Above all, long-expected Messiah, do come! Your ancient people who despised you once are waiting for you in your second coming, and we, the Gentiles, who knew you not, neither regarded you, we, too, are watching for your advent. . . . Earth travails for your coming. The whole creation groans in pain together until now. Your own expect you; we are longing till we are weary for your coming. Come quickly, Lord Jesus, come quickly. Amen and Amen.   *Charles Spurgeon*

Further Petition
- Personal
- Church
- World

Lord's Prayer
Pray the words that Jesus taught us to pray:

Our Father in heaven,
    hallowed be your name;
    your kingdom come;
    your will be done, on earth as it is in heaven.
    Give us this day our daily bread.
    And forgive us our debts, as we forgive our debtors.
    And lead us not into temptation but deliver us from evil.
    For yours is the kingdom, and the power,
    and the glory, forever. Amen.

Benediction
Receive by faith this blessing from God:

Now to him who is able to do far more abundantly than all that we ask or think, according to the power at work within us, to him be glory in the church and in Christ Jesus throughout all generations, forever and ever. Amen.   *Ephesians 3:20–21*

Postlude

In closing, say or sing this praise to God:

His Name for ever shall endure,
    last like the sun it shall;
Men shall be blessed in Him, and blessed
    all nations shall Him call.

Now blessèd be the Lord, our God,
    the God of Israel,
For He alone does wondrous works,
    in glory that excel.

And blessèd be His glorious Name
    to all eternity;
The whole earth let His glory fill.
    Amen, so let it be.   *Based on Psalm 72:17–19*

January 6

Epiphany

Meditation
Reflect on these words about the incarnation of the Lord Jesus:

It is because of His humanity and His incarnation that Christ becomes sweet to us, and through Him God becomes sweet to us. Let us therefore begin to ascend step by step from Christ's crying in His swaddling clothes up to His Passion. Then we shall easily know God. I am saying this so that you do not begin to contemplate God from the top, but start with the weak elements. We should busy ourselves completely with treating, knowing, and considering this man. Then you will know that He is the Way, the Truth, and the Life.
Martin Luther

Call to Worship
Hear God call you to worship through his word:

And behold, the star that they had seen when it rose went before them until it came to rest over the place where the child was. When they saw the star, they rejoiced exceedingly with great joy. And going into the house, they saw the child with Mary his mother, and they fell down and worshiped him. Then, opening their treasures, they offered him gifts, gold and frankincense and myrrh.   *Matthew 2:9–11*

Adoration

Say or sing the words of this Epiphany hymn:

Earth has many a noble city;
Bethl'hem, thou dost all excel:
out of thee the Lord from heaven
came to rule his Israel.

Fairer than the sun at morning
was the star that told his birth,
to the world its God announcing
seen in fleshly form on earth.

Eastern sages at his cradle
make oblations rich and rare;
see them give in deep devotion,
gold and frankincense and myrrh.

Sacred gifts of mystic meaning:
incense doth their God disclose,
gold the King of kings proclaimeth,
myrrh his sepulcher foreshows.

Jesu, whom the Gentiles worshipped
at thy glad Epiphany,
unto thee with God the Father
and the Spirit glory be.   *Aurelius Prudentius*

Reading of the Law
Hear God's law as his will for your life:

The words of our Lord Jesus Christ:

Unless your righteousness exceeds that of the scribes and Pharisees, you will never enter the kingdom of heaven. . . . You therefore must be perfect, as your heavenly Father is perfect. . . . Beware of practicing your righteousness before other people in order to be seen by them, for then you will have no reward from your Father who is in heaven. . . . Seek first the kingdom of God and his righteousness, and all these things will be added to you. . . . So whatever you wish that others would do to you, do also to them, for this is the Law and the Prophets.   *Matthew 5:20, 48; 6:1, 33; 7:12*

Confession of Sin
Confess your sins to God:

O God the Father of heaven, *have mercy upon us.*
O God the Son, Redeemer of the world, *have mercy upon us.*
O God the Holy Spirit, *have mercy upon us.*
Be merciful to us and spare us, O Lord.
Be merciful to us and deliver us, O Lord.
From all sin, from all error, from all evil—*deliver us, O Lord.*
From the wiles of the devil and from everlasting death—
       deliver us, O Lord.

Lord Jesus, by the mystery of your holy incarnation,
by your holy nativity,
by your baptism, fasting, and temptations—*deliver us, O Lord.*
By your agony and bloody sweat,
by your cross and passions,

by your death and burial,
by your resurrection and ascension,
by the coming of the Holy Spirit, the Comforter—
        deliver us, O Lord. Amen.   *Martin Bucer*

Assurance of Pardon
Receive these words of comfort from God:

They shall not defile themselves anymore with their idols and
their detestable things, or with any of their transgressions. But
I will save them from all the backslidings in which they have
sinned, and will cleanse them; and they shall be my people,
and I will be their God. "My servant David shall be king over
them, and they shall all have one shepherd. They shall walk in
my rules and be careful to obey my statutes."   *Ezekiel 37:23–24*

Athanasian Creed, Part 3
Confess what you believe about the Christian faith:

Whoever desires to be saved should above all hold to the catholic faith. Anyone who does not keep it whole and unbroken
will doubtless perish eternally. Now this is the catholic faith:

that we worship one God in Trinity and the Trinity in unity,
neither confounding their persons nor dividing the essence. . . .

But it is necessary for eternal salvation that one also believe
in the incarnation of our Lord Jesus Christ faithfully.

Now this is the true faith:

> that we believe and confess that our Lord Jesus Christ,
>   God's Son,
>   is both God and man, equally.

He is God from the essence of the Father, begotten
      before time;
   and he is man from the essence of his mother, born
         in time;
   completely God, completely man, with a rational soul
         and human flesh;
   equal to the Father as regards divinity,
   less than the Father as regards humanity.
Although he is God and man, yet Christ is not two,
      but one.
He is one, however, not by his divinity being turned
      into flesh,
   but by God's taking humanity to himself.
He is one, certainly not by the blending of his essence,
   but by the unity of his person.
For just as one man is both rational soul and flesh,
   so too the one Christ is both God and man.

He suffered for our salvation;
he descended to hell;
he arose from the dead on the third day;
he ascended to heaven;
he is seated at the Father's right hand;
from there he will come to judge the living and the dead.
At his coming all people will arise bodily and give an
      accounting of their own deeds.
Those who have done good will enter eternal life,
   and those who have done evil will enter eternal fire.

This is the catholic faith: that one cannot be saved without
believing it firmly and faithfully.

Praise

Say or sing this praise to God:

Glory be to God the Father,
Glory be to God the Son,
Glory be to God the Spirit,
God Almighty, Three in One!
Hallelujah! Hallelujah!
Glory be to him alone.   *Gloria Patri*

Catechism

Receive this instruction from the Westminster Shorter Catechism:

Q. 32. *What benefits do they that are effectually called partake of in this life?*
A. They that are effectually called do in this life partake of
justification, adoption and sanctification, and the several
benefits which in this life do either accompany or flow from
them.

Prayer for Illumination

As you read his word, ask God to enlighten your mind and heart:

Almighty God, I earnestly ask you for such deeper fellowship
of the Holy Spirit, who speaks in the blessed Scriptures, that
when I open them, I may perceive his mind in what I read,
and immediately hear in them his voice to myself. I ask you
for a quicker understanding in spiritual things, for more
desire to understand, a fuller perception of your promise in
the church, that I may become teachable, and may love that
by which you will teach me. Amen.   *Henry Wotherspoon*

Scripture Reading

Read this portion of God's word: Matthew 2

Praise

Say or sing this praise to God:

Corde Natus

He is found in human fashion,
Death and sorrow here to know,
That the race of Adam's children
Doomed by law to endless woe,
May not henceforth die and perish
In the dreadful gulf below,
Evermore and evermore!

O that birth forever blessèd,
When the virgin, full of grace,
By the Holy Ghost conceiving,
Bore the Saviour of our race;
And the Babe, the world's Redeemer,
First revealed His sacred face,
Evermore and evermore!

O ye heights of heaven adore Him;
Angel hosts, His praises sing;
Powers, dominions, bow before Him,
And extol our God and King!
Let no tongue on earth be silent,
Every voice in concert sing,
Evermore and evermore!

Christ, to Thee with God the Father,
And, O Holy Ghost, to Thee,
Hymn and chant with high thanksgiving,
And unwearied praises be:
Honour, glory, and dominion,

And eternal victory,
Evermore and evermore!   *Aurelius Prudentius*

Prayer of Intercession
As you make your requests to God, pray this prayer:

O God, who by the leading of a star did manifest your only
begotten Son to the Gentiles—mercifully grant, that we who
know you now by faith, may after this life have the perfection of your glorious Godhead; through Christ our Lord.
Amen.   *Book of Common Prayer (1552)*

Further Petition
- Personal
- Church
- World

Lord's Prayer
Pray the words that Jesus taught us to pray:

Our Father in heaven,
    hallowed be your name;
    your kingdom come;
    your will be done, on earth as it is in heaven.
    Give us this day our daily bread.
    And forgive us our debts, as we forgive our debtors.
    And lead us not into temptation but deliver us from evil.
    For yours is the kingdom, and the power,
    and the glory, forever. Amen.

Benediction

Receive by faith this blessing from God:

Now may the God of peace himself sanctify you completely, and may your whole spirit and soul and body be kept blameless at the coming of our Lord Jesus Christ. He who calls you is faithful; he will surely do it.   *1 Thessalonians 5:23–24*

Postlude

In closing, say or sing this praise to God:

His Name for ever shall endure,
    last like the sun it shall;
Men shall be blessed in Him, and blessed
    all nations shall Him call.

Now blessèd be the Lord, our God,
    the God of Israel,
For He alone does wondrous works,
    in glory that excel.

And blessèd be His glorious Name
    to all eternity;
The whole earth let His glory fill.
    Amen, so let it be.   *Based on Psalm 72:17–19*

APPENDIXES

Appendix 1

Tunes for Hymns and Psalms, *Gloria Patri* and Doxology Versions

Hymns and Psalms
*Traditionally chanted

Angels from the realms of glory
Iris · 87 87 47 Extended

As with gladness men of old
Dix · 77 77 77

*Blessed be the Lord God of Israel, for he has visited (*Benedictus*)

"Comfort, comfort all my people"
Blaenwern · 87 87D

Come, Thou long-expected Jesus
Hyfrydol · 87 87D

Creator of the starry height
Puer Nobis · LM

Down in yon forest there stands a hall
Trad. English carol tune: Down in yon forest · 9 10 11 12

Earth has many a noble city
Stuttgart · 87 87

Endow the king with justice, Lord (*Sing Psalms: 72:1–9, 11–14*)
Church Triumphant · LM

*Glory to God in the highest (*Gloria in Excelsis*)

Hail to the Lord's anointed
Crüger · 76 76D

Hark! A thrilling voice is sounding!
Merton or Stuttgart · 87 87

Hark! the herald angels sing
Mendelssohn · 77 77D with refrain

He is found in human fashion
Corde Natus · 87 87 877

Hills of the North, rejoice
Little Cornard · 66 66 88

His Name for ever shall endure
Effingham · CM

*Holy, holy, holy, Lord God of hosts (*Sanctus*)

Jesus came, the heavens adoring
Regent Square · 87 87 87

Joy to the world, the Lord is come!
Antioch · CM

Let all mortal flesh keep silence
Picardy · 87 87 87

Lift up the Advent strain!
Carlisle · SM

Lo, how a rose e'er blooming
German Melody: Es ist ein Ros entsptrungen · 76 76 676

Lo! He comes with clouds descending
Helmsley · 87 87 47 Extended

*Lord, now let your servant depart in peace according to your word (Nunc Dimittis)

May God arise, and may his foes (Sing Psalms: 68:1–6, 32–35)
Melita · 88 88 88

*My soul magnifies the Lord (Magnificat)

*O Adonai, and Captain of the house of Israel (O Adonai)

O come, all ye faithful, joyful and triumphant!
Adeste Fideles · Irregular with refrain

O come, divine Messiah
Venez Divin Messie · 78 76 with refrain

O come, O come, Emmanuel
Veni Emmanuel · 88 88 88

*O Dayspring, splendor of light eternal and sun of righteousness (O Oriens)

*O Emmanuel, our King and our Lawgiver (O Emmanuel)

O heavenly Word, Eternal Light
Puer Nobis · LM

O holy night, the stars are brightly shining
Adolphe C Adam

*O Key of David and scepter of the house of Israel (*O Clavis David*)

*O King of the nations, and their desire (*O Rex Gentium*)

O little town of Bethlehem
Forest Green · CMD

O radiant light, O sun divine (*Phos Hilaron*)
Walton · LM

*O Root of Jesse, standing as a sign among the peoples
(*O Radix Jesse*)

O Savior, rend the heavens wide!
Winchester New or *Vom Himmel Hoch* · LM

*O Wisdom, coming forth from the mouth of the Most High
(*O Sapientia*)

Of the Father's love begotten
Corde Natus · 87 87 877

Once in royal David's city
Irby · 87 87 77

People, look east. The time is near
Old Besancon Carol Tune · 87 98 87

Prepare the way, O Zion
Bereden Väg För Herran · 76 76 77 Refrain

Savior of the nations, come
Lübeck · 77 77

See in yonder manger low
Humility · 77 77 and refrain

Silent night, holy night!
Stille Nacht · Irregular

The advent of our King
Carlisle · SM

The darkest midnight in December
Trad. Irish melody · Irregular

The King shall come when morning dawns
Ellacombe · DCM

The tree of life my soul hath seen
Jesus Christ The Apple Tree (Elizabeth Poston)

The world and all in at are God's *(Sing Psalms: 24:1–10)*
Richmond · CM

This is the truth sent from above
Herefordshire Carol · LM

To earth descending, Word sublime
Vom Himmel Hoch · LM

"Wake, awake, for night is flying"
Wachet Auf · 898D 66 4 88

We three kings of Orient are
Kings Of Orient · 88 44 6 with refrain

What star is this, with beams so bright
Morning Hymn · LM

Why do the heathen nations rage? *(Sing Psalms: 2:1–12)*
Winchester New · LM

Zion's King shall reign victorious
Abbot's Leigh · 87 87D

Gloria Patri and Doxology Versions

Gloria Patri (Traditional)
Words:

Glory be to the Father,
    and to the Son,
    and to the Holy Spirit:
As it was in the beginning,
    is now and ever shall be,
    world without end. Amen.

Tune: Gloria Patri (Greatorex)
Meter: Irregular

Gloria Patri (Alternative I)
Words:

Glory be to God the Father,
Glory be to God the Son,
Glory be to God the Spirit,
ever three and ever one:
As it was in the beginning,
now and evermore shall be.

Tune: Regent Square
Meter: 87 87 87

Gloria Patri (Alternative 2)

Words:

Glory be to God the Father,
Glory be to God the Son,
Glory be to God the Spirit,
God Almighty, Three in One!
Hallelujah! Hallelujah!
Glory be to him alone.

Tune: Regent Square
Meter: 87 87 87

Doxology (Traditional)

Words:

Praise God from whom all blessings flow;
Praise him all creatures here below;
Praise him above you heavenly host;
Praise Father, Son, and Holy Ghost. Amen.

Tune: Old Hundredth or Tallis's Canon
Meter: LM

Doxology (Alternative)

Words:

Praise and honor to the Father,
Praise and honor to the Son,
Praise and honor to the Spirit,
Ever three and ever one:

One in might and one in glory
While unending ages run!

Tune: Westminster Abbey
Meter: 87 87 87

Doxology (Psalm 72:17–19)
Words:

His Name for ever shall endure,
    last like the sun it shall;
Men shall be blessed in Him, and blessed
    all nations shall Him call.

Now blessèd be the Lord, our God,
    the God of Israel,
For He alone does wondrous works,
    in glory that excel.

And blessèd be His glorious Name
    to all eternity;
The whole earth let His glory fill.
    Amen, so let it be.

Tune: Effingham
Meter: CM

Advent to Epiphany
Bible Reading Plan

November
28 Genesis 3:1–15
29 Genesis 22:1–19
30 Genesis 49:1–12

December
1 Numbers 24:1–19
2 Deuteronomy 18:1–22
3 2 Samuel 7:1–16
4 Psalm 2
5 Psalm 16
6 Psalm 45
7 Psalm 68
8 Psalm 89
9 Psalm 110
10 Psalm 118
11 Job 19
12 Isaiah 7:10–17 and 9:1–7
13 Isaiah 11
14 Isaiah 40

15 Isaiah 42
16 Isaiah 49
17 Isaiah 50
18 Isaiah 52:13–53:12
19 Jeremiah 23:1–6 and 33:14–26
20 Micah 5
21 Zechariah 9:9–17; 13:1–9; and Malachi 3:1–4
22 Luke 1:26–56
23 Luke 1:57–80
24 Luke 2:1–21
25 Luke 2:22–40
26 Matthew 1:1–25
27 John 1:1–18
28 Colossians 1:1–20
29 Ephesians 3:1–12
30 Romans 1:1–17
31 Philippians 2:1–11

January

1 Isaiah 60
2 Hebrews 1
3 Hebrews 2
4 John 5
5 Psalm 72
6 Matthew 2

Appendix 3

Author, Hymn, and
Liturgy Index

Cecil Frances Alexander (1818–1895)
Irish hymnwriter; best known for her hymns "All Things Bright and Beautiful," "There Is a Green Hill Far Away," and "Once in Royal David's City."

Ambrose (339–397)
Bishop of Milan renowned for his preaching and defense of orthodox Christian doctrine; combatted paganism and Arianism and fought for independence of the church from the state.

Anselm (1033–1109)
Archbishop of Canterbury renowned for his godly character and sharp intellect; his *Cur Deus Homo* ("Why God Became Man") was a vital contribution to the church's understanding of the person and work of Christ.

Athanasius (c. 296/298–373)
Noted Egyptian Christian theologian who served the Greek church, especially in his defense of Trinitarianism over against Arianism.

Augustine (354–430)
North African church father and key founder of Western theology; forerunner of the Protestant Reformation; author of *Confessions* and *The City of God*.

Aurelius Prudentius (348–413)
Christian poet, lawyer, and provincial governor of Tarraconensis (northern Spain); his poetry was influenced by Tertullian and Ambrose.

Theodore Baker (1851–1934)
American musicologist; compiler of the well-known *Baker's Biographical Dictionary of Musicians*; translated several hymns into English.

Basil of Caesarea (330–379)
Monk who later became bishop of Caesarea; combatted heresy, including Arianism, and was known for his eloquence, holiness, organizational skill, and acts of mercy.

Herman Bavinck (1854–1921)
Dutch theologian in the Reformed tradition; taught at Kampen Theological Seminary and Free University of Amsterdam; best known for his four-volume work *Reformed Dogmatics*.

Richard Baxter (1615–1691)
English Puritan pastor known for his piety and quest for moderation amid the tumultuous English Civil War; author of *The Reformed Pastor*, a classic handbook on ministerial care.

Thomas Becon (1511–1567)
English Protestant Reformer who enjoyed the protection of Edward VI and Elizabeth I but fled to Europe during the reign of Mary I; penned popular writings in support of Protestantism.

Benedictus (6th century)
Ancient Latin hymn based on the opening words of Luke 1:68–79: "Blessed be the Lord God of Israel"; also known as the "Canticle of Zachary."

Bernard of Clairvaux (1090–1153)
French Cistercian monk who served as an able administrator, promoter of asceticism, champion of mysticism, defender of the faith, and advocate for the Second Crusade.

Book of Common Prayer (1552)
The Book of Common Prayer authored by Archbishop Thomas Cranmer (1489–1556), leader of the English Reformation during the reigns of Henry VIII and Edward VI.

Book of Public Prayer (1857)
Anonymous compilation of liturgies for church services in the Presbyterian Church in the United States of America.

John Bradford (1510–1555)
English preacher and Reformer; chaplain to Edward VI; burned at the stake for his Protestant convictions.

Richard Brooke (1840–1926)
South African priest who served as the longtime archdeacon of Cape Town and also fulfilled roles in parochial education.

Phillips Brooks (1835–1893)
Anglican minister in Philadelphia and Boston; later bishop of Massachusetts; known for writing "O Little Town of Bethlehem."

John Brownlie (1857–1925)
Free Church of Scotland minister and hymnologist.

Martin Bucer (1491–1551)
German Protestant Reformer who ministered in Strasbourg and influenced John Calvin during his three-year exile there; he wrote Church Practices (1539), which became a seminal liturgy for Calvin.

Heinrich Bullinger (1504–1575)
Swiss German Protestant Reformer who ministered in Zürich; he authored Christian Order and Custom (1535) to shape his church's liturgy.

John Calvin (1509–1564)
French theologian and longtime pastor in Geneva, Switzerland; key figure of the Reformation and forefather of Reformed theology and Presbyterianism; author of Institutes of the Christian Religion, a classic systematic theology.

Edward Caswall (1814–1878)
Anglican minister and hymnwriter; later became a priest in the Roman Catholic Church.

Stephen Charnock (1628–1680)
English Puritan divine in the Presbyterian tradition; best known for his work *Discourses upon the Existence and Attributes of God*.

John Chrysostom (347–407)
Patriarch of Constantinople whose powerful preaching combined careful and literal exegesis with practical application ("Chrysostom" means "golden-mouthed").

Clement of Alexandria (c. 150–c. 215)
Theologian in the early church who taught in Alexandria.

Clement of Rome (?–99)
One of the first apostolic church fathers and bishop of Rome (AD 88–99); his epistle to Christians in Corinth (known as *1 Clement*) provides insight into early church government, ministry, and theology.

Charles Coffin (1676–1749)
Rector of the University of Paris; composed a number of Latin hymns that appeared in the Paris Breviary in 1722; a larger collection of his hymns was published in 1736 under the title *Hymni Sacri Auctore Carolo Coffin*.

Corde Natus (4th/5th century)
Ancient Latin poem by Aurelius Prudentius, now associated with Christmas; known in English as "Of the Father's Love Begotten" (most popular translation by John M. Neale).

Cyril of Jerusalem (313–386)
Early church theologian who served as bishop of Jerusalem; known for his involvement in catechesis and liturgy formation.

Divine Liturgy of Saint James (4th century)
Ancient Christian liturgy attributed to James, the brother of Jesus; also known as the patriarch of Jewish Christians in Jerusalem. The hymn Sileat Omnis Caro Mortalis was originally part of the Eucharist section for Holy Saturday.

W. Chatterton Dix (1837–1898)
Manager of a marine insurance company in Glasgow, Scotland; also a capable lay Christian hymnwriter.

Jonathan Edwards (1703–1758)
Congregationalist theologian who ministered in Massachusetts and later became president of the College of New Jersey (later Princeton) just before his untimely death.

Es ist ein Ros entsprungen (1599)
Christmas carol of German origin based on the prophecy in Isaiah 11:1; known in English as "Lo, How a Rose E'er Blooming"; author unknown.

Frans Michael Franzén (1772–1847)
Finnish-Swedish poet who ministered in the Swedish church, most notably as the bishop of Härnösand.

Gloria in Excelsis (4th century)
Ancient Latin hymn based on the opening words of Luke 2:14: "Glory to God in the highest"; also known as the "Angelic Hymn" or the "Greater Doxology" (the "Minor Doxology" being *Gloria Patri*).

Gregory of Nazianzus (330–390)
Archbishop of Constantinople whose eloquent preaching promoted orthodox theology as espoused at the Council of Constantinople in 381; his formulations on the Trinity have been especially influential.

Gregory of Nyssa (335–394)
Bishop of Nyssa whose writings strongly defended orthodox theology, especially concerning the nature of the Trinity and the two natures of Christ, human and divine.

Gregory the Great (540–604)
Bishop of Rome, known as the "Father of Christian Worship," through his liturgical reforms; Calvin said that he was the last good pope; the "Gregorian Chant" is named after him.

Johann Habermann (1516–1590)
German theologian and pastor known for his Old Testament scholarship and especially for his book of prayers, written in accessible and biblical prose.

George Herbert (1593–1633)
English curate and poet whose verse, published posthumously, is considered some of the earliest and finest devotional poetry in Anglicanism, with skillful rhyme and rhythm.

Hippolytus of Rome (170–235)
Early church father and priest considered the most important Western theologian of the third century AD; very little is known of his personal life or background.

John H. Hopkins (1820–1891)
Ecclesiologist in the Episcopal Church in Vermont; viewed as a significant developer of hymn writing in the Episcopal Church in the mid-nineteenth century.

John Howe (1630–1705)
Puritan writer and minister who served as domestic chaplain under Oliver Cromwell; sought to bridge denominational divides and to unite Presbyterians and Congregationalists.

John Hunter (1848–1917)
Scottish Congregationalist minister, serving primarily in Glasgow; wrote a volume of devotional services and another volume of hymns, focusing on the social implications of the gospel.

Richard Hutchins (1700–1800)
Calvinistic Baptist minister in Northampton, England.

Irenaeus (c. 130–c. 202)
Early church Greek father who served as bishop of Lyon; defender of Christian orthodoxy; best known for his book *Against Heresies*.

William Jay (1769–1853)
English nonconformist pastor known for his revivalist preaching as well as his writing and counseling ministries.

Samuel Johnson (1709–1784)
British scholar whose 1755 *Dictionary of the English Language* set the standard for English lexicography; devout Anglican who periodically wrote sermons for friends.

Thomas Kelly (1769–1855)
Irish independent preacher and minister who seceded from the Church of Ireland; known best as a prolific hymnwriter.

C. S. Lewis (1898–1963)
Professor of English literature at Oxford and Cambridge Universities; Christian apologist; best known for his children's series The Chronicles of Narnia.

Wilhelm Loehe (1808–1872)
German evangelical pastor known for his fervent preaching and for sending Lutheran missionaries around the world; founding sponsor of the Lutheran Church, Missouri Synod.

Martin Luther (1483–1546)
Leading voice of the Protestant Reformation due to his insistence on the biblical doctrine of justification by faith alone;

voluminous writer and preacher who founded the Lutheran Church.

Magnificat (6th century)
Ancient Latin hymn based on the opening words of Luke 1:46–59: "My Soul Magnifies the Lord"; also known as the "Canticle of Mary" or "Ode of the Theotokos."

George Matheson (1842–1906)
Scottish pastor and hymnwriter, blind from youth, whose writings and lectures were well received, including by Queen Victoria.

Middelburg Liturgy (1586)
Liturgy penned by English Puritan Thomas Cartwright (1553–1603) after he and his congregation were exiled to Middelburg in the Netherlands.

Joseph Mohr (1792–1848)
Roman Catholic priest who served in Austria; known for penning "Silent Night."

James Montgomery (1771–1854)
Scottish-born poet and newspaper editor in Sheffield, England; viewed by some as an equal to Isaac Watts and Charles Welsey, he published at least four hundred hymns.

John Murray (1898–1975)
Professor of systematic theology at Westminster Theological Seminary (1930–1966); among other writings, known for his commentary *Epistle to the Romans.*

Philipp Nicolai *(1556–1608)*
German Lutheran pastor, known best for his hymnody.

Nunc Dimittis *(4th century)*
Ancient Latin hymn based on the opening words of Luke 2:29–32: "Lord, now you are letting your servant depart in peace"; also known as the "Canticle of Simeon."

O Antiphons *(6th century)*
Short ancient Latin hymns traditionally used at Vespers (Evensong) on the last seven days of Advent (December 17–23); also known as the "Great Advent Antiphons" or "Great Os"; each Antiphon is a name of Christ: *O Sapientia* (O Wisdom) | *O Adonai* (O Lord) | *O Radix Jesse* (O Root of Jesse) | *O Clavis David* (O Key of David) | *O Oriens* (O Dayspring) | *O Rex Gentium* (O King of the Nations) | *O Emmanuel* (O God with Us); these form the basis for the hymn *Veni, Veni, Emmanuel* (O Come, O come, Emmanuel).

Charles E. Oakley *(1832–1865)*
Anglican minister who served at St. Paul's, Covent Garden, London.

John Oecolampadius *(1482–1531)*
German Protestant Reformer who ministered in Basel; he wrote two liturgies: The Testament of Jesus Christ (1523) and Form and Manner (1526).

Old Palatinate Liturgy *(1563)*
Liturgy penned mainly by Zacharias Ursinus; it formed, along with the Heidelberg Catechism, the Palatinate Church Order

(the Palatinate was a historical region in Germany near the Rhine river).

Johann Olearius (1611–1684)
German minister and professor; author of a commentary on the whole Bible; compiler of one of the largest German hymnbooks in the seventeenth century.

John Owen (1616–1683)
English nonconformist minister and theologian at University of Oxford; known for his multivolume works, among which is his famous *The Death of Death in the Death of Christ*.

Blaise Pascal (1623–1662)
French philosopher, mathematician, and theologian whose *Pensées* argue forcefully for the truth of the Christian faith; his deep faith combined love of Christ with love of reason.

Saint Patrick (5th century)
British-born missionary to Ireland who felt called to the island after being captured by Irish pirates as a teenager; followed a strict rule of faith, combined with intimate knowledge of the Latin Bible.

Simon-Joseph Pellegrin (1663–1745)
French cleric and librettist; known for his collection of French carols published 1708–1711.

Phos Hilaron (late 3rd, early 4th centuries)
Ancient Latin hymn originally written in Greek (Φῶς ἱλαρόν); earliest known Christian hymn used in worship; Basil of

Caesarea (329–379) wrote of the aged tradition of singing the Phos Hilaron.

E. B. Pusey (1800–1882)
English priest and Hebrew scholar known for his powerful preaching, support of high church Anglicanism, and quest for rapprochement with the church of Rome.

Sanctus (5th century)
Ancient Latin hymn, commonly associated with Preface to the Lord's Supper; known in English as "Holy."

Diebold Schwarz (1485–1561)
German Reformer in Strasbourg who was one of the first ministers to begin reforming the German Mass; Schwarz's reforms were seen in his German Mass (1524) liturgy.

Richard Sibbes (1577–1635)
Moderate English Puritan theologian who worked to fund Puritan ministers and theologians in the early seventeenth century; well respected for his devotional writings and sermons.

Sileat Omnis Caro Mortalis (3rd century)
Ancient Greek hymn based on the words of Habakkuk 2:20 ("Let all the earth keep silence before him") and Zechariah 2:13 ("Be silent, all flesh, before the LORD"); known in English as "Let All Mortal Flesh Keep Silence." Originally part of the Liturgy of Saint James.

Henry Smith (1560–1591)
Puritan preacher during the reign of Elizabeth I; the immense popularity of his sermons led to the nickname "Silver-Tongued Smith."

Charles Spurgeon (1834–1892)
Calvinistic Baptist preacher known for his powerful preaching at the Metropolitan Tabernacle in London; strong supporter of Christian charity, especially orphanges, and the abolition of slavery.

Jeremy Taylor (1613–1667)
Anglican bishop who served as chaplain to Charles I and was well known for his devotional writings, which stressed piety and were valued for their clear prose and vivid imagery.

Gerhard Tersteegen (1697–1769)
German Protestant mystic who dedicated his life to devotional writing, including poems, hymns, and biographies, as well as translations of French mystic writings.

Thomas à Kempis (1380–1471)
German-Dutch priest known for his devotional writings, especially those concerning the imitation of Christ.

Henry Thornton (1760–1815)
English economist and politician who served as a founding member of the Clapham Sect, a society of Anglicans who fought for evangelical values, such as the abolition of slavery.

Godfrey Thring (1823–1903)
Anglican minister and hymnwriter.

Augustus Toplady (1740–1778)
Anglican minister known for his extensive writings, including essays, hymns, letters, theological polemics, and reflections on the natural world.

Zacharias Ursinus (1534–1584)
German Protestant Reformer who taught at the University of Heidelberg; along with others, he wrote the Heidelberg Catechism (1563), at the back of which was the Palatinate Church Order liturgy.

Friedrich von Spee (1591–1635)
German Jesuit priest and professor; following the Reformation, he was the first significant writer of sacred poems in the Roman Catholic Church in Germany.

Geerhardus Vos (1862–1949)
Dutch-American theologian at Princeton University, holding the chair of biblical theology from 1893–1932.

John Francis Wade (1711–1786)
Catholic layman and hymnwriter; the suspected author of "O Come, All Ye Faithful."

Waldensian Liturgy (16th century)
Waldensians were part of an ascetic movement of the twelfth century in France and Italy that was brought into the Prot-

estant church through the influence of German, Swiss, and French Reformers in the sixteenth century.

B. B. Warfield (1851–1921)
Princeton theologian who taught New Testament and systematic theology; also served as the last principal of Princeton.

Thomas Watson (1620–1686)
English Puritan who was ejected from the Church of England as a nonconformist preacher; best known for his work *Body of Practical Divinity*, a series of sermons based on the Westminster Catechism.

Isaac Watts (1674–1748)
English nonconformist minister and hymnwriter; in his lifetime he wrote more than eight hundred hymns.

Charles Wesley (1707–1788)
Anglican minister who cofounded the Methodist Church in England with his brother John; a prolific hymnwriter, composing over 6,500 hymns.

John Wesley (1703–1791)
Anglican minister and theologian who cofounded the Methodist Church with his brother Charles; committed to biblical preaching, evangelism, personal holiness, and social ministry.

George Whitefield (1714–1770)
English Anglican minister; traveling evangelist in Britain and the American colonies during the First Great Awakening.

William Wilberforce (1759–1833)

English evangelical orator and member of Parliament who provided leadership in the successful crusade to abolish the slave trade, and later slavery itself, in the British Empire.

John Witherspoon (1723–1794)

Scottish-American Presbyterian who served as the sixth president of the College of New Jersey (later Princeton University) from 1768–1794; also a founding father of the United States.

Henry Wotherspoon (1850–1930)

Scottish minister at St. Oswald's, Edinburgh; known for his devotional prayers and contributions to contemporary understandings of Presbyterianism and of spiritual gifts.

Huldrych Zwingli (1484–1531)

Swiss German Protestant Reformer who ministered in Zürich; he wrote two liturgies: Act or Custom of the Supper (1525) and Form of Prayer (1525).